YOU ARE HERE

Y⊙U ARE HERE

A DOSSIER

by

Rory Bremner,
John Bird *and*
John Fortune *with*
Geoff Atkinson

to Emma Jennifer + Madeleine! Rory Bremner

Weidenfeld & Nicolson
LONDON

First published in Great Britain in 2004
by Weidenfeld & Nicolson

Fifth impression 2004

A CIP catalogue record for this book
is available from the British Library.
ISBN 0 297 84778 3

Typeset, printed and bound in Great Britain
by Butler and Tanner Ltd, Frome and London

Weidenfeld & Nicolson

The Orion Publishing Group Ltd
Orion House
5 Upper Saint Martin's Lane
London, WC2H 9EA

www.orionbooks.co.uk

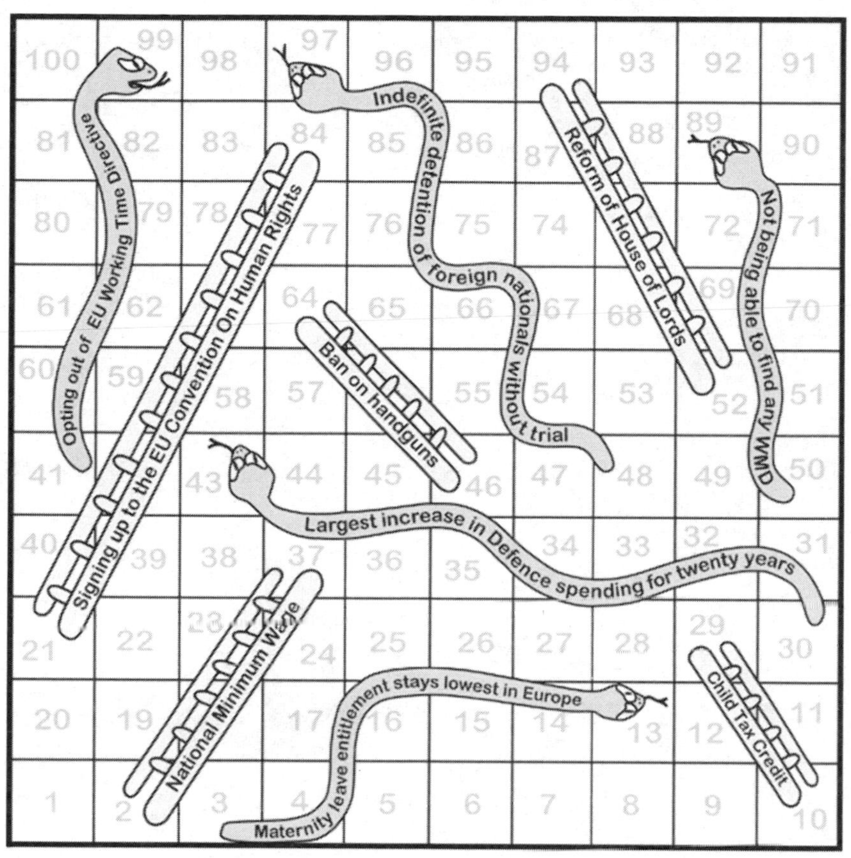

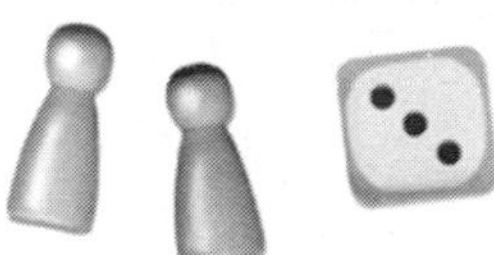

Snakes and Ladders

A selection of Labour's ups and downs

Contents

PART IV *There's a whole world out there*

PART V *So here's the bill . . .*

Preface

BY RORY BREMNER

In November 2003, our Channel 4 programme *Bremner, Bird and Fortune* received an award from the Political Studies Association for the Best Political Satire on Television – an accolade that should clearly have gone to Fox News for their coverage of the Gulf War that year. It's an enduring feature of so-called satirical programmes that we constantly struggle to match the levels of absurdity displayed by governments and the media on an almost daily basis. At the Establishment Club in the 1960s, John Bird and John Fortune would frequently reduce audiences to helpless laughter merely by reciting government policy. They continue to do so today.

Shortly after the first Gulf War, the two were struck by the apparent discovery that, under the Export Credit Guarantee Scheme, Britain had not only sold weapons to Saddam Hussein, but supplied him with the money to pay for them. Feeling this was too ridiculous an idea, even by their standards, they contacted a friend from university who was now a senior civil servant. He confirmed the story, adding that it was even worse than they'd imagined: 'it's all part of the fog of hypocrisy that surrounds this place'.

Over the course of the last ten years – and particularly the last two – the show has been inspired by a fascination with the absurdities of actual policies, many of them beyond parody. We've been fortunate to have the assistance of a dedicated team of researchers who have uncovered some truly extraordinary material. They in turn have been assisted by experts in many fields who have freely shared their knowledge with us. The results appear, in sketch or monologue form, a few days later.

The process throws up some strange ironies. It was odd to think that as we were sitting in a room trying to work out the ins and outs of government policy, Her Majesty's Official Opposition were sitting in a room at Westminster trying to write jokes for Prime Minister's Questions.

Some years ago, we wrote a song about the then Conservative chancellor (D'ye Ken Ken Clarke, to the tune of John Peel). The last verse went as follows:

> But I have to say, you'd still pay the tax
> Under Labour or Liberal Democrats
> *We may be a bunch of sleaze-ridden prats*
> *But you know where you are with the To-ries.*

Soon after, I received a call from former Tory Minister Alan Clark asking if he could use the last two lines in a speech. 'We should use it as our election slogan' he said. For all their faults, he felt his party could at least claim the virtue of consistency. Reading through the statements of Tony Blair and his ministers before 1997 and comparing them with subsequent Labour policy, you can see his point.

I've often thought that Blair is like the girl in the poem: 'there was a little girl, who had a little curl, right in the middle of her forehead. And when she was good, she was very, very good; but when she was bad, she was horrid.' The last year has been a bad one: August saw him holed up in Sardinia with Berlusconi, his closest ally. (The choice was narrow: him or Gaddafi). A socialist government in Spain and the possibility of a Democratic victory in America cause him considerable embarrassment. Despite some undeniable achievements, such as rising employment and the minimum wage, his credibility is on the line. Many of those who began as believers have since become agnostic to the point of wondering if there really is a Blair.

In the meantime, this book brings together some of our individual and collective observations on New Labour, the New World Order, and what used to be known as 'the discipline of the market'. For the most part, though, it's a compendium of some of the remarkable material that has come our way over the last few years. A commonplace book, in a way, of facts, figures and comments that have caught our attention, reduced us to laughter or driven us to anger and despair.

It's not a book about how much we know: rather how little we know, and how even that little knowledge continues to trump our wildest fantasies.

Rory Bremner, October 2004

Acknowledgements

The authors would like to record their thanks to all those individuals or organisations who contributed, wittingly or unwittingly, to the making of this book and the television programme from which it stems.

The television series *Bremner, Bird and Fortune* is recorded on a Friday night and transmitted the following Sunday. On Monday morning we begin preparing a new show; the writers are the three named in the title together with John Langdon and our producer Geoff Atkinson. But none of it would be possible without the work of our researchers: Jack Cheshire, Susan Foulis, Elissa Phipps, and Abigail Fielding-Smith. This book is based on material gathered over the years by them and has been put together by Geoff Atkinson. The primary credit goes to him (together with, hopefully, all writs for libel).

John Bird and John Fortune

This book has been several years in gestation, and several months in the writing, but it was really only in the final weeks with deadlines looming that it finally took the shape we all wanted. The fact that we got through this period intact was down entirely to the wonderful, kind, and tireless support of our editor Tom Wharton. Without him we would have been truly sunk. And without the total support of Alan Samson at Weidenfeld & Nicolson whose unwavering enthusiasm and understanding was there from day one, it's fair to say we wouldn't even have got started. We are very lucky to have such great bookends and to be at such a perfect home.

Geoff Atkinson

FOREWORD

*A personal message from the Prime Minister, the Relatively Honourable Tony Blair**

Hello. Like me you're probably a pretty regular sort of guy. Just popped into Waterstone's or W. H. Smith's or Books *etc.* to see what's cooking (note to self: have I named them all? Better check, don't want to lose out on any bulk orders). Y'know, normal thing, Saturday morning, you've dropped the kids off at sport, you've got ten minutes to spare before you're due back to pick the eldest up from t'ai chi, and you wouldn't mind a quick coffee but there's a queue at Starbucks and by the time your tall skinny latte's cooled down it will be time to go, so instead you've drifted into your local bookshop/newsagent/stationer's/coffee shop/wild bean café/lap dance club (God, isn't it amazing how cross-branding has really caught on? Must try and do something about twinning the National Executive with Jimmy Choo shoes or something like that) and are now surfing the shelves looking through the lifestyle section for a cheap paperback to read now you've just finished the Wayne Rooney autobiography.

And it's then that you spot this little volume. Hmmm, looks interesting, might learn the odd thing . . . Gosh! I didn't know that . . .

. . . but hang on, just think about it.

Isn't that a spy camera up in the roof that's looking over at you? And what about back at the car park, wasn't that a CCTV camera filming you there as well . . . Now, let's see, which car's yours? What? You left it there? In the street? Wait, it's not the people carrier, the one sticking out from the pavement? Yes, look, the back end's at least 50 centimetres out from

* Correct at time of going to press. Office subject to status. Past performance is no guarantee of future success.

the kerb. No, no, it's too late now, they'll have ticketed it.[1] No, no, just leave it. Look, I mean it. What good will it do having a go at the warden? Because there's a camera out there too, and if you get caught . . . No, look there, you can see it. Yes, of course I'm sure, they're everywhere . . . when you came into town, down the bypass, those speed cameras, you know, the big yellow ones, the ones you slow down for, then speed up again as soon as you've cleared the white lines (what d'you mean, you didn't know that's what they're there for? Crikey, I thought everyone did that! At least, that's what my driver tells me. Gosh, things have changed since I was a lad and had lessons in my dad's old Volvo). So how many cameras is that all together? About ten? Then the petrol station. And the shop. I'd say you've been on film practically all the way.

You see, my government is interested in people. Interested in you. Particularly you, actually.

In fact, under my government, I'm actually quite proud to say you're now living in the most closely monitored country in the world, with more CCTV cameras per head than anywhere else, including North Korea.[2] And soon the cameras will all be digitized, which makes it so-o-o-o much easier. Plus we have powers to look into your bank accounts. And tap your phone. And monitor you if you try to pay in cash.

And still people bang on about ID cards. I mean, come *on.* That's just *so* September 10th. I really, honestly, think all this civil liberties stuff is just a playground for all those namby-pamby, smart-arse, overpaid human rights lawyers (oops! Not you, Cherie!). I'm serious about this. In fact, I know you can't see me, but I'm so serious about this I've actually taken my jacket off now. What I'd say to you is simply this. You have nothing to fear unless you're a terrorist. Or obese. Or both. Or David Blunkett doesn't like you. Actually, that's quite a big list.

Look, the point is, you don't seriously think you can buy this book you're now reading and get it home without us knowing, do you?

Not that, on the face of it, that means anything too terrible. A note on your file perhaps. Another little cross on the bottom of a form somewhere.

Not that anything is actually going to happen. Well, not yet, and not that you'd notice. I wouldn't lie to you. Well, not about this. Be a shame, though, if you missed out on that promotion. Or if that mortgage application got turned down. It's not like you can do a Peter and borrow £375,000 from one of your Cabinet colleagues. But then, well . . . No, no, it's your right. Go on . . . You want to live dangerously, you go ahead.

Actually, to be honest with you (note: is this strictly necessary?), I really don't want to interfere in what you do or don't do (actually, yes I do), but you've probably already had a file opened on you by just picking the book up. They're watching all the time. Look now, yes now, look over your shoulder, the spy cam, it's staring right at ... Oops, no, no, it's turned away again. Saw you getting suspicious and spun round the other way.

Look, why not put it back on the shelf? That's right. Careful, that's it, try and hide it so they can't tell what it was.

OK, OK, calm down, you're fine, just move away. Slowly. That's it. Go on, that's right, past the Jilly Coopers. That's good ... No, no, ignore the Tom Clancys, you don't want them thinking you're into all that corporate scandal blockbuster stuff – have you down as a potential troublemaker. That's it ... No, you're safe by the Harry Potters. OK, that's good, keep walking, now pick up a newspaper ... No, not the *Mirror*, idiot, d'you want them thinking you're a leftie? That's better, go with one of those part-work collections on the bottom shelf. OK, now just stand casually in the till line and wait to pay.

Phew! Good. Made it.

And in return, we can make life a little better for you. I don't mean the mundane things like health and jobs and safe streets. Though that would be nice. I mean other things. Little things I can fix for you – oh yeah, I know people. Grand Prix tickets? Free meals in Indian restaurants? Holiday villas? Think about it.

Hang on, what the hell are you doing? You're still reading it, aren't you? Look, what are you, a bloody idiot? Put it down right now ... Yes, put it down there ... Yes, there with the reduced price stationery items, and walk away.

Honestly, the things I do to get you out of trouble.

Tony Blair, Barbados, 2004

PART I

Things can only get better?

I
In the beginning...

'It will be a government that seeks to restore trust in politics in this country'

Tony Blair, Downing Street, 2 May 1997

When Tony Blair came to power on 2 May 1997, bringing down the curtain on the pantomime of the Major government, we thought, 'That's it. What on earth are we going to do now?' As it happens, Tony Blair must have been thinking much the same thing.

For New Labour, things actually *couldn't* get any better. Getting there wasn't half the fun, it was all of it. For the rest of us, though, there was a mood of optimism, of change. Let's face it, had we woken on that morning to hear John Humphrys congratulating Michael Howard on John Major's remarkable victory, we'd probably have shot ourselves. And Michael Howard. (Though not necessarily in that order.)

Amid the heady early achievements of a national minimum wage and an independent Bank of England, Robin Cook proudly announced his intention to bring an 'ethical dimension' to Britain's foreign policy. He can now look back and reflect, 'Just me, then.' Even as Foreign Secretary, Cook was left under few illusions that the Prime Minister's office shared his enthusiasm for an ethical dimension, let alone an ethical policy itself. Seeking a sponsor for the Foreign Office's prestigious Chevening scholarships, to allow overseas students to study in Britain, Blair's office rang Cook, who was out walking. How about British Aerospace? Cook's rage drove the birds from the trees and set seismograph needles quivering in Kyoto. He had to go, and eventually he did.

But when they said 'Things Can Only Get Better', did they really have Geoff Hoon in mind? Did they exactly mean Jack Straw?

And how have we got to the point where the arrival of a socialist government in Spain and the risk of a Democrat defeating George W. Bush can fill our own Labour leader with horror? After all, Labour leaders traditionally support the Democrat candidate. But then, Labour leaders traditionally support the Labour Party.

10 DOWNING STREET
LONDON SW1A 2AA

Bill Clinton, Nelson Mandela, Noel Gallagher, Geri Halliwell, Peter Gabriel, Ross Kemp, Mick Hucknall, Paul Smith, Richard Branson, Judi Dench, Waheed Ali, Chris Evans, Sting, Damien Hirst, Greg Dyke, Stella McCartney, Patrick Stewart, Sir Ian McKellen, Sir Cameron Mackintosh, Ben Elton, Eddie Izzard

10 DOWNING STREET
LONDON SW1A 2AA

~~José María Aznar~~ (please forward)
Silvio Berlusconi
George W. Bush
Vladimir Putin
Colonel Gaddafi

Tony Blair's two Christmas card lists, 1997 and 2004

'A new dawn has broken'

Tony Blair, Royal Festival Hall, 5.15 a.m.
2 May 1997

Last year we received a series of calls. From the Deputy Prime Minister's office. He'd seen an edition of our TV show in which we'd used an archive clip from 1997 – 2 May 1997 to be precise. The news clip showed John Prescott walking up Downing Street beaming, with the sun shining and a crowd cheering and clamouring to shake his hand. Given that this event had been carefully stage-managed by the Labour Party and these were party members bussed in by head office it didn't, perhaps, represent quite the moment of spontaneous adulation John believed it did, but nevertheless, we were told that he had been looking for this particular image for years. His request was simple: could we direct him to the original source of the footage so he could make a still from it to hang in pride of place on the wall back home in Hull. A fond memory of happier times when the Deputy Prime Minister could walk down the street without feeling the overwhelming urge to punch someone.

Being a soft-hearted bunch, we duly indulged him.

Months later, I bumped into the very same John Prescott backstage at a *Frost on Sunday* programme. He wasn't expecting to see me. In fact, at

101 uses for a John Prescott
No. 57 – Long-distance coach driver

John Prescott's Brain (weekend-only version)

that moment he looked like he was going to be sick. 'Rory's just working on your script,' someone joked. 'I don't care a crap what he says,' thundered the Deputy PM, and stormed out, almost taking the door with him. 'Was that crap with two ps?' we asked, as he stomped off down the corridor. 'Aye!' he said. 'And don't forget I always have the last word!'

Mercifully this book isn't just about John. It's about what happened next.

We can now imagine what was in Prescott's mind on that May day. He'd won the cup and this was his lap of victory. And we know what was on Alastair Campbell's mind, too. A few hours before John was doing a Nobby Stiles, jigging up and down Downing Street without his teeth, Alastair was leaping out of his car to hand Blair his victory speech, only to misjudge the speed of the PM's car which promptly ran over Campbell's foot. Things weren't only getting better, they were getting bigger and beginning to hurt. But even as Labour took office, perception and fact were parting company.

The record shows that Blair's predecessor, John Major, scraped back into Downing Street in 1992 with a majority of just twenty-one before losing in 1997 to a Labour landslide. Tony Blair swept to power with a 179-seat majority, the largest in the party's history.

But, as the former Conservative leader might have said, I fear that the voting figures tell a different tale, a rather remarkable one, if I may say so. For Tony Blair's landslide was actually achieved with *fewer* votes (13.5 million) than John Major's skin-of-the-teeth victory at the previous election (14 million).[3] Indeed, were there a parliamentary version of *Wisden*,

MAJOR: It would show that in 1992 I won the *largest ever* popular vote, *ever.* Oh yes.

1992 general election

	Votes	**Share**	**Seats**
Conservative	14.09m	41.9%	336
Labour	11.56m	34.4%	271
Liberal Democrat	6.0m	17.8%	20

1997 general election

	Votes	**Share**	**Seats**
Labour	13.52m	43.2%	418
Conservative	9.60m	30.7%	165
Liberal Democrat	5.24m	16.8%	46

Note too, the Liberal Democrats polled some 750,000 fewer votes in 1997, but more than doubled their seats in Parliament. So much for proportional representation.

So, as the psephologists mumbled into their beards, the door to power swung open, and in walked Prescott and co.: a Cabinet with no experience of governing the country (unless you count Jack Cunningham, former Under Secretary for Energy, but let's not go there), their sole qualification being years spent knocking successive Conservative governments. Much like us, come to think of it, which is presumably why Jonathan Powell, Blair's chief of staff, asked us to come up with some material for Tony's speeches. (We declined.)

On entering No. 10, Margaret Thatcher famously quoted St Francis of Assisi: 'Where there is discord, may we bring harmony.' Her words, like St Francis's, were strictly for the birds. Eschewing the words of the patron saint of Assisi ('Don't they make those rather cool metal cafetières Peter has?'), we can only guess at Blair's thoughts.

Our party
Which art in government
New Labour be our name.
Our kingdom's come
My will be done
In power, as it was at conference.
Praise us this day, o *Daily Mail*
As we give out our press passes
And forgive those who use their press pass against us.
Lead us not into complacency
But deliver us a second term.
For ours is the kingdom
In power, we're Tory
For ever and ever,
Our men
(And, of course, our women).

So what sort of government would it be? The people had voted for change (or not – see above). The Establishment certainly hadn't. After eighteen years of Conservative government, they looked at Tony Blair and they thought: let's have *another* Conservative government. And Blair was determined not to let them down. 'Trust me', was his pitch, 'I may be a Labour leader, but actually you don't need to worry about all that, because really I'm on *your* side.' You have to feel sorry for the word 'Trust' here, being stretched just as hard as could be in the opposite direction. Luckily, Blair had a phrase that would paper over the cracks:

> We were elected as New Labour, we shall govern as New Labour.
>
> Royal Festival Hall, 2 May 1997

Far from removing his centre-right mask to reveal true Labour colours, he was going to keep it on. Soon we realized it wasn't a mask at all. What became striking about his premiership was that when the chips were down (tuition fees, foundation hospitals, war) he defined himself not by taking on the Right but by taking on the Labour Party.

So what did New Labour mean, back then?

As far as government spending went, it meant they would govern as Old Conservatives. Ken Clarke, the outgoing Tory Chancellor, was always fond of a joke, and one of his biggest was the Tory spending levels in the year leading up to the 1997 election. Clarke himself memorably described them as 'eye-watering tight'.[4] The spending targets were deliberately, ludicrously low, on the basis that Labour couldn't possibly undercut them and would therefore look like the old tax-and-spend Labour Party we knew and didn't vote for.

To New Labour, though, that looked like a challenge – like the card game misère, where each player seeks to declare a worse hand than the player before. As it happens, misère is Gordon Brown's middle name, and he duly trumped Ken Clarke. ('I'll see your hand and halve it!') And just to prove they could, Gordon and his press spokesman Charlie Whelan announced they'd stick to Tory spending limits for two years. ('Make it two – what the hell!')

> BROWN: In return for no jam today, we are promising you the reward of no jam tomorrow.

And so, at a time of considerable economic success, instead of turning on the taps and investing, Gordon turned them off so hard that he practically broke the thread. By 2001, Labour were still spending proportionately less on health and education than the Conservatives had (government spending in 1996/7 was 41.2 per cent of GDP; in 2000/1 it was 38.8 per cent). When Labour eventually decided to spend money, many departments had forgotten how to. In 2000/2001 they *underspent* by £6.2 billion.

The idea was to convince people (or rather, business people, those being the ones that count) that Labour could be trusted. Old Labour went along with this, presumably realizing that before you betray someone's trust you have to gain it in the first place. As it was, it was in many ways the Left's trust that was to be betrayed.

Either way, government was an act, and in Blair they had the consummate actor.

2
Labour Day

So, seven years ago, a young Labour leader, born in Bethlehem, under the star of Neil, came among us, and anointed us with his wisdom, and spoke freely to us in words we could understand, telling us that indeed things could only get better.

He was young, popular, engaging, everybody liked him – it was like Will Young before the album came out. So what happened? What went on between 1997 and 2002? Well, imagine if you condensed that whole period of Labour government into just one day. It would start, like 2 May 1997, with Blair going into Gordon Brown's office at six in the morning – you know, hit the ground running –

BLAIR: Right, come on Gordon, early start, let's get going!

To which Gordon bright and breezily replies,

BROWN: Where have you been for the last three hours?

And straight away a whole load of things are happening. Devolution.

BLAIR: Promise delivered. Sorted. National minimum wage, sorted. House of Lords reform, sort of.

Everyone's working away. John Prescott looking for an integrated transport policy, Robin Cook looking for an ethical foreign policy, Peter Mandelson looking for a flat in Notting Hill (willing to share). Over in Northern Ireland Mo Mowlam's doing the Good Friday agreement, and everything's buzzing. And then, at around 10.30, Peter Mandelson sticks his head round the door,

MANDELSON: Tony, fancy a coffee?

And he takes Tony off to Starbucks.

MANDELSON: Come on, I'll get you a Tazo Chai latte with a vanilla shot.

And Blair's amazed,

BLAIR: Gosh, we never got this under John Smith.

To which Mandy replies,

MANDELSON: Forget John Smith. From now on it's Paul Smith. Ah, yes. Coffee's the new politics. Wake up and smell the macchiato. Ask not what your country can do for you, ask for a tall skinny latte. Look, Tony, there's a whole world out there, I've met some wonderful people. Not politicians, real people. With real money. Come on, I'll take you out to lunch.

So they book a table and go off for lunch. Everyone's there: the Hinduja brothers, Lakshmi Mittal, Bernie Ecclestone, Geoffrey Robinson. Blair's eyes are wide open.

BLAIR: Gosh! You guys are just great. Wow! Is that a real Rolex Oyster?

The lunch bill comes to about £3000 at which point Blair starts to panic.

BLAIR: How are we going to pay?

But Mandy just flicks his tail and says,

MANDELSON: Don't you worry. It's all taken care of.

So Tony reels back towards Downing Street, feeling all light-headed, and when you're feeling like that nothing is too much of a problem. He wanders past the Home Office.

JACK STRAW: Tony, what are we going to do about juvenile crime?
BLAIR: Er ... Just take them off to the cashpoint machine![5]

He staggers on past the Department of Health.

ALAN MILBURN: Tony, what about health spending?
BLAIR: Put it up to the European average![6]

Then, finally back in Downing Street, Gordon Brown opens the window and shouts out,

BROWN: What about scrapping the Dome?
BLAIR: No! It's a fabulous idea! Let's have lots of fireworks! I'm going for a nap. And for God's sake don't spend any money or people will think we're Labour.

And he spends the rest of the afternoon fast asleep, only to be woken about four by a call from George Bush saying,

BUSH: Tony, we've been attacked. Can I count on your support?
BLAIR: I don't know, George, can you count?

And Bush says,

BUSH: Will you help us in the War on Terror?

But Blair is still drowsy and can't concentrate.

BLAIR: Look, just have whatever you want, George.

And he rolls over and goes back to sleep. And he has this fantastic dream where he flies across the world like an angel and all these great people appear to him. Gandhi. Mother Teresa. Jackie Milburn. He hears Nelson Mandela saying,

MANDELA: Thank you for saving Africa.

David Attenborough's saying,

ATTENBOROUGH: I don't know how the planet survived without you.

There's the Queen,

QUEEN: Arise, Sir Tony.

Then he hears Bill Clinton,

CLINTON: Arise, Sir Tony.

Which wakes him up pretty quickly.

Then John Prescott bursts in . . . well, bursts . . .

PRESCOTT: Bloody 'ell, Tony, the transport system's gridlocked, education's going backwards, the health service is in a terrible state, Byers has gone, Estelle Morris has gone, Mandy's gone twice, we've got gun crime and drug culture and terrorists and asylum seekers and top-up fees and the euro debate and the stock market's collapsed and housing's through the roof – what are we gonna do?

So he runs in to see Gordon and asks how much it will cost to put right. And Gordon says

BROWN: five hundred and eleven billion, seven hundred and thirty million, two hundred and eighty thousand pounds and thirty-eight pence.[7]

Which was the spending figure announced in Gordon Brown's spending review of July 2002. Give or take a few pence.

Five years on from those first days in office, as New Labour began its second term, a backbench MP took the opportunity of Prime Minister's Questions to ask, in light of 'unflattering or even malevolent descriptions of his motives'

> Will [the Prime Minister] provide the House with a brief characterization of the political philosophy that he espouses and which underlies his policies?
>
> Tony McWalter
> 27 February 2002

The question came from one of his own side, and was meant to give him a chance to spell out his beliefs. Maybe that was the problem.

Cut-out-and-keep instant Blair speech

Caught in a hurry and need to knock up a quick speech for TB? Then use the amazing Blair-o-lite speech writer to create the perfect address for any occasion. Cut out the ten pictures along with the text, put them in a hat, then pull them out at random and assemble them in the order they appear. Infinite possibilities. Perfect for every occasion.

I think it's important

I really do

And I'm passionate about this

Gosh

Look

It's time to move on

It's a tough choice

And all that I ask is that you trust me on this

Thanks

> First, I should thank my Honourable Friend for his question, which has evinced such sympathy in all parts of the House, about the criticism of me [*sic*]. The best example that I can give is the rebuilding of the National Health Service today under this government – extra investment. For example, there is the appointment today of Sir Magdi Yacoub to head up the fellowship scheme that will allow internationally acclaimed surgeons and consultants from around the world to work in this country. I can assure the House and the country that that extra investment in our NHS will continue under this government. Of course, it would be taken out by the Conservative Party.

It was nice, presumably, for Magdi Yacoub to know that he is now a branch of political philosophy, and the PM quickly managed to get round to announcing his new initiative and 'extra' investment (still below Conservative levels). And he got in a dig at the Tories. But another opportunity to set out what it was that he believed in had been lost.

3
1945 and All That

Prior to 1997, Labour's finest hour had been the election victory of 1945 – all the more remarkable for the fact that it followed the Second World War and removed the leader credited with winning it, Winston Churchill.

Exhausted after six years of fighting, the country might have been forgiven a desire to tread water – to have a lie in. Instead, Labour's 1945 Manifesto was bold and ambitious. From the provision of libraries and concert halls to full employment, a National Health Service and international solidarity, it sought to provide 'a high and rising standard of living, security for all against a rainy day, an educational system that will give every boy and girl a chance to develop the best that is in them'. Fine words – we still hear them from New Labour today – but no more than that, as Labour specifically said in 1945, without a plan and the will to see it through.

The public embraced their vision. Labour was elected by a genuine landslide, and set about a massive period of house building to do away with slums and tenements, industries were nationalized, and health and education were made free at the point of delivery for everyone.

All this despite rationing, despite a huge national debt, despite an infrastructure still crippled by war damage, despite the threat of further war in Russia and the Far East, despite a snowbound winter that brought the country to a standstill. They even managed to throw in the hugely popular Festival of Britain, with packed-out attractions all along the Thames. The class of 1997 managed a £750 million tent which became a national joke and closed down after a year.

But the effort proved too great and in 1951, exhausted and disillusioned, Labour was defeated and the Tories returned to Downing Street. But in those six years most of what had been demanded, and which would underpin the rest of the century's political landscape, Tory or Labour, was in place.

Amongst Blair's achievements, one of the proudest is that he has lasted longer than Attlee. An entry in the *Guinness Book of Records*, although sitting alongside the man with the largest feet, and the most eggs consumed in a minute, isn't perhaps the greatest achievement to which a politician should aspire.

The 1945 Labour Government was responsible for creating the National Health Service, the welfare state, universal education and full employment. And in their spare time, they granted independence to India and helped to form both NATO and the United Nations. By contrast, New Labour thought 'never again!', decided to transform Britain, and then said, oh no, let's go to war instead.

From Labour's 1945 Manifesto

After the ~~First~~ gulf World War, the "hard-faced men" and their political friends kept control of the Government. They controlled the banks, the mines, the big industries, largely the press and the cinema. They controlled the means by which the people got their living. They controlled the ways by which most of the people learned about the world outside.

Great economic blizzards swept the world in those years. Norman Lamont sang in the bath. John Major clung to power ~~The great inter-war slumps were not acts of God or of blind forces.~~ They were the sure and certain result of the concentration of too much economic power in the hands of too few men. These men had only learned how to act in the interest of their own bureaucratically-run private monopolies which may be likened to totalitarian oligarchies within our democratic State. They had and they felt no responsibility to the nation.

OOPS! CUT

But the new war in the East is not yet over. There are grand pickings still to be had. ~~A short boom period after the war can make a profiteer's paradise. But this will happen only if the people voted into power let the profiteers and racketeers have that freedom.~~

CUT THIS – MUST ASK GEORGE WHY UK COMPANIES CUT OUT

The Labour Party makes no ~~baseless~~ promises! The future will not be easy. It wants a reasonable ~~high and rising st~~andard of living, increased security for Heathrow ~~all against a rainy day~~, a properly costed educational system that will give every boy and girl a chance to ~~develop the best that is in them.~~

PHILIP – CAN WE INSERT LATEST INITIATIVE IN HERE?

These are the aims. In themselves they are no more than words. All parties may declare that in principle they agree with them. But the test of a political programme is whether it is sufficiently in earnest about the targets ~~objectives~~ to adopt the means needed to realise them. It is very easy to set out a list of bench marks ~~aims~~. What matters is whether it is backed up by a genuine workman-like plan based on prudent economic planning ~~conceived without regard to sectional vested interests and carried through.~~

DO WE HAVE TO KEEP GOING ON ABOUT THIS ALL THE TIME?

Point by point these national aims need analysis. Point by point it will be found that if they are to be turned into realities the nation and its ~~post-war~~ Governments will be called upon to put the nation's ~~above any sectional~~ interest, alongside ~~above any~~ free enterprise.

SUGGEST WE REPLACE THIS WITH A JOKE!

The Labour Party will ~~put the community first and the~~

sectional interests of private business after. Labour will plan from the ground up – giving an appropriate place to constructive enterprise and private endeavour in the national plan, but dealing decisively with those interests which would use high-sounding talk about economic freedom to cloak their determination to put themselves and their wishes above those of the whole nation. * WHO CAN WE NAMECHECK HERE? POTENTIAL DONORS!

~~They say,~~ "Full employment. Yes! If we can get it without interfering too much with private industry." ~~We say,~~ "Full employment ~~in any case, and if we~~ needs ~~to keep~~ a firm ~~public~~ on the public sector, not hand ~~on industry in order to get jobs for all, very well. No more dole queues, in order to let~~ the Czars of Big Business who ~~remain kings~~ bring much-needed in their own ~~castles. The price of so-called~~ 'economic freedom' ~~for the few is too high if it is bought at the cost of idleness and misery~~ for millions." CAN SOMEONE CHECK THIS AND FILL IT IN? MUST BE WRITTEN DOWN SOMEWHERE!

The Labour Party is a ~~Socialist Party, and proud of~~ it. Its ultimate purpose ~~at home~~ is ~~the establishment of the Socialist Commonwealth of Great Britain~~ – ~~free, democratic, efficient, progressive, public-spirited~~ passionate, non-interventionist, pro-business, better than the Tories, its material resources organised in the service of the British people. *

~~But~~ Forget Socialism! ~~cannot come overnight, as the product of a week-end revolution~~ Forget the ways of the past. The members of the Labour Party, like the British people, ~~are practical-minded men and women.~~ aren't interested in that

I'M SORRY – DON'T UNDERSTAND THIS BIT.

Let us remember that the great purpose of education is to

?

give us individual citizens capable of thinking for themselves.

modems internet cafes downloads

By the provision of ~~concert halls~~, ~~modern libraries~~, ~~theatres~~ and

wap technology

~~suitable civic centres~~, we desire to assure to our people full

a website

access to ~~the great heritage of culture in this nation.~~

America Spain

We must join with ~~France~~ and ~~China~~ and all others who have

finding some form of

contributed to the common victory in ~~forming an International~~

role that a modern, slimmed down UN can perform

~~Organisation capable of keeping the peace in years to come~~. All

* IS IT POSSIBLE TO SLIP SOMETHING IN HERE ABOUT

~~must work together in true comradeship to achieve continuous~~

MY ROLE AS A WORLD STATESMAN?

~~social and economic progress.~~

supported be backed up by

An internationally ~~protected~~ peace should ~~make possible a~~

increased

~~known~~ expenditure on armaments as our contribution to the

LEAVE THIS TO HOON.

protection of peace; ~~an expenditure that should diminish as the~~

~~world becomes accustomed to the prohibition of war through~~

~~an effective collective security.~~

Your

~~The~~ economic well-being ~~of each nation largely~~ depends on

us staying in power

~~world-wide prosperity~~. The essentials of this prosperity ~~for the world~~

less red tape more

~~as for individual nations~~ are ~~high production~~ and ~~progressive~~

digital technology

~~efficiency~~, coupled with steady improvement in ~~the standard of~~

disposable income holdings

~~life~~, an increase in ~~effective demand~~, and ~~fair~~ shares for all ~~who~~

~~by their effort contribute to the wealth of their community~~. We should build a new United Nations, allies in a new war on hunger, ignorance and want.

I FIND THIS LAST BIT VERY WORRYING AND SUBVERSIVE. CAN WE JUST DROP IN A FEW CELEBRITY NAMES INSTEAD?

In February 1994 Blair told a gathering of Fabians, traditionally guardians of the Labour flame, that he would offer the country

> Principle liberated from particular policy prescriptions.

Whatever that meant (though you have to admire the alliteration).

Nine years later, again at a Fabian event, he explained:

> For much of the twentieth century, left-of-centre governments have agonized over a series of false choices. To be principled and unelectable or electable but unprincipled.
>
> Address to Fabian Society 17 June 2003[8]

Luckily, Blair supplied the answer:

> New Labour are attempting to break out of that bind. We are attempting to take traditional values – equality, liberty, solidarity, democracy, justice – but find modern means to give them expression.[9]

Blair wanted to give these concepts new meaning. And to be fair he has. He's given them a completely new set. Ones we'd never even thought of. 'I have taken from my party everything they thought they believed in,' he was reported to have said. 'I have stripped them of their core beliefs. What keeps it together is success and power.'[10]

Glossary of New Labour terms

Equality Widening the gap between rich and poor[11]

Liberty Introducing ID cards and internment

Solidarity Ignoring the Labour Party at home and ignoring the United Nations abroad

Democracy Trying to fix elections in Wales and London, and avoiding elections to the House of Lords

I passionately believe in this You don't trust me, do you?

I think the people of Iraq understand why we did what we did I think the people of Iraq understand *exactly* why we did what we did

Push for peace Table a resolution authorizing war[12]

Calm tensions between India and Pakistan Sell arms to both sides[13]

Aid to Third World Become the world's biggest arms supplier to developing countries

Mass destruction, weapons of *See* Weapons of Mass Destruction

Time to move on I stopped listening five minutes ago

I respect your point of view La la la la la la la la

Forces of conservatism The *Daily Mail*

The *Daily Mail* A. A paper I passionately despise
B. A paper with a readership of several million that could win us the next election

Traditional values in a modern context John Prescott in Armani

Prudence Now don't *you* start as well

Weapons of Mass Destruction *See* Mass destruction, weapons of

Y'know No, we don't

Blair, Tony See under Bush

Legal ruling A ruling that has no bearing in law

Announcement Re-announcement

Reform Opportunity for presentation

Imminent threat The BBC

The BBC Axis of evil

Trust Hospital that is run as a business

I just think we should draw a line in the sand I just think I'm right and you're wrong

Resource unit Anything that we can get off the balance sheet

Regime change Put our guy in

Of course you have the right to disagree with me Do you really want Michael Howard in charge?

I believe I am right and will be proved right I don't care what you say, I'm going to keep saying this until you ask me another question

We are living in dangerous times John Prescott is dealing with it

101 uses for a John Prescott Landfill

I really do believe in this I really do believe in this today

Cynics Anyone who disagrees with me

> **Totality** Something that when put together as a whole contradicts what was first said

But this wasn't New Labour's only attempt at modernization.

Clause Four

1 To ~~organise and maintain in parliament and in the country a political Labour Party~~ win elections!

2 To cooperate with ~~the General Council of the Trades Union Congress~~ Bernie Ecclestone, or other~~s~~ s like him, sums to be paid in cash, by cheque, direct debit, or by regular ~~kindred organisations, in joint political or other action in harmony with the party constitution and~~ standing order~~s~~.

3 To ~~give effect as far as possible to the principles from time to time approved by the~~ keep John Prescott occupied between party conferenceS

4 To secure for the ~~workers~~ ruling class by hand or by brain the full fruits of their industry and the most equitable distribution thereof that may be possible upon the basis ~~of the common~~ that they own~~ership of~~ the means of production, distribution, and exchange, and the best ~~obtainable system of popular administration and control of each industry or service.~~ we can hope for is to strike a deal where we can

5 Generally to promote ~~the political, social and economic emancipation of the people~~ my mates, and more particularly ~~of~~ those who

aren't going to disagree, or rock the boat, or
~~depend directly upon their own exertions by hand or by brain for~~
give me a hard time
~~the means of life.~~

6 To cooperate with the labour and socialist organisations ~~in~~ *if* the *cash starts to dry up*
~~commonwealth overseas with a view to promoting the purposes~~
~~of the party~~, and to take common action for the promotion of a*n*
appropriate office for Peter Mandelson
~~higher standard of social and economic life for the working pop-~~
~~ulation of the respective countries.~~

7 To cooperate with *George Bush* ~~the labour and socialist organisations in other~~
~~countries and to support the United Nations and its various agencies and other international organisations for the promotion of peace, the adjustment and settlement of international disputes by conciliation or judicial arbitration, the establishment and defence of human rights, and the improvement of the social and economic standards and conditions of work of the people of the world.~~

4
The court of King Tony

> The problem is centralization of power in the hands of a Prime Minister and an increasingly small number of advisers who make decisions in private without proper discussion.
>
> Clare Short, 12 May 2003

Blair has gone further than any Prime Minister since Churchill in overriding advice of those outside his court. He has surpassed Margaret Thatcher in establishing his own diplomatic staff at No. 10 and promoting his own favourites, assembling a court based one-third on suffrage, and two-thirds on patronage.

FRIENDS

There's a fable, dating back a hundred years or so, that tells the story of a man who had been to market and set off back home somewhat the worse for wear after a pleasant afternoon in the alehouse.

As he staggered slowly down the road, his feet weary and blistered, the poor man spotted a patch of soft ground by the side of the path and sat for a few minutes to rest. Well, a few minutes turned into an hour or more during which he drowsed peacefully, and as he slept a pig came by and wandered over to lay down beside him. In due course the man woke up. Still under the influence, he looked at the pig alongside, wrapped his arm around it and sang songs of happy times and fine friends – to which the pig, with nothing better to do, sat happily listening.

In due course, a smart lady walked by and, spotting the man and the pig sat together by the side of the road, gave a haughty sigh and scoffed 'You can tell a man who boozes from the company he chooses'. Whereupon the pig rose slowly, looked around, and walked off.

In his first term Blair assembled around him an unprecedentedly close-knit circle of unelected confidantes and advisers. These included Cherie, Jonathan Powell (Blair's chief of staff), Alastair Campbell, Anji Hunter (his old friend and diary secretary), her successor Sally Morgan (Blair's political secretary and subsequently director of government relations), Charlie Falconer (his old flatmate), the pollster Philip Gould and Peter Mandelson. Their collective influence was such that cabinet ministers (not just Short) complained that their own access to the Prime Minister was limited and their influence on policy less than that of Tony's inner court.

Much later, in the build-up to war in Iraq, the consequence of Blair's inner-circle style of government (widened to include John Scarlett, head of the Joint Intelligence Committee), was that sceptical, independent-minded advice simply could not get through. Instead, meetings went on, decisions were made and policy was decided on the hoof between friends, often with little or no record. Jonathan Powell himself admitted to the Hutton Inquiry that, even in the midst of the unfolding crisis over the naming of David Kelly,

> about three written records for seventeen meetings a day is the sort of average you get.[17]
>
> Hutton Inquiry transcript, 18 August 2003

A career diplomat, Powell was recruited by Blair in 1995 from his job as first secretary in the Washington Embassy. He is the brother of Margaret Thatcher's principal private secretary Charles, though they have less in common than you might think. As if to prove the point, while Jonathan pronounces his surname to rhyme with 'towel', Charles pronounces his to rhyme with 'coal' (or 'dole' if you're a miner). Jonathan and his wife Sarah Helm, a former journalist, caused a stir in May 2000 when they reportedly handed their eight-week-old child to a cloakroom attendant while they dined at the Groucho Club.

Not that the Prime Minister's advisers lacked qualifications. His Middle East envoy, Michael (now Lord) Levy, came highly recommended as Tony's tennis partner and the former manager of pop acts Alvin Stardust, Dollar, Darts and Bad Manners. Blair also handpicked two senior personal diplomatic advisers in Number 10, Sir David Menning and Sir Stephen Wells.

Over the years (as with any government) some ministers fell out of favour, and either resigned or were consigned to the back benches. These outcasts now comprise a useful 'B' team, whose members doubtless hope that one day they might reclaim their places and kick out the manager. They include Robin Cook, Clare Short, Frank Dobson, Chris Smith, Nick Brown, and

Gordon Brown. Except that Gordon Brown is considered too big a player to drop, so he plays for the 'A' team but keeps in with the 'B' team as well.

A mathematical history of New Labour

First law of Labour

Tony + Cherie + Gordon + Peter = Tony + Cherie + Peter – Gordon

First law of Mandelson

Tony + Cherie + Mandy + Geoffrey + mortgage = Tony + Cherie – Mandy – Geoffrey – Charlie

Second law of Mandelson

Tony + Peter + Hindujas + Mike O'Brien = Tony – Peter – Hindujas – Mike O'Brien

Brown's universal dictum

Tony + Cherie + Peter + Gordon = Tony + Cherie + Gordon – Peter

First law of Caplin

Tony + Alastair + Cherie + Fiona + Carole + Peter F. + flats in Bristol = Tony + Cherie + flats in Bristol – Alastair – Fiona – Carole – Peter F.

First law of Cook

Robin + Margaret + Alastair = [Robin + Gaynor – Margaret] + [Tony + Alastair – Robin]

Labour law of permanency

Tony + Clare + Robin + Ron + Harriet + Mo + Harriet + Alastair + Anji + Peter + . . . = Tony – Clare – Robin – Harriet – Mo – Harriet – Alastair – Anji – Peter – . . .

Ken's law

Tony > Ken = Tony – Ken
Tony < Ken = Tony + Ken

Blair's final law

Tony + Cherie – everyone = Tony + Cherie + George + Silvio + Rupert

BLAIR AND POP STARS

Tony Blair, as he has revealed in interviews from Des O'Connor to Richard and Judy, used to be in a pop band called Ugly Rumours. From the beginning Blair liked to associate himself with the world of contemporary rock. Hence the stream of pop stars through his door in the early days in power and the strange can't-quite-believe-it expression on his face when he handed out Brit awards at the 1996 ceremony. George Michael, who has since spoken out against the war and the PM, was once a guest at the Islington residence before Blair was elected. There he was solemnly shown the Blair electric guitar, and at that moment knew there might be an ego problem about to burst on the country. Likewise, Led Zeppelin were fêted by the PM in his early days. A few years later, Robert Plant publicly attacked Blair over plans to close down a local hospital in Kidderminster, and Blair took the trouble to reply personally.

> Dear Robert,
> I am certainly a Led Zeppelin fan,

he wrote, before dealing with an invitation to visit Kidderminster, enthusing,

> I would be delighted to come if my diary allows it, and my diary secretary will be in touch if we can arrange something. I can't tell you how many memories of you I have.

(Hey, I'm one of you guys – let's not let a little thing like closing a hospital come between us!)

Pop stars were welcome in the Blair court in the early days. All part of Cool Britannia. Oasis, Mick Hucknall, that kind of thing. By the gala dinner of 2002 he was down to Lesley Garrett and Petula Clark. In 2003 he holidayed in Barbados with Cliff Richard, though this may have been because both the Pope and the Archbishop had given him a hard time about the war, and Tony needed to talk to someone who had a more direct line to the Almighty. He's always had a personalized view of God, has Tony. When Cardinal Hume advised him that as a Protestant he couldn't attend Catholic mass regularly with Cherie, Blair's response was, 'I wonder what Jesus would've made of that.'[18]

BLAIR-FACED LAWYERS

Shortly after Blair's victory his good friend Charlie Falconer held a birthday party at the Middle Temple. There was much laughter and ribaldry among a group of people who had once been students together and were now running the country. It was as if they themselves couldn't believe it and found the whole thing a complete joke.

Lawyer, lawyer

Among those trained at the bar are Blair, Geoff Hoon, Jack Straw, Derry Irvine, and Charlie (Lord) Falconer. Add to this, Lord Goldsmith, the Attorney General, and Harriet Harman, Solicitor-General, and, of course, at night there is always lawyer Cherie to run through the case notes again.

Law is inbred in Blair. His father, Leo, was a lawyer, and his little-mentioned elder brother, William (Bill) Blair, QC, is a part-time judge and professor of law specializing in business law, international law, and conflicts of law (now that could be useful). Bill was appointed head of the highly influential Commercial Bar Association in 2004, and no doubt can fill in for those nights when Cherie is out at a Bar Council function and Tony wants someone to run through the finer points of case law.

Lord Derry Irvine

Former Lord Chancellor. Came to public attention after £600,000 of public money was spent tarting up his Westminster pad. With £59,000 spent on the £350-a-roll wallpaper alone, and much talk of his famous four-poster bed, the knee-breeches-wearing, wine-loving, frock-coated peer was a perfect advert for New Labour's go-ahead look which sought to shed itself of charges of waste, pomposity, and fuddy-duddyism. Irvine acted as general counsel to the PM and wrote the 1997 manifesto in his chambers with David Miliband, son of Ralph Miliband, founder of *New Left Review*. Both Blairs are former pupils of Derry, and met in his chambers.

Charles Falconer

Childhood friend and former flatmate of Blair. Fellow lawyer. Failed to win selection as a Labour Party candidate when his refusal to withdraw his children from private school irked Labour supporters. Blair wanted him in government, so made him a lord in 1997, thereby getting around any electoral objections. Married to Marianna Hildyard, another successful barrister whose diplomat father had been British ambassador to Mexico.

Silvio, Tessa, David, and Barbara

Should Silvio Berlusconi want to move into the British TV market he would have to get the approval of Tessa Jowell, Secretary for Culture, Media and Sport (Berlusconi's favourite things). But should the Italian PM want formal legal advice, he would have to find a lawyer, such as (for example) Ms Jowell's husband, David Mills, who has acted as Berlusconi's offshore adviser for over twenty years. Naturally, the Italian premier might want to take further advice. For that, he could try David's sister, the formidable Barbara Mills, herself the former Director of Public Prosecutions.[19]

Tessa, David, Bernie, and Tony

Soon after Blair came to power in 1997 a scandal broke out over a £1 million donation made to the Labour Party by motor-racing supremo, Bernie Ecclestone. That Labour should take funds from a controversial figure raised eyebrows, but a little more detective work revealed a more alarming PR problem. Blair had met Ecclestone while in opposition, and had been his guest, along with his family, at Silverstone, watching the Grand Prix and posing for the cameras in a racing car.

With a promise to ban tobacco advertising in the Labour manifesto, Ecclestone visited the freshly elected PM. The day after the meeting between Blair and Ecclestone – both having no doubt confined their conversation to the relative fuel compression ratios of the Ferrari and the McLaren – Health Secretary Tessa Jowell received a note from the Prime Minister's office informing her that motor racing was to be exempted from the tobacco ban.

Doubtless this put Ms Jowell in a tricky position, and she would surely have sought advice. We obviously don't know if she spoke to her husband David Mills. If she did, she could have made an awkward situation even worse. For when he wasn't advising Berlusconi, Mr Mills had been a director of the Benetton Formula One racing team and also their legal advisor. There has never been a suggestion of any impropriety, but by unfortunate connections such as these, the press was given a chance to question the new government's squeaky-cleanness, and in turn, the public perception of potential conflicts of interest that had dogged the Tories now began to land at Labour's door.

Blair naturally protested his innocence, pointing out he had written to the chairman of the Committee on Standards in Public Life about the donation. Although the letter had only been written after the press took an interest in the matter.

Either through guilt or outraged innocence, Labour quickly repaid the money to a grateful Bernie Ecclestone; a decision not made easier by the fact that Labour had already spent heavily to get elected and had little left in the coffers to reimburse anyone for 'faulty goods'. While an apology of sorts was made (albeit for the PR failure, not for the ethics), tobacco advertising remained in motor racing. Ecclestone got his wish *and* his money back – a great deal even by his standards, and certainly no advert for Labour's business acumen.

But the lawyers would come into their own over the war in Iraq. In the Spring of 2003 Katherine Gunn, a translator at the GCHQ listening centre, came across an email from the American government asking allied intelligence agencies – that means us – to increase surveillance of UN Security Council members, so that the US could gain leverage in persuading wavering countries to back the war. Even Kofi Annan's conversations were allegedly recorded (the one with Clare Short should be prescribed to insomniacs).

UN sources shrugged their shoulders and claimed their New York headquarters is so riddled with bugs that the only safe place to hold a meeting was in the noisy basement coffee shop. So now you know why every time you talk to Kofi Annan he does a passable impression of a cappuccino machine.

Back home, Gunn was detained and charged under the Official Secrets Act, the government refusing her the right to brief her own defence team for fear that this too would breach the Act. Then, at the eleventh hour, with court proceedings due to start the following day, the government dropped all charges. No explanation, no apology, just a statement blaming the risks posed by a potentially over-liberal jury.

If the case had gone ahead, Gunn's team could have applied to the courts for disclosure of the Attorney General's written advice to Tony Blair on the legality of the conflict.

In the end it seems that, as far as the government was concerned, the legal case was strong enough to go to war, but not strong enough to go to court.

And while it's true that Lord Goldsmith did publish a brief summary of his findings in 2003, ever since he has steadfastly refused to publish the full opinion on which it was based.

5
What happened next

Prisons

> I find it morally unacceptable for the private sector to undertake the incarceration of those whom the state has decided need to be imprisoned.
>
> Jack Straw,
> 1996

> The private sector has played and will continue to play a significant role in the delivery of high-quality correctional services.
>
> Paul Boateng,
> 2001

Schools

> Watch my lips – no selection, either by examination or interview, under a Labour Government.
>
> David Blunkett,
> Labour Party conference, 1995

He later said that this was a joke.[191]

> I'm not hunting grammar schools. I'm desperately trying to avoid the whole debate in education concentrating on the issue of selection when it should be concentrating on the raising of standards. Arguments about selection are a past agenda.
>
> David Blunkett,
> *Daily Telegraph*, 2000

Grammar schools still select pupils, whose numbers have increased considerably, while the new specialist schools can select up to 10 per cent of their pupils. Blair's own children were admitted to Oratory by selection.

Higher Education

> Labour has no plans to introduce tuition fees for higher education.
>
> Tony Blair,
> April 1997

In fact, tuition fees were first introduced later that year. In January 2004, after intense pressure from the whips, Labour managed to get its controversial education bill, which includes provision for universities to charge top-up fees, through the Commons. With total student debt standing at some £14.5 billion, the bill was passed in July 2004.

Human Rights

> The [Human Rights] Bill marks a major step forward . . . it will enhance the awareness of human rights in our society. And it stands alongside our decision to put the promotion of human rights at the forefront of our foreign policy.
>
> Tony Blair,
> Human Rights Bill White Paper, October 1997

In 2003, appearing on the BBC's *Breakfast with Frost* programme, Blair responded to questions about the current perceived crisis in asylum and immigration, by suggesting that

> If [the current] measures don't work, then we will have to consider further measures, including fundamentally looking at the obligations we have under the Convention of Human Rights . . . the problem with removing people is that under the obligations we have you cannot remove someone to a country where they might be subject to torture.

Foreign Policy

And having set the no 'soft touch' tone, Tone continued to walk the walk, notching up five wars in five years: in Iraq, Kosovo, Afghanistan, Sierra Leone and Iraq (again).

All this, having previously declared at the NATO–Russia summit in Paris in May 1997 that

> Mine is the first generation able to contemplate the possibility that we may live our entire lives without going to war or sending our children to war. That is a prize beyond value.

It's remarkable that Blair's appetite for war seems to have outstripped even that of the army. In April 2003 Sir Michael Boyce, chief of defence staff, warned the Prime Minister, 'If you asked us to go into a large-scale operation in 2004 we couldn't do it without serious pain. We must allow ourselves time to draw breath.'

Under New Labour, the British Army was said to be strung out across the world like a line of washing. This isn't quite true. They're strung out across the world like a line of washing *without any pegs*.

But we do have music.

See the world

In 2004 Britain had an active military presence in Germany, Kuwait, Iraq, Afghanistan, Cyprus, the Congo, Ethiopia, Kosovo, Eritrea, Georgia, Bosnia, Saudi Arabia, Kenya, the Falkland Islands, Gibraltar, Belize, Brunei, Northern Ireland, Sierra Leone, Macedonia and the Ascension Islands.

And the largest? Germany with 22,500, compared with 13,500 in Northern Ireland and 7500 in Iraq. Rather like relatives at Christmas, it seems the British army is rather too slow to leave once it's been invited in. Of course, the German operation is partly explained by the fact that the Germans, as part of the Second World War settlement, pay for the privilege of having us there. And it's a lot cheaper to get someone else to feed, water and pay for the troops if you can. Which is what the Iraqis could end up doing when their oil revenue starts to flow again.

But before everything starts to sound rather bleak, there is one little thing that might put some cheer on your face. As well as all their other duties, our hard-pressed armed forces provide one of the few sources of employment for musicians in the country. Apart from tribute bands. As well as walking the streets, keeping the peace, refereeing civil wars and a million and one other jobs, at the last count, the army found work for nearly 1200 musicians in thirty bands. Funny to think that the place you are most likely to spot a 'Keep Music Live' sticker is on the back of an army personnel carrier in the middle of a war zone.

Household Cavalry	70 musicians	2 bands
Grenadier Guards	49 musicians	1 band

Coldstream Guards	49 musicians	1 band
Scots Guards	49 musicians	1 band
Welsh Guards	49 musicians	1 band
Irish Guards	49 musicians	1 band
Royal Artillery	49 musicians	1 band
Royal Engineers	35 musicians	1 band
Royal Signals	35 musicians	1 band
Royal Logistic Corps	35 musicians	1 band
REME	35 musicians	1 band
Adjutant General's Corps	35 musicians	1 band
Army Air Corps	35 musicians	1 band
Royal Armoured Corps	140 musicians	4 bands
Scottish Division	70 musicians	2 bands
Queen's Division	70 musicians	2 bands
King's Division	70 musicians	2 bands
Prince of Wales's Division	70 musicians	2 bands
Light Division	49 musicians	1 band
Parachute Regiment	35 musicians	1 band
Royal Irish Regiment	35 musicians	1 band
Royal Gurkha Rifles	35 musicians	1 band

Having achieved victory at the polls, Blair dominated his party and his government like few others before him, a style of leadership described in 1997 as 'Napoleonic'. Those (like Mandelson) who have complained that Blair's critics go for the man and not the ball missed the point: this is a man who will not pass the ball. Time and time again in his conference speeches he has personalized government, spoken of the scars on *his* back. By 2000, he had successfully reduced the whole government, the whole Labour movement, to a reflection of his personality – what he called his 'irreducible core'.

By the eve of the war in Iraq, his identification of the national interest with his own beliefs had hardened. The judgement was made not on facts and evidence, but on what he believed ('I may be wrong about this, but it's what I believe' he told Jeremy Paxman). It had become a faith-based Premiership.

But the country needed him. Who else was there? Young(ish), without any previous, fit(ish), without any major noticeable tics or annoying mannerisms (they would come later), and with the huge grin of the confident alpha male.

And what he lacked in specifics he has certainly made up for in passion.

The passion of Blair

I am . . . *passionately* committed to the idea that education must be available throughout people's lives.

Ruskin School, December 1996

I *passionately* believe in the equal worth of every individual. I hate the squalor and idleness that shames our rich societies.

Guardian/Nexus conference, March 1997

I am in politics because I believe *passionately* in Britain, and I believe *passionately* in education as the key to the success of an individual and of a nation.

Morpeth School, Tower Hamlets, August 1997

I reflect on the sheer waste of children taught to hate when I believe *passionately* children should be taught to think.

Irish Parliament, November 1998

I believe *passionately* that we will all benefit hugely from a thriving Russia making use of its immense natural resources, its huge internal market, and its talented and well-educated people.

Economic Club of Chicago, April 1999

I really *passionately* hope that whatever has happened in the past we are able, Britain and Argentina, to work together, not just as two countries, but internationally with other countries to solve the problems that confront us all.

Press conference with Argentine prime minister, August 2001

Because we believe in our values of justice, tolerance, and respect for all regardless of race, religion, or creed just as *passionately* as they believe in fanatical hatred of Jews, Christians, and any Moslems who don't share their perverse view of Islam.

Welsh Assembly, October 2001

We are emerging from a long period in which Tory values held sway: elitism, selfish individualism, the belief that there is no such thing as society and its international equivalent, insularity and isolationism, which led Britain to turn its back on Europe and the world. I *passionately*, profoundly, reject these values.

March 2002

We believe *passionately* in giving people the chance to get off benefit and into work.

June 2002

I buy completely into the notion – because I believe that *passionately* – that it is the low-level antisocial crime that you have to deal with in order, in fact, to be able to deal with the high-level organized crime as well.

Press conference with Rudy Giuliani, February 2002

Africa and the environment. I believe *passionately* that these issues, combined with those to do with terrorism and WMD, are the critical challenges confronting today's world.

Mozambique, September 2002

The thing I would say *passionately* to people in the Arab world today is, you don't have to choose between dealing with the threat that Iraq poses with weapons of mass destruction and dealing with the question of the Palestinians and the Middle East peace process, we should actually be dealing with both issues, we should be strong against international terrorism, strong against weapons of mass destruction, and equally strong in making sure there is justice, based on the two-state solution, for people in the Middle East.

Press conference with president of Syria, December 2002

I *passionately* believe if we don't ensure Saddam disarms, if we don't stand up for the authority of the UN, the result will not be peace but more bloodshed and devastation – not just for the people of Iraq but, in the longer term, for those in neighbouring countries and the wider world including this country.

Sunday Herald, March 2003

My *passionate* belief in Europe is not born of any diminishing of my belief in Britain ... And in the past months, there has been division between Europe and the United States. There's no disguising it. And even for those of us who have supported the United States and believe *passionately* in that support, it has divided our nations.

Warsaw, May 2003

> Take either [the European or the transatlantic alliance] away and I believe *passionately* Britain is weaker for it.
>
> Guildhall, 11 November 2003
>
> I believe *passionately* that the progressive cause is the best to lead our country and our world at this time.
>
> The Big Conversation, in Newport, Wales, November 2003
>
> I feel so *passionately* that we are in mortal danger of mistaking the nature of the new world in which we live.
>
> Sedgefield, March 2004

How passionate can one man be? If this was a Jilly Cooper novel he'd have burst out of his riding breeches and squired every lady in the local hunt, and all before page three.

Yet, curiously, in policy terms, that passion did not manifest itself in idealism but in pragmatism. Idealism was reserved for speeches and manifestos, where his rhetoric would carry him away: Blair the campaign socialist.

It was as if he was trying to convince himself, and having done that, convince us. Winning impossible arguments on passion alone became a challenge, a hobby. By the time of Iraq, such was his self-belief that he felt confident history would forgive him: history for Blair not being something in the past, but something in the future which will judge him favourably.

> It's not a day for sort of soundbites, really. We can leave those at home. But . . . I feel the hand of history upon our shoulder . . . I really do.[20]
>
> Tony Blair on the Northern Ireland Peace Process, 7 April 1998

The actor and lawyer in him revelled in taking on difficult briefs: selling the new clause four, foundation hospitals, tuition fees. And when George W. Bush turned up, looking for a top lawyer to prosecute his case for war, he found a willing advocate in Blair.

PART II
Drawing a line

I think what this does now is allow us to draw a line and move on.

Tony Blair, following publication of the Hutton Report[21]

Right, but before we do . . .

Invitation

The President of the United States of America invites

TONY BLAIR

to a pre-emptive strike against Iraq

Bring an Army

Carriages 2035

6
Bush Cassidy and the Sundance Kid

WHEN BUSH COMES TO SHOVE

On 11 September 2001 Tony Blair was due to address the Trades Union Congress at Brighton. It was to be a keynote speech, the first salvo in the battle to reform the public services which was to define his second term.

The speech was never delivered. Neither was the reform of public services (but more of that later).

At 1.46 BST that afternoon, the first hijacked plane smashed into the North Tower of the World Trade Center in New York.

Almost two years later, on 17 July 2003, the Prime Minister boarded a flight from Washington to Japan with the applause of the US Congress still ringing in his ears. He had received an unprecedented seventeen standing ovations and, it was reported, eighteen 'applause breaks'. He must have wondered how his critics back home were going to come back at him after a success like that.

And his performance in Washington that night was one of his finest. On the podium, Blair responded to his warm welcome by gushing,

> That's more than I deserve and more than I'm used to, quite frankly.

There were cheers and there was laughter.

Having apologized for the British burning the books of the Library of Congress (in 1814), he went on to claim that history would forgive him for invading Iraq, before building to a conclusion some forty minutes later with a rousing celebration:

> Members of Congress, don't ever apologize for your values. Tell the world why you're proud of America. Tell them, when the 'Star-Spangled Banner' starts, Americans get to their feet – Hispanics, Irish, Italians, Central Europeans, East Europeans, Jews, Muslims, white, Asian, black. Those who go back to the early settlers and those whose English is the same as some New York cab drivers I've dealt with, but whose sons and daughters could run for this Congress.
>
> Tell them why Americans, one and all, stand upright and respectful. Not because some state official told them to, but because whatever race, colour, class or creed they are, being American means being free.

Twelve hours later, now halfway across the Pacific, the plane was hit by severe turbulence. Not from outside, but from within. News had come that David Kelly, the weapons inspector outed by the government as the source for a report critical of the government's claims about Saddam's WMD, had been found dead.

Between those two dramatic events, Tony Blair embarked on an adventure that was to divide Europe, the world, and the Labour Party, and shake his government to its foundations. Some eighteen months after September 11th, a coalition of three countries – the United States, Britain, and Australia – more if you include the Marshall Islands and Micronesia, as did Colin Powell[22] – was involved in a full-scale invasion of Iraq. For the first time, journalists spent the war embedded with front-line troops, and the British Prime Minister spent the war embedded in the president.

Once the decision to invade Iraq had been taken, nothing – not Hans Blix, not the UN, not international opinion – was going to stop it. On the eve of war, the former Foreign Secretary, Robin Cook, resigned from the Cabinet, saying,

> Only a year ago, we and the United States were part of a coalition against terrorism that was wider and more diverse than I would ever have imagined possible. History will be astonished at the diplomatic miscalculations that led so quickly to the disintegration of that powerful coalition ... Tonight the international partnerships most important to us are weakened: the European Union is divided; the Security Council is in stalemate. Those are heavy casualties of a war in which a shot has yet to be fired.[23]

It was worse than even he thought. As mentioned earlier, such was the desperation to get a second UN Security Council resolution authorizing war that council members and even the Secretary-General, Kofi Annan, had their conversations bugged.[24] Voting members felt the full weight of diplomatic pressure to back Bush. Doubtless they were reminded that Yemen's 1990 decision not to support Resolution 678 (authorizing the previous Gulf War) cost it at least US$70 million in US aid. 'The most expensive "no" vote you ever cast', as an American diplomat put it.[25]

Having invested his faith in the United Nations, Blair then told Jeremy Paxman that if the Security Council vetoed war he'd regard such a veto as unreasonable and go to war anyway.

All this was a far cry from the Blair who had declared in his 1997 manifesto that:

> Labour wants Britain to be respected in the world for the integrity with which it conducts its foreign relations.

Having exhausted its supply of Ferrero Rochers ('Mr Ambassador, with these strong-arm tactics you are spoiling us!'), Britain acknowledged it wasn't going to get a second UN resolution and resorted to the legal profession in this country.

Fearing the legal implications of an illegal war, Britain's chief of defence staff, Admiral Sir Michael Boyce, had been seeking clarification. The British government had serious trouble getting it. Elizabeth Wilmhurst, senior legal adviser at the Foreign Office, resigned. It was clear that most legal opinion was either dubious or against a war. The Americans had little time for this. 'Get another lawyer', they said; and, sure enough, round the back of the LSE the government found Christopher Greenwood, Professor of International Law who, in a masterpiece of creative interpretation, knitted together the previous UN resolutions into a fig leaf big enough to hide the embarrassment of the Attorney General, Lord Goldsmith.[26]

For Bush and Blair, the necessity for the Mother of All Wars was the Mother of All Inventions. Blair's government ran through reasons for war like a man falling through a tree, desperately grabbing on to new branches as the previous one gave way. In the end they went for weapons of mass destruction, which sounded good, and for which you could find some pretty scary and persuasive evidence if you knew which PhD thesis to copy, which bits of evidence could be stretched to fit, and who could spice it all up into a dossier. And if you had a compliant head of the Joint Intelligence Committee.

So how did Blair get to this position? How did the all-things-to-all-men populist of the 1990s become the resolute ally of George W. Bush?

To put a new spin on an old phrase, some are born with convictions, some acquire convictions, and some have convictions thrust upon them.

In this case, the convictions were George Bush's. He has a number of them (including one for drink-driving in 1976, but more of that later.) Post-September 11th, Blair embraced Bush's Manichaean belief in good versus evil and signed up to it with religious fervour. But such were his powers of self-belief that he thought he could persuade Bush to do things by the book and go through the UN.

BLAIR: Look, George, it would help a lot if you could at least look as if you give a flying fuck about the United Nations.

Blair would then win round the UN and Europe. He was to be the bridge between George Bush and the rest of the Western allies. And to be fair, in this he was totally successful. George Bush walked over him.

A very special relationship

One of the striking features of the special relationship is that, for Tony Blair, it illustrates two of his greatest qualities: courage and humility. In this case, the courage to stand up to the Bush administration and tell them what he wants, and the humility to accept that he won't get it.

Maybe it was simply that the whole Iraq business brought out the lawyer in him. What's more, Blair has that quality, essential to both barristers and compulsive liars, of absolutely believing in the truth of everything he says at any particular time. Thus

BLAIR: Look, black is white.

In Blair's world becomes:

BLAIR: No, look, hang on, I may be wrong about this, but what I'm saying to you is that, at the time I said that, on the basis of the intelligence available to me, I honestly believed that black was white.

An election problem

If Tony Blair is always right and we are usually wrong – unless we agree with him, when, by definition, we are right as well – this causes a dilemma for the Prime Minister. What if he were to call an election at the wrong time in our cycle, at a time when our judgement couldn't be trusted? What then?

The answer is that in addition to deciding the timing of an election, Tony Blair must also find a mechanism to decide the result.

This special relationship with the truth is characteristic of the British PM.

The crazy, mixed-up world of Tony Blair

Some time back, in a moment of endearing honesty, tear in his eye, onion up his sleeve, Blair reminisced with one reporter as to how as a teenager he would sit behind the goal at St James's Park in Newcastle and watch Jackie Milburn play – forgetting that Milburn had retired from the game when the keen-to-impress PM was aged just four, and that seats didn't appear till much later.

Blair's teenage years must have been an unusual time. In December 1996 he told Des O'Connor (there he goes again with the heavyweight hitters) in a searching political interrogation that as a fourteen-year-old he had run away to Newcastle airport and boarded a plane for the Bahamas: 'I snuck on to the plane, and we were literally about to take off when the stewardess came up to me ...' he confessed. Leaving to one side the obvious question of how he was able to do this without a boarding card or passport, what surprised many people, including his own father who first raised the point, was the fact that there has never been a flight from Newcastle to the Bahamas. Even more alarming, though, was that this wasn't said around the dinner table in an attempt to impress a few supper guests, but on national television with millions watching and his words consigned to tape.

A few years later, in another moment of candour Downing Street confirmed the story of how when he first came to London, on his gap year, he lived rough for a while, and therefore knows just how it feels to be down and out in a big city. Maybe it's just long-term memory playing tricks. We all get things wrong. But that wouldn't explain another strange porky in which Blair cast himself as the hero as he dived into the sea while on a family holiday in the Seychelles, and rescued a man from drowning. The story made the headlines again. Blair modestly declined to speak about it – as, too, did the swimmer, who remained something of a mystery until eventually tracked down a few days later, only to confess to being a little bemused, pointing out that he hadn't been drowning and the PM certainly hadn't rescued him.

7
The new world order

(AMERICA FIRST, REST LAST)

> Creative destruction is our middle name. We do it automatically, and that is precisely why the tyrants hate us, and are driven to attack us.
>
> Michael Ledeen, neo-conservative academic[29]

On 11 September 2001, a group of determined fanatics succeeded in hijacking four airliners and crashing them into the Twin Towers and the Pentagon. Minutes after the third plane hit the Pentagon, George Bush launched his own attack, calling Dick Cheney and announcing, 'We're at war.'[30] He didn't know who with. But there were others in his administration who had a pretty clear idea. It was one they'd held for years.

The nineteen terrorists were not the only hijackers at work that day. For September 11th also saw the hijacking of American foreign policy by an equally determined group of fanatics with a fundamentalist agenda. What's more, they held key positions in the Bush administration. They *were* the administration.

Their masterstroke was to link al-Qaeda to Saddam Hussein when the two had no proven connection. (The pair were like Nancy Dell'Ollio and Ulrika Jonsson. They can't stand each other; they just like fucking the same bloke.) But at one time 70 per cent of Americans polled believed Saddam Hussein was behind September 11th. By June 2004, that figure had shrunk to 40 per cent.

THE LEAGUE OF EXTRAORDINARY GENTLEMEN

In January 1998, a group of individuals, under the auspices of the Project for the New American Century, wrote to the then president, the then Bill

Clinton, saying that if Saddam acquired the capability to deliver weapons of mass destruction:

> The safety of American troops in the region, friends and allies like *Israel*, and the moderate Arab states, and a significant portion of the world's supply of *Oil* [oops!] will all be put at hazard.[31]
>
> (Our emphasis. Though, to be fair, it was their emphasis as well.)

No mention of terrorists, of course; that came later. They then went on to announce:

> Removing Saddam Hussein and his regime from power needs to become the aim of American foreign policy. A policy, which cannot continue to be crippled by a misguided insistence on unanimity in the United Nations Security Council.

Note how they'd already anticipated that the UN, being the ultimate authority on world opinion, might be something of a problem.

So the impulse to go after Iraq in 1998 wasn't about terrorism, it wasn't about humanitarian concerns, it was:

> What do we want? Saddam out. When do we want it? Now!

Fair enough, we know Saddam was a brutal dictator. We'd known it for years – in fact for all those years when he'd been our kind of brutal dictator.

But as William Kristol, director of the Project said,

> The mission begins in Baghdad, but it does not end there . . . it is so clearly about more than Iraq. It is about more even than the future of the Middle East and the war on terror. It is about what sort of role the US intends to play in the twenty-first century.
>
> William Kristol, neo-conservative academic[27]

The strategy had been in development for thirty years. First under Kissinger, then under Donald Rumsfeld and Dick Cheney and a bunch of other neo-conservatives itching for the main chance. Cheney had co-ordinated a similarly hawkish briefing group for George Bush senior on 21 May 1990. Advisers included Paul Wolfowitz, whose 1992 policy statement 'Defense Planning Guidance' argued that the number one objective of American post-Cold War political and military strategy should be to prevent the emergence of a rival superpower.[32]

The 1998 letter was signed by prominent members of the Project – a collection of academics, writers, businessmen, and politicians. Donald Rumseld, Paul Wolfowitz, Richard Perle, William Schneider, were all there. All in all, eighteen people signed, including seven with interests in arms, or oil, or arms and oil, as well as Elliot Abrams, a convicted liar. And they succeeded in making the removal of Saddam an objective of American foreign policy, as declared in the Iraq Liberation Act of 1998.

Then in September 2000, the Project published a new report, 'Rebuilding America's Defenses'. It said:

> At present the United States faces no global rival. America's grand strategy should aim to preserve and extend this advantageous position as far into the future as possible.[33]

But it didn't end there. By the time September 11th happened, this group, and its disciples, gathered within a few blocks of each other in Washington, had come to dominate the Bush administration. Far from being a bunch of wacky fantasists on the fringe of things, these people were now a bunch of wacky fantasists dictating policy – everything from a US$48 billion increase in defence spending to the development of small battlefield nuclear weapons.

Rumsfeld, Wolfowitz, Perle, and Schneider had become, respectively, Defense Secretary, Deputy Defense Secretary, chairman of the Defense Policy Board, and chairman of the Defense Science Board.

Lewis Libby, another leading neo-con, was now Dick Cheney's chief of staff, and Elliot Abrams was special assistant to George Bush on the Middle East (having been convicted of withholding information during the Iran Contra scandal but pardoned by George Bush senior).

Donald Kagan, Sterling professor of classics and history at Yale, was a former co-chairman of the Project and a key member of its inner circle. How does he describe the American foreign policy they were hoping to shape? With a reference to Tacitus? A historical insight, a gem of ancient Greek philosophy? No, writing in the *Atlanta Journal and Constitution* in September 2002, he chose a slightly more direct approach and spelt it out thus:

> You saw the movie *High Noon*. Well, we're Gary Cooper.
>
> Donald Kagan, neo-conservative academic[28]

The group had support in the Pentagon and the White House. More than that: they were now *running* the Pentagon and the White House.

They had the means, the motive, and the opportunity to put their plan ('world domination' for short) into action. But they lacked one thing: the public appetite to support their aims. Winning the public round would take time, they explicitly acknowledged:

> The process is likely to be a long one, without some catastrophic and catalysing event – like a new Pearl Harbor.[34]

On September 11th 2001, it happened. For Jo Moore back in England, it was an opportunity to bury bad news. For Rumsfeld, Wolfowitz, and Cheney, it was Christmas Day. As the *New Yorker* later reported, Condoleezza Rice called together senior staff at the National Security Council and asked them to think about 'how you capitalize on these opportunities [*sic*].'[35]

Given that the September 11th hijackers were from Saudi Arabia, trained in Afghanistan, and planned their operations in America and Germany, it was obvious where the blame lay: Iraq. It didn't matter that there wasn't a connection between Iraq and September 11th. With the wind behind them, they'd find one.

When Bush's counter-terrorism czar Richard Clarke pointed out that Osama Bin Laden and al-Qaeda were the most likely culprits and they were based in Afghanistan, Defense Secretary Donald Rumsfeld, with his characteristic grasp of the essentials, said that '. . . there were no decent targets in Afghanistan and [they] should consider bombing Iraq.'[36]

They may not have been decent targets, but they were easy ones. And on 7 October 2001 the US-led coalition launched their attack on Afghanistan. The Americans knew Osama Bin Laden had used bases in that country to train al-Qaeda terrorists. They knew, because the CIA had originally helped build some of those bases, including one at Khost (or was that at cost?).[37] This was back in the good old days when Bin Laden was America's best general, leading the 'Arab Afghans' in their resistance against the Russians.

When Saddam originally invaded Kuwait, Bin Laden, a sworn enemy of Saddam, offered his sizeable guerrilla army to his native Saudi Arabia to fight the Iraqi invader. The Saudis rejected him and sent for the cavalry, in the shape of the US Army. Bin Laden never forgave this slight, and ten years later took his revenge on the Americans for their infidel presence in Saudi Arabia.

And so the 'coalition' attacked Afghanistan first. Rude not to, considering that's where al-Qaeda trained, and the Taliban had been causing a problem with their ruthless fundamentalist Islamic regime and their

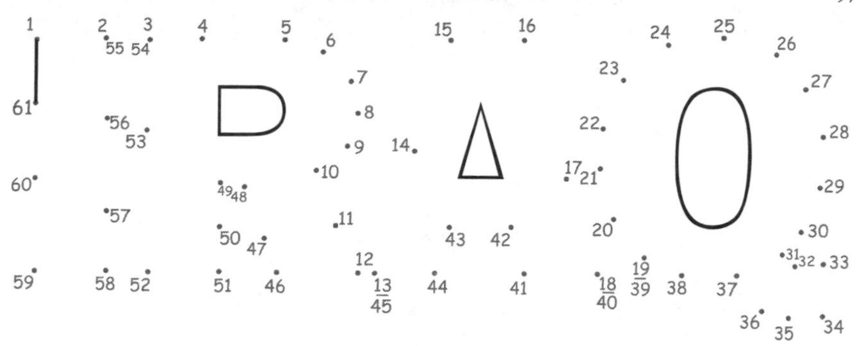

Join up the dots

Pin it on Saddam

reluctance to play ball with the Americans over building an oil pipeline. Not that this influenced the Americans. Having installed as president Hamid Karzai, who worked for the Californian oil company Unocal, and, as US special envoy Zalmay Khalilzad, who also worked for Unocal and shared with Karzai an interest in constructing a pipeline from Turkmenistan to Pakistan via Afghanistan – the Americans moved on. But not before Tony Blair had promised, 'We will not walk away.' Which they didn't. They ran. They had bigger fish to fry . . .

8
Iraq II: This time it's personal

A flag, a Constitution, and a National Assembly
Each one a distortion of the true meaning
Names of which we have only utterance
But as to their true meaning we remain in ignorance
He who reads the Constitution will learn
that it is composed according to the Mandate
He who looks at the flapping banner will find
that it is billowing in the glory of aliens
He who sees our Assembly will know
that it is constituted by and for the interests of any but the electors
He who enters the Ministries will find
that they are shackled with the chains of foreign advisors

Ma'ruf al-Rasafi
Written during the British mandate of the 1920s

Iraq was always going to be tougher. The Americans even admitted it themselves.

> I think if we had [finished off Saddam in 1991] that we would have been bogged down there for a very long period of time with the real possibility we might not have succeeded . . . it would have needed a very large force for a long time in Iraq to run him to ground, and then you've got to worry about what comes after. You're gonna take a lot more casualties if you're gonna muck around in Iraq for weeks on end trying to run Saddam to ground and capture Baghdad and so forth and I don't think it would have been worth it.

The worries were quite specific:

'If you're going to go in and try to topple Saddam Hussein, you have to go to Baghdad. Once you've got Baghdad, it's not clear what you do with it. It's not clear what kind of government you would put in place of the one that's currently there. Is it going to be a Shia regime, a Sunni regime or a Kurdish regime? Or one that tilts toward the Baathists, or one that tilts toward the Islamic fundamentalists? How much credibility is that government going to have if it's set up by the US military when it's there? How long does the US military have to stay to protect the people that sign on for that government, and what happens to it once we leave?'[38]

Wise and, as it turned out, prescient words – all the more remarkable for the fact that they came from Dick Cheney, speaking after Gulf War I. Remarkable, when you consider what he told *Meet the Press* on the eve of Gulf War II:

> I really do believe that we will be greeted as liberators. The read we get on the people of Iraq is there is no question but what they want to get rid of Saddam Hussein and they will welcome as liberators the United States when we come to do that.[39]

Whatever's in those heart pills must be pretty strong stuff.

THE REPETITION OF HISTORY

Iraq has a history – an ancient one (Babylon lies some sixty miles south of Baghdad), and a modern one, in which we British feature rather heavily. Here's the view from 1922. Spot the similarities:

> The whole of the Islamic world is in a distracted state. Turkey, Arabia, Persia, Afghanistan, Turkistan, and India are all fermenting with unrest. Great Britain has a special reason to fear a great Islamic combination throughout Asia directed against the West. Iraq, for its geographical position may be regarded as a key position ... the existence there of a strong Arab state, friendly to the British government, breaking the chain of possibly hostile influences, may be of immense importance to us in the difficult times ahead.
>
> British Colonial Office memo, 11 December 1922

If you replace the words 'Great Britain' with the word 'America', you have today's solution to a problem we thought we'd solved eighty years ago.

What is striking about the whole Iraq adventure is the constant parallels with history, together with the refusal of any of the major players to learn from it. As we've discussed, for Tony Blair history is not something in the past to be learnt from, but something in the future that will judge him favourably. Is he on the same medication as Dick Cheney?

Iraq was created by the British during the break-up of the Ottoman Empire in the 1920s. Formerly part of Mesopotamia, it had never previously been a country. Rather, it was a collection of tribes: Kurds, Marsh Arabs, Shiites, Sunnis, Turcomans, Jews, Assyrians. Mostly they detested each other, so you would think it would be a tough job for Britain to unite them.

But we did it. Less than three years after we took over in 1924 they all got together and threw us out. That revolt was put down by British troops, but the Arab tribesmen and the Kurds kept on causing trouble. How did we deal with that? The same way Saddam Hussein dealt with the same problem sixty years later: we bombed them.

The RAF had a big airbase at Habbaniya, outside Baghdad, from where they sent Handley Page biplanes to blitz the tribesmen at the first sign of trouble. In fact, there didn't need to be any trouble at all before a place was bombed. Perfectly peaceful villages got the treatment if the tribesmen were thought to be slow paying their taxes. This was the first systematic bombing of civilians in history. And who was the man behind this policy? The Colonial Secretary, Winston Churchill. He said,

> I look forward to the country being in the condition of an independent native state, friendly to Great Britain, favourable to her commercial interests, and costing hardly any burden on her Exchequer.

That last bit was certainly true, as the Iraqis not only endured the effects of the RAF's bombing raids but were forced to pay for the privilege. But as for the policy itself, the Secretary of State for War, Sir Laming Worthington-Evans, had his doubts, stating,

> If the Arab population realized that the peaceful control of Mesopotamia ultimately depends on our intention of bombing women and children, I'm very doubtful if we shall gain that acquiescence of the fathers and husbands of Mesopotamia to which the Secretary of State for the Colonies looks forward.

Shame he never met Donald Rumsfeld.

Churchill didn't agree. On 29 March 1919 he ordered:

> Gas bombs are required by the 31st Wing for use against recalcitrant Arabs.

At the Air Ministry, Lieutenant Colonel Gossage worried about the effects of gas on the innocent. But those qualms were not shared by Churchill, then Secretary of State for War and Air, the future Colonial Secretary, Prime Minister, and Greatest Briton of All Time.

> I do not understand this squeamishness about the use of gas. I am strongly in favour of using poison gas against uncivilized tribes.[40]

Churchill felt what was required was to arouse in the local population what he called, 'a lively terror'.

Which is a neat phrase, bearing in mind the ongoing War on Terror we're now fighting. But there were still worries at the Air Ministry:

> I understand that the Secretary of State has approved the general policy of using poisonous gas on uncivilized tribes. So far, although considerable time and trouble was expended on research during the war, we have not yet evolved suitable and practical gas bombs for use from aircraft.

So there we are, another good idea goes down the tube. Not because we didn't have the heart, but because we didn't have the technology.

The intention throughout the 1920s was to create an independent country and leave with honour. Where have we heard *that* before?

In the end, the British didn't leave Iraq, with or without honour, until 1958, when we were finally kicked out by Arab nationalists, and the king, the crown prince, and the prime minister were all slaughtered. So much for constitutional monarchy.

Having thus seized power, the new ruler, Abd al-Karim Qasim, began a bloody and repressive regime. But that was OK because Iraq was still a buffer against the Soviet Union, so we tolerated the killings and turned a blind eye to the bloodshed. It was only when Qasim changed his allegiances the following year and started to deal with the Russians that the CIA finally sat up and declared Iraq 'the most dangerous spot in the world'.

With enlightened self-interest in mind, it was time to step in again and engineer a little regime change, and a CIA plot was hatched to assassinate the prime minister. The man at the centre of the plot being a twenty-two-year-old thug, described as having no class. After a series of bungled opportunities, the attempt ended in farce. The young assassin killed the wrong man, winged the prime minister, and was accidentally shot in the leg by a fellow gunman. He then had to be bundled out of Iraq and shunted around Beirut and Cairo under CIA protection. So who was the CIA's bungling henchman and would-be assassin? Saddam Hussein. Whatever happened to him?

It's a recurring characteristic of American foreign policy that, having installed or shored up a foreign dictator, the relationship then goes sour and they have an awful lot of trouble getting him out. It happened in Somalia with Said Barre, in Haiti with Baby Doc and in Panama with Noriega. And so it was with Saddam.

Of course, it would be wrong to think that in the past the West has always been Saddam's friend. On 15 February, George Bush said,

> There is another way for the bloodshed to stop, and that is for the Iraqi military and the Iraqi people to take matters into their own hands, to force Saddam Hussein to step aside.[41]

That was George Bush senior by the way, speaking after the first Gulf War (Operation Desert Storm) on 15 February 1991, when he was in the White House, Saddam was in retreat and George W. didn't know where he was. The Iraqi people duly rose up, but they'd reckoned without Dick Cheney and the US State Department. No sooner had the 1991 uprising started than the Americans began to equivocate, State Department spokesman Richard Boucher stating,

> We do not think that outside powers should be interfering in the internal affairs of Iraq.

The American administration wavered about whether or not Saddam should be allowed to use his helicopter gunships against civilians. Saddam had no such doubts and used them to crush the rebellion. Tens of thousands of civilians were killed and nearly two million forced to flee while American troops were ordered not to intervene.[42] The White House refused to be drawn, repeating,

> We cannot police what's going on in Iraq.

And George Bush became angrier. Not with Saddam, but with the Kurds and others who accused him of turning his back.

> I have not misled anybody. I don't think the Shiites or the Kurds ever felt the United States could come to their assistance to overthrow this man.

In Britain, John Major was equally offended:

> While I hope very much that the military in Iraq will remove Saddam Hussein I do not recall asking the Kurds to mount this particular insurrection.

The US-inspired (but sadly not US-backed) uprising duly crushed, Saddam survived, until 1995, when the CIA backed another attempted coup. Well, we say backed, but on the eve of the raid the Americans smelt trouble and ordered their key man out. He returned to the United States where he was promptly arrested by the FBI for conspiracy to murder a foreign leader. Which is, of course, exactly what he thought he was supposed to be doing.

He was later released, but the others weren't so lucky. The coup failed and many were killed. But memories die hard, and that of Saddam taking his revenge while the Americans looked on goes a long way to explain the reluctance of Iraqis to trust Uncle Sam in 2003, when, in his State of the Union Address, George W. Bush told them, as his father had before:

> Your enemy is not surrounding your country. Your enemy is ruling your country. The day he is removed will be the day of your liberation.

To which the Kurds must have responded, 'By us and whose army?'

9
Which just leaves the small matter of weapons of mass destruction

'You need to make it clear Saddam could not attack us at the moment.'
Jonathan Powell, Chief of Staff to Tony Blair,
email to Alastair Campbell, 17 September 2002[44]

In the ultra-neo-conservative Defense Science Board, George W. had a true friend. What they still needed was a reason to go after Iraq – something else around which a coalition of the willing could unite, something the UN would accept, and most importantly, something that would convince Tony Blair.

Regime change was obvious, but the legality was questionable. Vile and obnoxious as Saddam's rule was, it was by no means clear that it was worse than many other torturing dictatorships around the world. America could hardly go after all of them.

No matter how hard Bush and Rumsfeld pushed to link al-Qaeda to Saddam, the intelligence community just couldn't come up with what was required and place the Iraqis at the scene of the crime.[45]

There was really only one thing that pressed all the buttons: weapons of mass destruction. If Saddam had them, he would pose a clear and immediate threat. It would prove, too, that he was in material breach of previous UN resolutions demanding that he hand over any stockpiles. And it was easy to sell to the public. A madman with a big bomb is easy to sell.

In the words of that great German neo-conservative Hermann Goering,

> Voice or no voice, the people can always be brought to the bidding of the leaders. That is easy. All you have to do is tell them they are being attacked and denounce the peacemakers for lack of patriotism and exposing the country to danger; it works the same in any country.
>
> Nuremberg, 1946

Leading hawk and neo-con, Paul Wolfowitz, was later honest enough to admit the truth when he conceded in an article in *Vanity Fair* that all this was just a convenient hook to bring the others on board, admitting,

> For bureaucratic reasons we settled on weapons of mass destruction because it was the one issue everyone could agree on.[46]

Did Saddam have them? He must have. For one thing, we'd sold them to him in the first place. In the 12,000 page dossier submitted by the Iraqis to the UN Security Council in 2003 (8000 pages of which were never made public, after appeals by the US), twenty-four American firms were listed as supplying arms to Saddam. Germany, which objected to the war on moral grounds and refused to back a UN motion supporting an attack, proved to be the biggest arms-trading partner, with eighty companies supporting the Baghdad government by supplying components used in the gas attack on the Kurds.

Britain, meanwhile, put in a very creditable performance of its own with sixteen companies named in the Iraqi list, a spokesman for one of them explaining that he had merely sold a consignment of magnets to a German middleman who in turn had sold them on to Iraq. Responding to the suggestion that these could be used in a nuclear programme, he said that

> I've no idea if this is the case. I couldn't tell one end of a nuclear bomb from the other.

And so WMDs became the rallying cry of the faithful and the centre point of Tony Blair's case. All that was needed was to find the evidence. It later emerged (in the Butler report[48]) that the West's human intelligence in Iraq was seriously lacking and what they did know was sporadic and patchy. Emails made public during the Hutton Inquiry made clear how desperate the Blair camp had been to find enough evidence to support the case.

By the summer of 2003 that intelligence was looking seriously shaky. Many of the claims made in the Government's September dossier were outdated and the new information depended on untested and subsequently discredited sources. This did not concern the Prime Minister at the time.

> There is no doubt whatever that he is continuing with the WMD programme.
>
> 23 September 2002

> His WMD programme is active, detailed and growing ... It [the intelligence service] concludes that Iraq has chemical and biological weapons, that Saddam has continued to produce them, that he has existing and active military plans for the use of chemical and biological weapons, which could be activated within forty-five minutes, including against his own Shia population.
>
> 24 September 2002

> We are asked now seriously to accept that in the last few years – contrary to all history, contrary to all intelligence – Saddam decided unilaterally to destroy those weapons. I say that such a claim is palpably absurd.
>
> 18 March 2003

[Hans Blix now believes that that is precisely what happened around 1995, just as General Hussein Kamal, Saddam's son-in-law, revealed to UN weapons inspectors when he defected to Jordan that year.]

But, as the war came and went with nothing found that matched the description 'weapons of mass destruction', the PM's language became more defensive ...

> Before people crow about the absence of weapons of mass destruction, I suggest they wait a little bit. I remain confident they will be found.
>
> 28 April 2003

> As I have said throughout, I have no doubt that they will find the clearest possible evidence of Saddam's weapons of mass destruction.
>
> 4 June 2003

> I have absolutely no doubt at all that we will find evidence of weapons of mass destruction programmes.
>
> 8 July 2003

Seasoned Blair watchers will spot the elision from 'weapons' – hard evidence – to 'programmes' – the intention to have weapons one day.

And, as time passed, so Blair passed the blame for his original claims:

> I remember having conversations with the chief of defence staff and other people were saying well, we think we might have potential WMD finds here or there.
>
> 11 January 2004

> I can only tell you I believed the intelligence we had at the time.[49]
>
> 25 January 2004

The Hutton Inquiry revealed to everyone (except, curiously enough, Lord Hutton) how No. 10 had seized on every piece of intelligence to hand and stretched it to the limit to make their case. This meant disregarding any caveats and exaggerating any threats. As Hans Blix memorably described it, they put exclamation marks where they should have put question marks.

And they did have some circumstantial evidence. We certainly know Saddam used to have WMDs; he had enough to kill the world's population four times over at one point. We know that because we sold him most of it. But the last team of UN inspectors claimed they had destroyed 95 per cent of Saddam's weapons.

During those inspections Saddam used every trick in the book, including moving biological weapons material around in a fleet of red and white vans, on which he painted Tip-Top Ice Cream Company. So we had every right to be suspicious.

But how much of a threat did he represent in 2003? Well, one way to find out was to attack him and see what happened. Which is what we did.

Over in America, the WMD argument followed a similar course.

> Simply stated, there is no doubt that Saddam Hussein now has weapons of mass destruction.
>
> Dick Cheney
> Speech to VFW national convention, August 2002
>
> Right now, Iraq is expanding and improving facilities that were used for the production of biological weapons.
>
> George W. Bush
> Speech to UN General Assembly, September 2002

If he declares he has none, then we will know that Saddam Hussein is once again misleading the world.

Ari Fleischer
Press briefing, December 2002

We know for a fact that there are weapons there.

Ari Fleischer
Press briefing, January 2003

Our intelligence officials estimate that Saddam Hussein had the materials to produce as much as 500 tons of sarin, mustard gas, and VX nerve agent.

George W. Bush
State of the Union Address, January 2003

We know that Saddam Hussein is determined to keep his weapons of mass destruction, is determined to make more.

Colin Powell
Remarks to UN Security Council, February 2003

We have sources that tell us that Saddam Hussein recently authorized Iraqi field commanders to use chemical weapons – the very weapons the dictator tells us he does not have.

George W. Bush
Radio address, February 2003

So has the strategic decision been made to disarm Iraq of its weapons of mass destruction by the leadership in Baghdad? . . . I think our judgement has to be clearly not.

Colin Powell
Remarks to UN Security Council, February 2003

Intelligence gathered by this and other governments leaves no doubt that the Iraq regime continues to possess and conceal some of the most lethal weapons ever devised.

George W. Bush
Address to the nation, March 2003

Well, there is no question that we have evidence and information that Iraq has weapons of mass destruction, biological and chemical particularly . . . all this will be made clear in the course of the operation, for whatever duration it takes.

Ari Fleischer
Press briefing, March 2003

There is no doubt that the regime of Saddam Hussein possesses weapons of mass destruction. And . . . as this operation continues, those weapons will be identified, found, along with the people who have produced them and who guard them.

General Tommy Franks
Press conference, March 2003

I have no doubt we're going to find big stores of weapons of mass destruction.

Defense Policy Board member, Kenneth Adelman
March 2003

One of our top objectives is to find and destroy the WMD. There are a number of sites.

Pentagon spokeswoman, Victoria Clark
Press briefing, March 2003

We know where they are. They're in the area around Tikrit and Baghdad and east, west, south, and north somewhat.

Donald Rumsfeld
ABC interview, March 2003

I think you have always heard, and you continue to hear from officials, a measure of high confidence that, indeed, the weapons of mass destruction will be found.

Ari Fleischer
Press briefing, April 2003

We are learning more as we interrogate or have discussions with Iraqi scientists and people within the Iraqi structure, that perhaps he destroyed some, perhaps he dispersed some. And so we will find them.

George W. Bush
NBC interview, April 2003

There are people who in large measure have information that we need . . . so that we can track down the weapons of mass destruction in that country.

Donald Rumsfeld, April 2003

We'll find them. It'll be a matter of time to do so.

George W. Bush, May 2003

I'm absolutely sure that there are weapons of mass destruction there and the evidence will be forthcoming. We're just getting it just now.

Colin Powell, May 2003

> We never believed that we'd just tumble over weapons of mass destruction in that country.
>
> Donald Rumsfeld, May 2003
>
> I'm not surprised if we begin to uncover the weapons program of Saddam Hussein – because he had a weapons program.
>
> George W. Bush, May 2003

Bush later quoted an International Atomic Energy Agency report which said that the Iraqis were six months away from developing a nuclear weapon, claiming,

> I don't know what more evidence we need.

Well, perhaps the evidence of a top IAEA spokesman who stated,

> There's never been a report like that issued from this agency.[50]

Add to that: the aluminium tubes that were just that; the drone aircraft which represented no threat at all; the mobile chemical weapons trucks which turned out to have nothing to do with chemical weapons (their purpose was to blow up weather balloons); and the so-called al-Qaeda terrorist camp in northern Iraq which was later downgraded to 'a dilapidated collection of concrete outbuildings'.

Although to be fair the camp did still pose a threat. Well, to local people at least. America attacked it with cruise missiles at the start of the war and killed forty-five villagers.

So, back to the question, did Saddam possess any weapons? Let's try Donald Rumsfeld. He should know, he met Saddam in Baghdad back in the 1980s when the Iraqi despot (then a valued friend) was on a buying spree and America was happy to sell to anyone who stood up to the fundamentalists – unless the fundamentalists were opposing the Russians, as in Afghanistan, which made them the good guys; or unless, like Iran, the fundamentalists happened to keep Saddam in check, in which case the US sold weapons to both sides.

On 14 March 2004 Rumsfeld was interviewed by Bob Schieffer on CBS's *Face the Nation*, who asked him why, if they didn't have weapons of mass destruction, the Iraqis posed an immediate threat. Rumsfeld went into denial.

RUMSFELD: Well, you're the – you and a few other critics are the only people I've heard use the phrase 'immediate threat'. I didn't. The president didn't. And it's become kind of folklore that that's – that's what's happened. The president went...
SCHIEFFER: You're saying that nobody in the administration said that?
RUMSFELD: I – I can't speak for nobody – everybody in the administration and say nobody said that.
SCHIEFFER: Vice-president didn't say that? The...
RUMSFELD: Not – if – if you have any citations, I'd like to see 'em.

Unfortunately for Mr Rumsfeld, the respected *New York Times* journalist Thomas Friedman, who was part of the discussion, happened to have a citation in front of him.

FRIEDMAN: We have one here. It says, 'some have argued that the nu–' – this is you speaking – 'that the nuclear threat from Iraq is not imminent, that Saddam is at least five to seven years away from having nuclear weapons. I would not be so certain.'
RUMSFELD: And – and –
FREIDMAN: It was close to imminent.
RUMSFELD: Well, I've – I've tried to be precise, and I've tried to be accurate. I'm – I suppose I've...

The ground was rapidly disappearing beneath his feet. And Friedman immediately produced a second direct quotation from Mr Rumsfeld.

FRIEDMAN: 'No terrorist state poses a greater or more immediate threat to the security of our people and the stability of the world than the regime of Saddam Hussein.'
RUMSFELD: Mm-hmm. It – my view of – of the situation was that he – he had – we – we believe, the best intelligence that we had and other countries had and that – that we believed and we still do not know – we will know. David Kay said we're about 85 per cent there. I don't know if that's the right percentage. But the Iraqi Survey Group – we've got 1200 people out there looking. It's a country the size of California. He could have hidden his – enough chemical or biol – enough biological weapons in that hole that – that we found Saddam Hussein in to kill tens of thousands of people. So – so it's not as though we have certainty today.[51]

Right, well, at least that's cleared that up.

Some of our weapons are missing . . .

It may be no surprise that the Americans have been unable to find weapons of mass destruction in Iraq. They have considerable trouble finding their own stuff. A couple of years ago they 'lost' US$900 million of their own kit, a sum not far off the entire Iraqi military budget for the same year. Items lost included an entire missile guidance system and a number of helicopters.

In 2003, reports suggested an even bigger problem when the Defense Department inspectorate found the Pentagon couldn't account for a part of its US$400 billion annual budget, including fifty-six aircraft, thirty-two tanks, and thirty-six Javelin missile command launch units, which had simply gone missing.[52]

With so much missing and unaccounted for, it might perhaps have been prudent for the Pentagon to start searching for their own weapons first, before they began looking for Saddam's.

So much for the stated reason for war. What of the unstated reasons? For these, we need to understand the people we're dealing with and what motivates them.

10
Meet the teams

So, with WMDs as the clarion call, and the idea of a clean war giving the mission a moral veneer which validated its integrity in the absence of UN support, Bush and Blair launched their crusade, maintaining that whenever they are given the choice, the poor and downtrodden of this world jump at the opportunity to embrace Western values. It was an upbeat vision of third-world consumers itching to embrace the Western economic model and desperate that the bombs might stop long enough for them to rush out to the local Share Shop and buy up stock in BP.

And, just out of interest, what were those values we felt sure the rest of the world (and a grateful post-invasion Iraq in particular) would want to take on? Well, democracy, of course, although it remains to be seen which model – the American one, where you add up the votes at the end and the one with the most votes loses, or the British one where few can be bothered to vote in the first place.

Then, of course, there were the ideals of freedom and justice, qualities the Americans were busy championing in Guantanamo Bay (later, the infamous Abu Ghraib prison would provide further instances of justice, US-style – the degrading and inhumane treatment of prisoners, under the regime of Team Rumsfeld). Not to mention the traditional American values of international co-operation (from an administration refusing to sign a list of international treaties) and economic strength (from the people who brought you Enron).

As if to prove the point, many of the key proponents of these values held top positions in the Bush administration.

American roll of honour

Thomas White

Former vice-chairman of Enron Energy Services. While he was in the job, Enron rigged and exploited California's electricity market, causing chaos, power cuts, and unemployment, in what the Senate investigator called 'a mob-style protection racket'. Subsequently appointed Secretary of the US Army.

Larry Thompson

Headed up the audit and compliance committee of Providian. This insurance firm was forced to pay US$300 million (the largest fine ever doled out by the Comptroller of the Currency) in fines and compensation after swindling its investors, the frail and elderly, of most of their savings. Larry later faced accusations of insider trading, after selling US$4 million of Providian stock just before the share price dropped. Went on to become George Bush's fraud buster, charged with restoring faith in American business ethics.

Dick Cheney

Sold US$35 million of his shares when chief executive of engineering company Halliburton after accounting changes allegedly inflated the share price by US$100 million. The shares later collapsed. Halliburton are now under investigation over a multi-billion no-bid contract in Iraq. Appointed head of the Republican committee to find a vice-presidential candidate, he duly found one: himself.

Whoever George W. Bush had in mind when he said:

> We [the SEC] should be able to punish corporate leaders who are convicted of abusing their powers, by banning them from ever serving again as officers or directors of a publicly held corporation,[53]

it certainly wasn't Tom, Dick or Larry.

Incidentally, George W. himself was arrested three times for different offences, and escaped a US$800,000 charge over the trading of oil shares courtesy of an investigator (appointed by his father), who claimed that despite looking everywhere he just couldn't find enough evidence to prosecute.

Meet the Bushes

The Bushes are a pretty law-abiding family. One was arrested for larceny. Another was arrested for prescription fraud. Another relative jumped a red light and killed a fellow driver who happened to be her boyfriend. Then there was a US$20,000 jewellery smuggling case. And cocaine abuse. And being drunk and disorderly at a football game. And arrests for under-age drinking. And sex in a parking lot. And stealing a Christmas tree (that was George W. by the way). But overall, they are pretty normal.

As far back as the 1930s the Bushes were raising eyebrows with their business dealings, not least in Nazi Germany. In 1942, a US government investigation found that the Union Bank, with Prescott Bush on the board, was an interlocking concern with the German Steel Trust, which produced 50 per cent of Germany's pig iron along with much of its heavy armour plate, wire, piping, and explosives. Little surprise, then, that George senior had few qualms about helping to arm another dictator, Saddam Hussein, in the 1980s.

George senior has been an adviser, ambassador, and stakeholder of the Carlyle investment group. The Carlyle group, whose main business is in the defence industry, specializes in breaking down barriers between business and politics. Reagan's Defense Secretary, Frank Carlucci, is its head, and Bush senior's Secretary of State, James Baker, is just one of the many high-profile ex-politicians it has signed up. They have confirmed that one of their investors used to be the Bin Laden Group – which itself insists that it has nothing more to do with Osama, estranged son and major-league terrorist. When Bush senior flew to Kuwait just after the end of his presidency, it seemed natural that Baker should go with him. Only later did it emerge that Baker was there to lobby for contracts on behalf of Enron. Enron's chief executive, Ken Lay, subsequently helped get George W. Bush elected by offering him his single largest campaign contribution.

George W. Bush's own business history was helped a great deal by such relationships. His grandmother, Dorothy Bush, along with other associates of his father, gave him the money to start up his own oil company, Arbusto, in 1978. Arbusto wasn't very good at producing oil and was tottering until a friend of James Baker's, Philip Uzielli, bought 10 per cent of the company in 1982. He paid US$1 million, although the whole company was valued at no more than US$382,376. This kept it alive long enough for it to be sold off to another company, Spectrum 7, which was in turn bought by Harken. Bush was compensated with shareholdings in Harken. Despite a lot of creative accounting to cover losses and bail-outs from people such as the Saudi financier Khalid Bin Mahfouz, Harken went bankrupt. Behind all the manoeuvrings, it was producing scarcely any actual oil. Fortunately, Bush managed to sell his stock at a huge profit in 1990, just before Harken tanked and its losses were made known to the other shareholders.

But if Dubya ever feels too bad about his shortcomings as a businessman, he can console himself that it's in the genes. His brother, Neil Bush, notoriously allowed the Silverado company, of which he was a director, to finance his disastrous enterprise, JNB Exploration, through a savings and loan company until Silverado went belly up, costing the US taxpayer US$1.3 billion in compensation payments. It's a good job these boys have friends in high places.

THE OILIGARCHY

But let's for once accept what George says. This was about getting rid of a bad man. It was as simple as that. Not about business opportunities, not about favouring a bunch of mates, and certainly nothing at all to do with oil.

Bush & co.: petroleum vitae

Bush, George W.
president

Founder of oil company Arbusto Energy. Former shareholder in oil company Spectrum 7 Energy. Former director of Harken Oil and Gas. Son of oil magnate George H. W. Bush.

Cheney, Richard 'Dick'
vice-president

Former chief executive of oil company Halliburton Industries. Customers included Unocal, Exxon, Shell, and Chevron. Also Saddam Hussein, Colonel Gaddafi, Ayatollah Ali Khamenei.

Rice, Condoleezza
head of national security

Former director of oil company Chevron. Chevron are partners in a massive new Caspian oil venture. Had a 129,000 ton oil tanker named after her.

San Francisco-based construction company Bechtel, which was responsible for laying down the backbone of the American nuclear industry, is one of the prime companies to benefit from the Iraq reconstruction programme, earning coveted 'preferred bidder' status.

While their present contract in Iraq is worth several hundred million dollars – small beer perhaps to a company with an annual turnover of over US$20 billion – in the long term they could earn up to US$100 billion rebuilding the country.

The name Bechtel may not be on everyone's lips in Britain, but you will know the company from some of the projects they have worked on: notably the ever so slightly late opening Jubilee Line extension, and the very slightly delayed Channel Tunnel rail link. Or perhaps you've come across one of the public-private projects they've been involved with. Most prominent is a joint share with Jarvis and Amey as one of the controversial PPP operators now running part of the tube. In their case the Jubilee, Northern and Piccadilly lines.[53i]

Bechtel enjoys cordial relations with the Labour government, although that is just a sideshow compared to their political leverage back in the States. There, they don't have to go too far to twist arms – just down the corridor in fact.

Former Secretary of State to George Bush senior, George Shultz, is a director of Bechtel and just happens to be chair of the advisory board to the Committee for the Liberation of Iraq (set up in late 2002 by Bruce Jackson, a director of the Project for the New American Century).

Jack Sheehan, a senior vice-president of Bechtel, is a member of the Defense Policy Board which helped to flatten the place and has a big say in what happens next.

Former Defense Secretary, Caspar Weinberger, was a company vice-president and general counsel to the Bechtel group.

And Bechtel's head of Middle East operations, Chuck Redman, is well known in political circles as a former US ambassador to Sweden and Germany.

To add even more muscle, Daniel Chao, another of Bechtel's senior vice-presidents, is on the advisory board of the highly influential Export–

101 uses for a John Prescott
No. 62 – Traffic-calming measure

Import Bank which provides credit for many of the schemes under tender in Baghdad.

But perhaps we're being a tad harsh. Bechtel have other strengths that qualify them for the work in Iraq, not least their previous experience in the region.

As well as an oil pipeline (see below), Bechtel signed contracts with Saddam back in the 1980s to build a huge dual-use chemical plant near Baghdad – this after Saddam had demonstrated his interest in chemicals by gassing his own people at Halabja.

Odd, then, that when they were awarded the post-war contract to rebuild Iraqi schools, Bechtel should proudly announce:

> We are honoured to have been asked to help bring humanitarian assistance and economic recovery to the Iraqi people.

That is, assuming economic recovery is possible. Bechtel projects having a nasty habit of coming with small cost overruns. The Big Dig road project in Boston, costed at US$2.5 billion, eventually ran up a bill of US$14.6 billion. In addition, their contract to clean up the mess after the Three Mile Island disaster led to the company being fined for safety breaches.

And once you have a contract with Bechtel, it's hard to get out of: when the company privatized the water supply to the city of Cochabamba, people took to the streets to protest against huge price rises. The Bolivian government cancelled a multi-million-dollar contract only to be hit by a US$25 million counter-lawsuit for loss of earnings.

Close to the President, tough on unions and wary of whistleblowers, Bechtel have much in common with New Labour.

Bechtel

In 1983 Bechtel had a number of projects in the pipeline. Including, funnily enough, a pipeline. This would run from Iraq to Jordan. They needed someone to discuss it with Saddam Hussein. That someone was Donald Rumsfeld, who happened to be in Baghdad as a peace envoy visiting the Iraqi leader. He reported back to George Shultz, who had previously been President of Bechtel, but left to become Secretary of State, only to rejoin the board after leaving political office.

Other companies – oil and construction supply firm Halliburton and construction giants Fluor, for example – had key people in the Bush administration and interests in the New Iraq:

Ray Hunt

Member of the Intelligence Advisory Board
Director of Halliburton

Lawrence Eagleburger

Secretary of State to George Bush senior
Vice-president of Fluor Construction Company

Kenneth Oscar

Former US Army Secretary, oversaw Pentagon procurement budget
Vice-president of Fluor Construction Company

Philip J. Carroll

Chair of new oil advisory board for Iraq
Former chief executive of Fluor Construction Company

A small fact

In 2000 and 2002 US$2.8 million of funding for Republican congressmen came from just five companies – by an amazing coincidence the same five companies that were originally shortlisted for reconstruction work in Iraq.

Top ten US contractors in Iraq and Afghanistan

KBR/Halliburton	US$2.329 billion
Bechtel	US$1.030 billion
International American Products	US$527 million
Perini Corporation	US$525 million
Contrack International	US$500 million
Fluor	US$500 million
Washington Group International	US$500 million
Research Triangle Institute	US$466 million
Louis Berger Group	US$300 million
Creative Associates International	US$217 million

US$0 · US$0.5 billion · US$1 billion · US$1.5 billion · US$2 billion

Creative Associates is a Washington-based, private, for-profit aid company. They hold contracts worth over US$200 million for desks, blackboards, chalk, textbooks, curriculum reform, academic standards, and teacher training in Iraq and Afghanistan. Unlike roads and airports and bridges, there is an extra edge to their work beyond just profiting from American intervention: they have access to the minds of the children in both countries.

Creative Associates was incorporated in 1979, its first account being to help the poor of Bolivia. In the 1980s it worked with the Defense Department, running a programme to retrain Contra rebels in Nicaragua. In Haiti it worked on an aid-backed radio show. Creative Associates has good contacts on Capitol Hill.

Among other things, Creative Associates has the job of helping to rewrite the two countries' history. In Iraq, this means the entirely proper business of taking out the Baathist propaganda from school textbooks. In Afghanistan it means expunging the equally dubious culture of violence.

The previous supplier of educational needs to Afghanistan was another US-based outfit, the Centre for Afghanistan Studies at the University of Nebraska at Omaha. This had been involved in Afghan educational projects for the previous thirty years, receiving support from USAID and attracting the interest of many parties in Washington.

During its time as schoolbook contractor, the centre was criticized for its ties with the Taliban, and also for producing books that used images of bullets as counting aids in its maths texts.

> We were providing education behind enemy lines,

The centre's director Thomas Gouttierre said.

> We were providing military support against the enemy lines. So this was a kind of co-ordinated effort indeed.

Education as military propaganda. That'll teach those ingrate mooslems.

As Bush and Blair are keen to say, history will judge them, and in Iraq and Afghanistan at least, with a strong handle on the history books, there's a chance that judgement may well be pretty favourable.

Iraqi quiz (1)

1. You have three places to protect. Which do you choose?
   a) The National Museum

b) The palace of Saddam
c) The Ministry of Oil

2. What did the US give Saddam Hussein after Rumsfeld's visit in 1983?
   a) A piece of its mind
   b) An ultimatum
   c) Anthrax

3. What did Britain do to Saddam after he gassed the Kurds at Halabja?
   a) Threatened sanctions
   b) Threatened military action
   c) Increased his credit rating

4. What did Rumsfeld discuss with Saddam at their meeting?
   a) The Kurds
   b) Saddam's WMD program
   c) An oil pipeline

Answers: 1, c; 2, c; 3, c; 4, a – no, only joking, it was c

11

War and peace and Tony Blair

Tony Blair's attitude to war is ambiguous. We have already noted his 1997 assertion that 'Mine is the first generation able to contemplate the possibility that we may live our entire lives without going to war or sending our children to war.'[54] (Oops!) Yet even while he was canvassing for his first seat during the 1983 election (post-Falklands) he had observed, 'Wars seem to make Prime Ministers popular.'[55]

He's now had so many that both Admiral Sir Michael Boyce and his successor as chief of defence staff publicly told him he couldn't have any more for the time being. But, as John Kampfner has brilliantly traced, Blair's philosophy on war has developed and hardened over the years, together with his taste for intervention. The subject has intrigued him for some time:

> For me, before September 11th, I was already reaching for a different philosophy in international relations from a traditional one that has held sway since the treaty of Westphalia in 1648; namely that a country's internal affairs are for it and you don't interfere unless it threatens you, or breaches a treaty, or triggers an obligation of alliance.[56]
>
> March 2004

The treaty, and the writings of the Dutch scholar Hugo Grotius, gave the PM much food for thought. Grotius argued that war should be legitimized by the whole human race and not just an elite council of ministers. Indeed, he went further, in an uncanny prediction of the policy of the pre-emptive strike:

> The possibility that violence that may some day be turned on us gives us the right to inflict violence on others is a doctrine repugnant to every principle of justice.

Maybe Blair didn't read that bit. In any case, the Americans were doing some thinking of their own:

> What you're seeing from this administration is the emergence of a new principle or body of ideas [about] the limits of sovereignty.
>
> Sovereignty entails obligations. One is not to massacre your own people. Another is not to support terrorism in any way. If a government fails to meet these obligations, then it forfeits some of the normal advantages of sovereignty, including the right to be left alone inside your own territory. Other governments, including the United States, gain the right to intervene. In the case of terrorism, this can even lead to a right of preventive, or pre-emptory, self-defense. You essentially can act in anticipation if you have grounds to think it's a question of when, and not if, you're going to be attacked.[57]
>
> Richard Haass, US Deputy Director of Defense

Needing a speech in a hurry, to give at the Economic Club of Chicago in April 1999, the PM's office contacted Lawrie Freedman, professor of defence studies at King's College, London, to prepare some thoughts to flesh out Blair's burgeoning doctrine of 'international community' – whatever that meant. As it happened, Blair didn't know what it meant either, but Professor Freedman obliged with some ideas on when and when not to intervene – Are we sure of our case? Have we exhausted the diplomatic options? Are the goals achievable? Are we prepared for the long term, including rebuilding? – and these went straight into the speech. He left out a key one – Does George Bush want to? – that came later, but already Blair was warming to a theme that would lead him to Iraq:

> We cannot turn our backs on conflicts and the violation of human rights within other countries if we want still to be secure.[58]

(China, anyone?)

By 2001, and his post-September 11th conference speech, he was on fire:

> This is a moment to seize. The kaleidoscope has been shaken. The pieces are in flux. Soon they will settle again. Before they do, let us reorder this world around us.[59]

But if Professor Freedman supplied the velvet glove for Blair's interventionism, others were working on the iron fist. His 2001 speech was heavily influenced by Robert Cooper, a senior Foreign Office diplomat on secondment to the Cabinet Office, where he had become Tony's personal foreign policy adviser. Robert Cooper's influential pamphlet, *The Post-Modern State and the World Order*, was published in 1996 by Demos, a left-wing think-tank founded by Geoff Mulgan, later Blair's head of policy at No. 10.

Cooper divided the world into zones of modernity: pre-modern states, such as Afghanistan and Somalia, which are incapable of establishing even basic governance; modern nation states such as China, the United States of America, or Brazil, which focus on acquiring the status of the classic great powers, like the European nation states of the nineteenth century; and postmodern states, interested in interdependence and mutual cooperation, exemplified by the European Union. In 1998 Cooper refined his argument in a book called (curiously enough) *Re-ordering the World*:

> The challenge in the post modern world is to get used to the idea of double standards. When dealing with more old-fashioned kinds of states we need to revert to the rougher methods of an earlier era – force, pre-emptive attack, deception, whatever is necessary to deal with those who still live in the 19th century world of 'every state for itself'. Among ourselves we keep the law but when we are operating in the jungle, we must also use the laws of the jungle. (Robert Cooper, *The Post Modern State*)[60]

By February 2002 our troops were busy with the Americans reordering Afghanistan, and Cooper had been appointed as the government's official adviser on the future of Afghanistan, reordering the country as Britain's representative at the Bonn summit which established the interim administration.

Who needs American neo-conservatives when we have our own?

12
Spin, Moore or less

At 2.45 p.m. BST on 11 September 2001, just two hours after four planes were brought down by terrorists and the World Trade Center collapsed with the tragic loss of 3000 lives, Jo Moore, a press officer in the DTI, sent out the following email:

From: Jo Moore
Sent: 11/09/01

It's now a very good day to get out anything we want to bury.
Councillors' expenses?
Jo

The following exchange then took place:

From: Tony Blair
Sent: 12/09/01

Jo,
Thank you for your email. Can I just confirm I have never seen it?
Tony

From: Jo Moore
Sent: 12/09/01

Tony,
God. Yes. Definitely.
Jo

From: Alastair Campbell
Sent: 13/09/01

Jo,
Tony just emailed confirming he hasn't seen your email. Can you confirm with me that this is the case?
Al.

From: Jo Moore
Sent: 13/09/01

c.c. Tony
Alastair,
Correct. I've never sent or received a single email from you or Tony.
Jo

From: Alastair Campbell
Sent: 14/09/01

Jo,
Thanks.
Al.

From: Jo Moore
Sent: 14/09/01

c.c. Tony
Alastair,
Sorry, does that include that last one as well?
Jo

From: Alastair Campbell
Sent: 15/09/01

c.c. Tony
Jo,
Yes.
Al.

From: Tony Blair
Sent: 15/09/01

Al/Jo,
Actually, I was going to raise that point too.
Tony

From: Alastair Campbell
Sent: 16/09/01

Tony/Jo,
For everyone's benefit, can we just get the following straight? There never was an email from Jo. There never have been any follow up emails from anyone to anyone. There never will be any emails between Jo and me or Tony. Ever. Including this one.
Can U confirm?
Al.

From: Alastair Campbell
Sent: 19/09/01

Jo/Tony,
Sorry. No reply. Can you confirm?
Al.

From: Jo Moore
Sent: 20/09/01

Alastair,
Sorry. Thought we were incommunicado.
Jo

From: Tony Blair
Sent: 21/09/01

c.c. Alastair
Jo,
I think what Al is trying to say is that the totality of our email correspondence should be nil.
Tony

From: Alastair Campbell
Sent: 21/09/01

Tony,
Shut up.
Al.

From: Tony Blair
Sent: 21/09/01

Al,
Oo-er, who's pinched your pillow?
Tony

From: Alastair Campbell
Sent: 22/09/01

Tony,
OK, look, it stops now. D'you understand?
Al.

From: Alastair Campbell
Sent: 23/09/01

Tony,
And don't respond to last email!
Al.

From: Tony Blair
Sent: 25/09/01

c.c. Alastair
Jo,
Sorry, Jo. Re your email of 12/09/01. What sort of bad news did you have in mind?
Tony

Jo Moore's was the first of many subsequently published emails to lay bare the cynical manipulation at the heart of the New Labour machine. More were to come to light in the Hutton Inquiry ('we're in serious trouble with this as it stand now', etc., etc.). Significantly, the government's first instinct was to protect her. She was, after all, only doing her job.

HUTTON DRESSED AS LAMB

As we have said, Blair is looking to the future, confident that it will forgive him.

Except, he didn't expect history to happen quite so quickly as the Hutton Inquiry.

The standing ovations and applause which Tony Blair received from Congress after war in Iraq had been declared over (by the Americans, at any rate) marked the high point for the Prime Minister. As the weeks passed, with still no sign of the weapons that had led Britain to join the war, the arguments refused to go away. On the contrary, they grew louder, and they went to the heart of Blair's Premiership. Alastair Campbell knew the stakes could not be higher. It was what motivated his attack on the BBC. He confided in his diary, made dramatically public during the Inquiry: 'Grim for me and grim for TB and there is this huge stuff about trust'.[61]

It was to protect Blair's integrity that Campbell took on the BBC with such force: the pent-up aggression of years of frustration with, and hostility to, a fickle and uncompliant media. In airing his reservations to a journalist, Kelly had sought to play the government at its own game. But he stood no chance against those who had invented it and would do whatever it took to win.

Ironically, the Hutton Inquiry produced two verdicts: Hutton's, which exonerated the government, and that of the public, which was astonished that a law lord should see fit to disregard the whole context in which Kelly was driven to suicide, namely the fierce battle to control the media. As the full scale of the government's desperation to convince a sceptical public was laid bare in the flurry of emails surrounding the publication of the weapons dossier ('very long way to go. Think we're in a lot of trouble with this as it now stands'; 'what will the headline be? What do we want it to be?' also Powell's concern: '... does nothing to demonstrate a threat, let alone an imminent threat from Saddam')[62], suspicions were confirmed that this was not so much an issue of integrity as of panic. Hans Blix later characterized the relationship between government and intelligence chiefs as one of mutual intoxication.

The fatal flaw was that the government was trying to make the facts fit their policy, not the other way round. And once this was exposed, trust in the Prime Minister's judgement was dealt a blow from which it may never recover. For if Blair's appeal in the arguments to come – over Europe, over public services, crime, asylum, all the important issues – is for us to trust him, Iraq has robbed him of his greatest weapon: his credibility.

When the Report, clearing the government of blame for the suicide of weapons inspector David Kelly, was greeted with disbelief, Blair went on the attack.

> We have seen one element – intelligence about some WMD being ready for use in forty-five minutes – elevated into virtually the one fact that persuaded the nation into war. This intelligence was mentioned by me once in my statement to the House of Commons on 24 September and not mentioned by me again in any debate. It was mentioned by no one in the crucial debate on 18 March 2003. In the period from 24 September to 29 May, the date of the BBC broadcast on it, it was raised twice in almost 40,000 written parliamentary questions in the House of Commons, and not once in almost 5000 oral questions. Neither was it remotely the basis for the claim that Saddam had strategic as well as battlefield WMD.[63]

The Hutton Report told a different story. Not in the judge's conclusion (as if), but in the appendices detailing the emails flying around Whitehall: Jonathan Powell's email, sent to Alastair Campbell in September 2002, when the dossier was at a critical stage, showed that the presentation issue was all important and the forty-five minute claim was central to that presentation. The memo from Jonathan Powell on 19 September 2002 read simply:

> Alastair, What will be the headline in the *Standard* on day of publication?[64]

The answer?

> 45 MINUTES from attack
> Dossier reveals Saddam is ready to launch chemical war strikes.
>
> *Evening Standard* front page, 24 September 2002

And just in case, like Andrew Gilligan, we stand accused of relying on a single source, here are a few more.

> 45 MINUTES from chemical war
>
> *Daily Star*

Saddam can strike in 45 MINUTES

Daily Express

While the *Sun* led with a more tempered

45 MINUTES FROM DOOM

before shrieking:

British servicemen and tourists in Cyprus could be annihilated by germ warfare missiles launched by Iraq, it was revealed yesterday. They could thud into the Mediterranean island within 45 MINUTES.

Not for the first time, the press had done the government's work for them and the impression of an imminent threat had been created. But, as the Butler Report later made clear in July 2004,

More weight was placed on the intelligence than it could bear.

Indeed,

Language in the dossier may have left with readers the impression that there was fuller and firmer intelligence behind the judgements than was the case: our view, having reviewed all of the material, is that judgements in the dossier went to (although not beyond) the outer limits of the intelligence available. The Prime Minister's description, in his statement to the House of Commons on the day of publication of the dossier, of the picture painted by the intelligence services in the dossier as '*extensive, detailed and authoritative*' may have reinforced this impression.[65]

By the Summer of 2003, that intelligence was looking seriously shaky. In fact, by the time of the Hutton Inquiry, some of the critical evidence they *did* have was being discredited or withdrawn as unreliable, something that John Scarlett failed to tell the Inquiry and the Foreign Secretary Jack Straw failed to tell the PM.

STRAW: I'm terribly sorry, Prime Minister, but could I just say – I'm sorry, let me finish, this is a very important point – what you don't know you can't be blamed for.

Characteristically, the government claimed the Butler report had cleared them, when in fact it did much to back up Gilligan's original story. The claim that the government knew the intelligence was wrong – the claim Campbell fought and Kelly died over – turned on the interpretation of 'wrong'.

As it is, Kelly is dead; John Scarlett is the newly appointed head of MI6 and Alastair Campbell is At a Theatre Near You. Eighteen months after a war sold to the public on a false premise, the only people to lose their jobs were a journalist, the chairman of the BBC and its Director General.

The sad postscript is that if a journalist sexes up his intelligence and the government goes on the warpath, one man dies. If the government sexes up its intelligence, 10,000 people get killed. But they're Iraqis, so they don't count. Or at least they're not counted, the coalition having felt no obligation to do so.[66]

YOU AND HOON'S ARMY?

But while Blair took a bullish line and felt no defence of the forty-five-minute claim and the lack of WMD was really necessary, his Defence Secretary, Geoff Hoon, took the opposite approach, offering not one explanation but two.

Speaking on Radio Four on 24 April, his views went something along the lines of

> HOON: The reason that we haven't found weapons of mass destruction are, is . . . are, Saddam Hussein had so much notice, so much warning, prior warning of our . . . er, invasion, that he had plenty of time to dismantle these weapons and, um, bury them in remote parts of the country.

But, asked John Humphrys, if he had such weapons, why didn't he use them when he was attacked? Barely pausing for breath, Hoon replied that Saddam had been so surprised

> HOON: . . . and had so little warning of our attack that he was unable to organize the use of these weapons.

A student of logic, which Geoff Hoon clearly isn't, might point out that these two statements appear to be mutually contradictory. But Hoon was alert to this one too. Asked which explanation we should believe, he replied,

HOON: Well, have the one you like, I don't mind, you choose, it's a free country.

A year later Hoon was reminded of the exchange. His response?

HOON: Hey – I'm a lawyer!

Accompanied by a laugh and a shrug of the shoulders.[67]

13
Reconstruction and beyond

They have elected a government. The Taliban are gone. The al-Qaeda are gone. The country is not a perfectly stable place, and it needs a great deal of reconstruction funds. There are people who are throwing hand grenades and shooting off rockets and trying to kill people, but there are people who are trying to kill people in New York or San Francisco. So it's not going to be a perfectly tidy place. But I'm hopeful, I'm encouraged. I wish them well.

Donald Rumsfeld,
Larry King Show, CNN December 2002

We will work to help Afghanistan to develop an economy that can feed its people in the best traditions of George Marshall.

George W. Bush,
17 April 2002

Since then:

1. The Taliban are back.[69]
2. al-Qaeda still controls large areas of the country.
3. Humanitarian agencies have pulled out of much of the country because of the danger.
4. Democracy extends to no more than limited local elections in one or two cities.
5. Opium production has soared and the region now produces 90 per cent of the world's heroin.
6. The warlords who control the trade, much of which reaches America and American kids, are now protected and funded by the American military.
7. Much of the country relies on aid and handouts to survive.
8. It is still safer to live in New York or San Francisco than Kabul.

ANOTHER VICTORY FOR MR RUMSFELD

Such have been the problems of rebuilding post-war Iraq that you'd be forgiven for thinking it wasn't properly planned. The common view is that if the coalition had put as much effort and resources into the aftermath of the war as into the war itself, things could have been better. In fact, it's worse than that. Plans were made, but they were then cast aside.[70]

A year before the invasion of Iraq, the American State Department set up the Future of Iraq Project. This was a very detailed and wide-ranging project, bringing together a lot of Iraqi exiles, Arabists, Middle East specialists, and moderates. It was a major exercise in post-war planning, discussing rebuilding, economic development, the prospects for democracy, everything except where to place the speed cameras. But they had one deadly enemy – no, not Saddam Hussein for once, but our old neo-con friends back in the Pentagon. They had their own ideas about post-war Iraq. Well, ideas is a bit of an exaggeration; they had one idea. And it could be summed up in two words: Ahmed Chalabi.

Ahmed Chalabi

We may never know who fed the information to Western intelligence about Iraq's alleged contacts with al-Qaeda and the readiness of its WMD programme. What we do know is that the Defense Policy Board chairman, Richard Perle, has said that Chalabi was the best single source of intelligence the United States government had on Iraq.

But was Chalabi right in whatever assessments he was offering?

> That tyrant Saddam is gone and the Americans are in Baghdad. What was said before is not important,

was his reply when questioned on this after the event. Except what was said before was the basis for going to war. So let's try the question the other way round: were Bush and Blair right to put so much trust in a man who had a twenty-two-year gaol sentence for fraud waiting for him in neighbouring Jordan since 1992?

Chalabi is a westernized businessman who dresses in Armani and has a base in Belgravia. A few months after Saddam was captured, it was announced that Chalabi's nephew would be the prosecutor. The Americans were sticking by their promise that the Iraqis would be allowed to try their own man, the only question being which particular Iraqis they had in mind.

A report later claimed that Chalabi had been fed information from sources close to Tehran. And wouldn't it be the ultimate irony if the invasion of Iraq had been partly initiated by Iran?[71]

Chalabi was the great hope of the Office of Special Plans, the Pentagon's own think-tank on Iraq, though once again the word 'think' is a bit misleading. Although, the word 'tank' is spot on.

For years, this group had been working with Chalabi, who had notions of returning as its new leader to the country he had left a mere fifty years earlier.

As it was, when he was flown into Iraq a few weeks into the war, with 500 men calling themselves the Free Iraqi Forces, the local Iraqis showed a singular lack of interest, gave a shrug, and said something that roughly translates as 'Who the fuck are you?'

So what happened to all the hard work of the Future of Iraq Project?

Well, that's what Jay Garner asked when he was put in charge of the reconstruction of Iraq. The answer was blunt. Responding to Rumsfeld's brief piece of advice to ignore all that had gone before, Garner struck out alone and set up his alternative Office of Reconstruction and Humanitarian Assistance from scratch, just eight weeks before the war – though, to be fair, according to one defence official, he did have three or four people to help him. And they did have a rehearsal for the post-war period; on the principle that Rome wasn't built in a day (it just looks like it), they set aside two days to rehearse plans for the reconstruction of Iraq.

On 25 February 2003 the US Army chiefs of staff warned that they'd need several hundred thousand troops to control the situation after the war. The Pentagon said it was hard to conceive they'd need that many, so they saved themselves the effort and didn't conceive it at all. When the looting started, the Americans could only stand and watch. Well, no, that's not true; they did protect the Ministry of Oil, and wondered later why the Iraqis thought that's all they were interested in.

Britain's role in reconstruction

In 2002 the cost of rebuilding Afghanistan was put at US$20 billion. Caught up in the frenzy of generosity, the British Treasury gave Clare Short, then head of international development, a fraction of that – £20 million – to help. While the chequebook was open, Gordon Brown then wrote out another cheque for double that amount – £40 million – as a post-war settlement for another poor country: America. Let's just clarify that: fifty-seven years after the Second World War ended, we paid twice as much to America in settlement of that debt as we paid to Afghanistan. The WW2 Debt (totalling $4,336 trillion) will finally be paid off on 31 December 2006.

But Paul Bremer did at least take one worry off the minds of the reconstruction companies: the fear that down the line the Iraqis might do a U-turn and take all the hard-won private contracts back into state control. Order 39 of the 100 Orders enacted by Bremer's Coalition Provisional Authority (transferred to the new administration) provides for the transition to a market economy, with provisions to favour foreign investment and privatization. While banning foreign ownership of 'natural resources' it allows foreign ownership of up to 100% of Iraqi businesses.[72]

But the Coalition Provisional Authority isn't a total control-freak. In a move of sweeping generosity, they at least acted quickly to hand back those parts of the country they felt the people of Iraq should run. The first ministry they returned as part of this renormalization was health. US advisers were withdrawn and the financially crippled and hopelessly under-resourced health service was put under the full authority of the Iraqis.

The US Health and Human Services Secretary, Tommy Thompson, was quick to offer them parting advice – telling the world that Iraq's hospitals would be fixed if the Iraqis

> just washed their hands and cleaned the crap off the walls.

Life in Iraq

Aware of the need for good stories in the early weeks of the peace, one of the first tasks the American occupying forces set themselves once they had settled in was to reopen Baghdad zoo. The reasoning appeared sound. Many of the animals were neglected and in poor health. It was good PR. And a zoo was a non-controversial family attraction. Half a million dollars were duly set aside for tarting the place up. With a lick of paint and some local TLC, courtesy of what remained of the previous workforce, the place reopened a few weeks later.

Alas, the amiable baboon that had been found roaming the grounds when the Americans arrived had to be shot when it attacked its keeper, and attendances were down on Saddam's day. One reason was the armed guards on the gates. It seemed few Iraqis felt the prospect of being frisked by armed officers on the ticket desk was quite the way to start a family fun day out. Strange how in little ways like this we find the world isn't that different wherever we live.

But at least the animals were safe. Well, until one night when a group of US soldiers, bored with the light duties at the zoo and with a few drinks inside, decided that the tigers looked in need of a little extra supper. Armed with a tray of meat, the soldiers tossed the scraps into the cage until one GI, convinced that the human touch was needed, poked his hand through the bars and held out a chunk of steak. The tiger, grateful for the offer, promptly took the meat in its mouth, along with half the soldier's arm. Luckily for the young recruit, though less so for the tiger, his colleagues reacted quickly to the incident and, drawing their guns, shot the creature dead.

Iraqi Democracy (a variation on a theme originally explored by Tom Lehrer)

All the Sunnis hate the Shias
And the Shias hate the Sunnis
And the Muslims hate the Christians
It's enough to make a general cry
But it's Iraqi Democracy
Something you've got to see –
Hundreds of hostile groups
Will live in perfect harmony, now
Saddam Hussein has gone, it's
Rule from the Pentagon
It's Iraqi as Big Mac and Apple Pie!

All the Shi-ites hate the Baathists
And the Saddamists hate the royalists
There's no room for the loyalists
Or anybody from Iran –
It's just Iraqi Democracy
Land of the young and free
Vote for any candidate
Whose name is Ahmed Chalabi
The best that you can do is
Vote how we want you to
We set you free now don't upset the plan.

All the Sadrists hate the Sistanists
And the Daawaists hate the Sciri-ists
The Americans hate the Islamists
And everybody hates the Kurds
Welcome Iraqi Democracy
A new theocracy
Instead of shouting 'USA'
They go to prayers five times a day
Hey! That doesn't fit the plan
It's like the Taliban

Look out 'cos when the Mullah's cry Jihad
We might prefer the government they had!

Iraqi quiz (2)

Who said the following?

1. We will not continue to tolerate the persecution of the minority, the killing of many, and their forcible removal under the most cruel conditions. I should despair of any honourable future for my own people if we were not, in one way or another, to solve this question.

2. He has led a reign of terror. He has hurled countless people into the profoundest misery. Through his terrorism he has succeeded in reducing millions of his people to silence. The maintenance of a tremendous military arsenal can only be regarded as a focus of danger. I am no longer willing to remain inactive while this madman ill-treats millions of human beings.

3. It is impossible to stand by and watch millions belonging to a great, an ancient civilized people be denied rights by their government. I have determined therefore to place the help of our country at the service of these millions.

Answers: 1, Adolf Hitler (on Poland); 2, Adolf Hitler (on Czechoslovakia); 3, Adolf Hitler (on Austria).

14
Brighter, cleaner, friendlier wars

At the time of the Pontiac rebellion in 1763, Sir Jeffrey Amherst, the commander-in-chief of the British forces in North America, wrote to Colonel Henry Bouquet requesting,

> Could it not be contrived to send smallpox among these disaffected tribes of Indians?

The colonel replied,

> I will try to inoculate the [Native American tribe] with some blankets that may fall in their hands, and take care not to get the disease myself.[73]

In the 1970s the Americans and the Soviets signed the Biological Weapons Convention, which finally outlawed biological warfare. The US effectively complied, but the Soviets embarked on a secret, illegal programme on an unprecedented and unimaginable scale. At the peak of their interest they produced 4500 tonnes of anthrax and 1500 tonnes of bubonic plague per annum, as well as botulinum toxin, Q fever, Marburg virus, and smallpox. Yeltsin supposedly stopped the programme in the mid-1990s. However, the collapse of the Soviet Union has left tens of thousands of scientists out of work and vast quantities of material – nuclear, biological, and chemical – unaccounted for and vulnerable to theft or to the black market.

Surprisingly little was ever done to track down this material or remove it from use.

Recently, the US has actually stepped up its biological weapons programme, building a factory capable of making and testing a bio-bomb, and coming up with Clear Vision, a biological weapons programme designed to build and test a simulated (rather than live) biological bomb.[74] Clear

Vision was funded by the CIA and went ahead without White House approval. As part of the programme, the US attempted to obtain equipment used in the Soviet germ warfare programme. The CIA found what appeared to be a bomblet-filling machine outside a reinforced bunker in Kazakhstan, and authorized US$150,000 for its purchase. However, the Kazakhs, somewhat puzzled by all the attention and secrecy, would only sell it for US$10,000. After it was shipped back to the US, numerous tests were conducted for all manner of deadly pathogens, only for it to emerge that the machine they had so carefully reassembled put caps on bottles, and the only substance that tested positive was powdered milk.

The US Defense Department also embarked on a study, codenamed Bacchus, to see if it could build a factory capable of making germ weapons from commercially available materials. By the summer of 2000, the team had built a functioning facility which turned out two pounds of anthrax stimulants. And the US also commenced a programme to create a 'superbug' – a vaccine-resistant strain of anthrax. This programme, somewhat inappropriately called Project Jefferson after a key founder of the free world, was funded by the Defense Intelligence Agency.

Not to be outdone, in 1998 the Israelis were alleged to have developed an 'ethnic bullet' – a chemical weapon that could distinguish between different ethnic types.[75] While the US is not actively studying such weapons, there is one exception. For the last few years the American military has been trying to develop 'malodorants' – foul-smelling bombs – and has conducted several studies designed to determine if different ethnic groups are differently affected by smells.[76]

It's not a new science. Almost sixty years ago, the US developed a nauseating 'bathroom odour' chemical for use as a weapon. But, according to the Army, the old malodorant will not work outside of the US and Western Europe, because 'it was found that people in many areas of the world do not find "faecal odour" to be offensive, since they smell it on a regular basis.' Therefore new agents are needed for overseas missions. These new malodorants are to be specifically adapted to their victims.

Who, me?

In 1944, the American National Defense Research Committee developed a mixture of chemicals that was called 'Who, me?' This material, which produced a faecal odour, was distributed to the French Resistance, with the aim of applying it to the German occupiers in order to make them into objects of derision.[77] In 1997 the Americans revived the idea and placed a US$100,000 order to develop

> A set of non-hazardous odoriferous compounds that can be applied against a population set around the world to influence behaviour. A hundred volunteer subjects shall be selected, based on a diversity of geographical origins and cultural heritage. This data will be used to develop culture response data for each odour.

Documents describe how the data is aggregated into 'odour response profiles' which suggest the types and quantities of malodorants necessary to 'elicit a favourable behavioural response' (incapacitation, panic, or flight) when used for crowd control on a particular ethnic group. Malodorants themselves generally do not cause serious injury or death, but their physical and psychological effects can be very powerful. Some experiments have been conducted outside the United States or on immigrants. An army report contained unexplained images of indigenous women and girls from Panama and Colombia, while another draft referred to testing on 'a group of South Africans'.

So there you have it. The latest hi-tech bio-weapon from the people who gave you the smart bomb – the giant stink bomb.

If your weapons were devastating enough to your opponents, war could become a ready instrument of foreign policy. The only brake would be public concern about the number of casualties on your side – something the Americans were particularly keen to avoid.

The official rules for military combat were spelt out in the Hague Conventions, the Geneva Conventions, and two additional protocols. These protocols, signed in 1977, go into some detail as to exactly how you can and cannot wage war, and, while most countries have signed up, America hasn't. Which meant that in Yugoslavia, American and Canadian pilots couldn't fly joint missions because the Canadians had to obey certain standards (for example, not attacking anti-aircraft guns stationed in schools) whereas US pilots had no such problems.

In a similar way, landmines are banned under the Ottawa Landmines

Convention, which, again, hasn't been ratified by America. So in Afghanistan, when Canadian soldiers refused to lay mines around their camp, the Americans did it for them.

But America has at least signed up to the main body of the Hague and Geneva Conventions – it would be awkward not to, having helped to draft them – so during the 1991 Gulf War, in order to reassure their coalition allies that they were obeying the rules, 200 military lawyers were dispatched to the Gulf from the US to advise the generals and give at least a veneer of respectability. A strike on a statue of Saddam Hussein was ruled out, for instance, because the statue couldn't be said to contribute to the Iraqi war effort. Unlike the war in 2003, when an attack on Saddam's statue pretty much became the war.

But there were still differences of interpretation, notably over the American use of cluster bombs and fuel–air explosives, whose effects on Iraqi soldiers were so appalling that at least five British officers resigned in horror, but which the American lawyers sanctioned.

Clean war league table

	US/ Western military killed in action	Local allies killed in action	Enemy military killed in action	Civilians directly killed in war	Civilians indirectly killed
Gulf War 1991	250	hundreds	50,000	few thousands	100,000
Kosovo	0	hundreds	1000	12,500	>1000
Afghanistan	60	few thousands	3000	10,000+	3200
Iraq War 2003	140		9200	>10,000	few thousands

The new way of fighting wars is linked to the new way of managing news media and public opinion. Unlike in Napoleon's day, when 'soldiers were made to be killed', modern military thinking seeks to transfer risk away from military personnel (a good example of this being the fast transfer of peacekeeping responsibilities to newly trained Iraqi soldiers and police). And key to it all is the idea of proportionality:

> The good act must be sufficiently good to compensate for the evil effect.

Maybe the neo-cons need to rethink things; you don't need lawyers to help you fight a clean war, just accountants.

In 1999, the Triangle Institute for Security Services tried to assess the appetite for war. The question they asked was a simple one:

> When American troops are sent overseas, there are almost always casualties. Imagine that a president decided to send military troops on one of the following missions. In your opinion, what would be the highest number of American military deaths that would be acceptable to achieve this goal:
>
> a) To stabilize a democratic government in Congo?
> b) To prevent Iraq from obtaining weapons of mass destruction.
> c) To defend Taiwan against invasion by China.

The questions were asked of three groups: the top brass of the military; a group of civilian policy makers; and the general public.

Congo

Military elite	284
Civilian elite	484
General public	6861

Iraq

Military elite	6016
Civilian elite	19,045
General public	29,853

Taiwan

Military elite	17,425
Civilian elite	17,554
General public	20,172

What was interesting is that a body count of nearly 30,000 was deemed tolerable for Iraq – way more than for the Congo, which was equally barbarous. Even more significant was that the public were far more tolerant than the military planners. Given this, even a moderately clean war looked plausible.

But all this was to change in 2003.

In October 2002, CIA operatives used a Predator drone to track the Taliban leader, Mullah Omar, to a building in a residential area of Kabul. An air strike was called off because a lawyer at US Central Command was concerned about the disproportionate risk of civilian casualties. According to a report in the *New Yorker*, the incident left Rumsfeld 'kicking a lot of glass and breaking doors'. Having learnt his lesson, the Secretary of State subsequently took all necessary steps to reduce the number of lawyers in uniform.

And then there is General Buster (we kid you not) Glossam who expressed clean war theory in the following robust terms:

> A major concern is that we don't get too preoccupied with Iraqi civilian casualties to the extent that we unnecessarily expose US and UK soldiers.

But that's just one man speaking. So here are two more. Michael Ledeen, the neo-con's neo-con, spelt it out thus:

> Creative destruction is our middle name. We do it automatically, and that is precisely why the tyrants hate us, and are driven to attack us.

It was a theme picked up by fellow neo-conservative torch-carrier Adam Mersereau. Who wrote,

> A total-war strategy does not have to include the intentional targeting of civilians, but the sparing of civilian lives cannot be its first priority. The purpose of total war is to permanently force your will onto another people group.

For any 'people group' lucky enough to get in the way, the non-lethal stink bomb can't come soon enough.

In the meantime, the American capacity for creative destruction is awesome.

Everything you need to know about American foreign policy in two paragraphs

Before the invasion of Iraq, George W. Bush argued that you couldn't have a situation where the world's worst leaders were in charge of the world's most powerful weapons.

Since the end of the Second World War, the Americans have spent US$19 trillion on what they call 'defense', which they spell differently. And define very differently. That means that if you were to spend US$26 million every day since the birth of Christ, you'd still have spent less than the Americans have spent on defence since the end of the Second World War. Put another way, if you had funded a small military invasion (helicopters, small arms, infantry support) each and every day for the last two thousand years – that's nearly 750,000 wars – you still would not have matched what the USA has spent on defence in the last fifty.

The axis of not very rich countries

Country	**Annual defence budget (US$)**
Iran	4.1 billion
Iraq	1.4 billion
North Korea	2.1 billion
Cuba	0.792 billion
Libya	1.2 billion
Syria	1.0 billion
Total	**10.6 billion**

Meanwhile, one US Nimitz-class aircraft carrier costs US$21.3 billion. So, like for like, as a trade-in, for half an aircraft carrier you could have the top six axis of evil countries' defence spending for an entire year.

The US had five carriers in the Gulf in 2003 – total cost US$106.5 billion. For the same money America could pay the annual defence budget for seventy-five countries the size of Iraq.

One US aircraft carrier has a fuel tank capacity of 3 million gallons and can travel 1 million miles without refuelling – that's fifty times round the world. At normal forecourt prices it would cost about US$40 million to fill up at the pumps. Fill it up a few times and you've got the total annual defence budget of Cuba, a country that America has long feared as one of the most dangerous and threatening in the world. Fill it up at a BP Select garage using a normal pump and it would take you seven years. Not including the time to collect all the free gifts and a cheese and coriander baguette from the Wild Bean Café.

And where are you going to get all that fuel from anyway? Or is that a silly question?

The legacy of war

Depleted uranium

By the end of the first Gulf War, US forces had left between 300 and 800 tons of depleted uranium 238, in anti-tank shells and other explosives, on the battlefields of Iraq.

Depleted uranium sounds fairly harmless, like an H-bomb that can't be bothered any more, but it is in fact almost twice as dense as lead and can cut through tank armour. When it hits a tank it explodes, producing clouds of tiny radioactive particles which get inhaled or ingested, causing cancer in the lungs, bones, blood, and kidneys. And with a half-life of 4.5 billion years, it's fair to say it will live on as the West's longest-lasting legacy to the region. In effect, the areas where it has been used will be radioactive for the rest of time.

Children are up to twenty times more sensitive to radiation than adults, and paediatricians in Basra reported an increase of up to 1200 per cent in the incidence of childhood cancer and leukaemia following the attacks. Yet because of the sanctions imposed on Iraq by the UN, they had little access to antibiotics or chemotherapeutic drugs.

But to be fair, not only Iraqis were exposed. One third of American tanks had uranium 238 in their construction. And even now, after nearly fifteen years, medical researchers are still reporting US servicemen passing uranium through their systems.

So one of the questions Blair had to answer when he sent the troops in in 2003 wasn't, could we risk a nuclear war in the Gulf? It was, could we risk another nuclear war in the Gulf?

The Voice of Reason

So is there a counterweight to all this? Astonishingly, there is. While the neo-cons were lobbying for war, another observer wrote,

> Why can this president not see that America's true power lies not in its will to intimidate but in its ability to inspire?

Who was the enlightened scribe? An academic? A journalist? A man of faith? No, these are the words of another politician. Step forward, Robert Byrd, American senator and former member of the Ku Klux Klan. He continued,

> We flaunt our superpower status with arrogance. We treat UN Security Council members like ingrates who offend our princely dignity by lifting their heads from the carpet. After the war has ended, the United States will have to rebuild much more than the country of Iraq. We will have to rebuild America's image around the globe.[78]

It comes to something when the most rousing words come from a man who used to wear a sheet over his head.

15
So what is so special about the special relationship?

Britain's foreign policy and, by extension, our defence, intelligence, and security policies are entirely dependent on our relationship with America. Everything dates back to the Second World War and the formalization of the (still secret) post-war 1958 UK/USA Agreement.

The cooperation extends across the board, from Star Wars to arms control and chemical and biological warfare. From nuclear cooperation . . .

Nuclear flights

Every few weeks a flight leaves RAF Brize Norton headed for America. On it are the components for a nuclear bomb. In kit form. These are parts prepared at the Atomic Weapons Research Establishment at Aldermaston returning for checks and tests in the US. The nuclear material is contained in flasks drop-tested to a safe height of nine metres (thirty feet) and shouldn't be carried above it. This is a bit difficult in an aircraft designed to fly at 35,000 feet, which to comply would be forced to fly the entire distance below the roof height of a normal semi. In America this niggly problem is overcome because the plane lands as soon as it reaches the eastern seaboard. Not so in this country, where the planes overfly the congested south-west corner of Britain, including Swindon, Bristol, Cardiff, Swansea, and all points in between.

. . . to intelligence cooperation. There may be a new GCHQ building, but the Americans still provide us with 90 per cent of its raw intelligence data . . .

Menwith Hill

Menwith Hill, just outside Harrogate – genteel land of Betty's cakes – is the biggest spy station in the world. We'll repeat that. On the moors above Harrogate, Britain has actually come first at something – spying.

Inside its vast perimeter fence (there is some confusion as to who actually owns the place since the original 1951 lease to the Americans has apparently lapsed, but the British, polite as ever, have refused to send the bailiffs in) are dotted over twenty-five satellite-receiving stations and accommodation for over 1400 American personnel.

Broken down into names such as Knobsticks, Moonpenny, Troutman, Ruckus, Silverweed, Pusher, Steeplebush, and Silkworth, the various pieces of surveillance kit dotted round the site sound more like the cast from a *Carry On* movie than the most sophisticated intelligence-gathering equipment on the planet.

But Menwith is as much a commercial listening station as a military one. How much it helps its commercial partners has never been disclosed (it's fair to say it comes somewhere between 'Oh, my God' and 'You could buy the entire Chelsea team for that'). And as a spy station, it's highly unlikely anyone will confirm any figures that might be suggested. Which does beg the question, how does Britain benefit from all this?

In the past, the argument was that it enabled us to stay one step ahead of the Russians. But, luckily, with the Cold War over, the War on Terror has given the whole operation renewed vigour.

Sucking in hundreds of thousands of calls a day – the major transatlantic telephone cables all run through Menwith – it is hard to filter and make sense of what's received. And terrorists these days are a lot more sophisticated than they used to be. Some may not use the words we think they are going to use, or perhaps they use the words and don't mean what we think they do. Just because we hear the word 'bomb', can we be sure they really intend to plant a bomb and aren't just referring to an ice-cream dish or particularly bad performance? If 'toothbrush' is the key word, how will we ever know? Unless someone tells us – but that would require local knowledge, and the last thing any spy wants is to spend weeks and months in the desert, eating revolting food, suffering the debilitating effects of dysentery, and living in fear of capture. Whereas a nice desk job, hunched over a mass of cables and speakerphones, with the occasional trip to Betty's tea rooms thrown in, must seem rather attractive.

Echelon

Thanks to this officially non-existent technology the staff at Menwith can hoover up thousands of telephone calls, faxes, emails, or radio transmissions and beam them back to America for decoding. The technology, Echelon, works by voice recognition, reputedly picking up keywords or patterns of messages. The journalist Duncan Campbell has spent much of his life investigating Echelon and a report he produced, commissioned by the European Parliament, revealed evidence that the US National Security Agency monitored phone calls from a French firm bidding for a contract in Brazil and passed on the information to an American competitor which won the contract. A number of other commercial spying activities were allegedly run in parallel with anti-terrorism work.

Despite the joint approach at Menwith, a parting of the ways does occur in the case of emergency plans, where the spirit of comradeship and equality doesn't quite seem to apply. Under US State Department priority designations, all non-combatants on American sites abroad are ranked in order to decide who gets on the first choppers out if they have to be evacuated. The ranking is numerical; then, where there is competition for places, alphabetical subdivisions apply. After that, it's stone–scissors–paper and a toss of the coin.

Category number	Major category	Minor category
I	US citizens with documentation	
II	Alien members of American families	
III	Certain alien employees	
IV	Other aliens	
A		Pregnant women
B		Women with children
C		Aged and infirm
D		Unaccompanied women eighteen years or over

So a British radio operator would come below an American radio operator, but would at least come before a pregnant alien.

Fylingdales explained

An anti-terrorism expert writes

What we have in Britain is a small group of anonymous individuals in shadowy corners of our cities, hell-bent on destroying the very fabric of our society. That is why in 2003 the government had no choice but to dispatch two aircraft carriers, four support ships, three landing ships, two minesweepers, three destroyers, a frigate, a nuclear-powered submarine, and 35,000 troops to the Gulf.

But, of course, we can't rely on an armada of battleships to totally eradicate the threat of an attack from somewhere like Tipton or Hackney. Which is where Britain's second line of defence comes in. By allowing the Americans to use the Fylingdales early warning radar installation as part of their National Missile Defence System, any missiles coming in from hostile countries can be immediately intercepted and destroyed.

Now, it's true that the people that benefit the most from this are not us but the Americans – but because Fylingdales itself will become a target, we can at least say that it acts as a decoy and protects London.

A few years ago George W. Bush revealed plans to increase the national ballistic missile defence system – the early warning 'shield' based in Britain. When he met the President, William Hague expressed his concern that Britons might not take kindly to this.

'I've got a secret plan', said the President. 'I'm going to do it anyway.'

Much the same as invading Iraq, in fact.

PART III
The home front

16

'The right environment for business'

On 12 December Tony Blair launched a stinging attack in Parliament on the electricity privatization bill:

> [The bill] staggers on, uncertain in its reasons, untested in its consequences and rejected even by those who gave it intellectual birth, because it is still sustained and propped up by the two most ancient principles of the Tory Party, prejudice and greed – greed for profits which are neither earned nor deserved, greed of a Treasury that has for so long paid the country's bills by selling the country's assets that it now knows no other way; and the simple and sinister prejudice that what is private is always right and what is public is always wrong. It is on that slender stem of dogma that the future of our electricity supply industry now rests. The Conservative Party can speak for the vested interests of City speculators and the irrational crusades of the ideologues. The Opposition will speak for the 22 million electricity consumers. We will speak up for a country that knows the good sense of a public industry in public hands.

That was 12 December 1988 by the way.

Nearly ten years later, a remarkable thing happened. Tony Blair became Prime Minister. And addressing the CBI conference in 2003, free from the responsibilities of opposition, he returned to the subject of public versus private:

> The role of government has to adapt ... it has to create the right environment for business: in skills, education, transport, and the system of healthcare. Most business people I speak to summarize the past few years as follows. They agree public sector investment is necessary but are unpersuaded that it is yielding sufficient results in health and

> education; and are profoundly concerned about transport [and] believe there is too much regulation and red tape. So how can we allay the concerns and change the failures?[79]

A question that he answered in a *Guardian* article where he explained:

> You've got to show people that it (PFI) is delivering public services within the public sector, not charging for them, but delivering in a better way.

Attacking Conservative plans to privatize the prison service in 1993, Blair tore into the government's 'obsession with the idea of privatization itself'. He continued,

> That is what the Conservative Party cannot understand. They believe that if something is not run for private profit it is not run properly – that private profit and the public interest are one and the same thing; but they are not.

All the more remarkable that the privatization programme has continued and expanded under his own government.

As Prime Minister, Blair is fond of justifying unpopular government policies by stressing the need for 'hard choices'. What doesn't seem so hard for him is that whenever the choice is between the public and private sector, he tends to side with the private sector. What was wrong with privatization, it seems, wasn't privatization itself: it was that it was the wrong *sort* of privatization. New Labour had to invent a new form of privatization. Hence the PFI (private finance initiative) and the PPP (~~piss-poor performance~~ sorry, public–private partnership), those two outriders of New Labour's reforms of the public services.

In its zeal to generate profit in traditional public services, Labour has continued the Tory tradition of privatizing anything that moves (air traffic control, the Tube) or doesn't (schools, hospitals, prisoners, the Tube) but under a different name (or names).

The deal is simple. Money for the new service is raised privately in the money markets and is thus kept off the country's balance sheet. So, nothing on the tax bill; but, like any free offer, it does come with small print.

The long-term value of PFI contracts may go down as well as up. Your public services are at risk if you do not keep up the repayments. The return for consortiums running PFI projects may go up and up and up. Standard terms include: cost-cutting, short-term employment contracts, high management costs, huge legal costs. Every element must be a profit centre. Please note that after expiry of contract (typically thirty-five years) the consortium is under no obligation to renew the terms of the lease and can renegotiate at more favourable rates or move out of the public service sector and turn the property into a hotel or office block.

PFI often means that an organization which previously worked to a single goal is now in competition with itself, as different parts of the same system strive to outbid each other, the primary goal being to enhance profitability rather than to deliver a service.

Far from rejecting the discredited Tory enthusiasm for privatization, New Labour embraced it, providing a new generation of buccaneers with a licence to print money.

The rationale was that private companies would take on and manage the risk involved in public service contracts. In reality, the risk remained with the government: faced with a failing electricity industry, nuclear programme, or air traffic control system, no government could stand by and let it collapse.[81] And no public service was beyond the reach of private initiative. The sky was the limit. Or rather, it wasn't, as the government proved when it sold off National Air Traffic Services (NATS), having previously pledged not to. Even prisons could be privatized.

You might find it morally unacceptable for the private sector to undertake the incarceration of those whom the state has decided need to be imprisoned. Indeed, as we have already noted, Jack Straw did, in those very words, in 1996, adding, 'almost all people believe that this is one area where a free market does not exist.'[82]

Those people included Tony Blair.

Tony Blair on prisons

The issue is not whether the prison system should be changed but whether change is best achieved by reforming the prison service or by privatizing it, by building a better public service . . . or by turning it over to private sector companies for profit, as is the government's case.

Privatization is not just a diversion from the agenda of prison reform; it is fundamentally flawed in principle and is now being pursued for reasons which have nothing to do with efficiency or prison reform but are simply an obsession with the idea of privatization itself.

Hon. Members say that they are not making a profit out of it, but of course they are – it is the very thing that they are there for; that is what they do as companies. Of course there are areas of national life where private profit is not suitable. That is what the Conservative Party cannot understand. They believe that if something is not run for private profit it is not run properly – that private profit and the public interest are one and the same thing; but they are not.

. . . We also say that it is fundamentally wrong in principle that persons sentenced by the state to imprisonment should be deprived of their liberty and kept under lock and key by those who are not accountable solely to the state. Those employed by security firms are primarily or solely accountable not to the state but to their shareholders.

[He then quoted former Home Secretary, Douglas Hurd:] I do not think that there is a case, and I do not believe that the House would accept a case, for auctioning or privatizing the prisons or handing over the business of keeping prisoners safe to anyone other than government servants.

[And went on:] Nothing has changed, except that the grip of dogma is rather stronger now than it was then.

. . . To allow a private security company, whose main motivation must be commercial, the coercive powers of detention, punishment, physical restraint, and influence on decisions about parole – powers of a real and harsh nature – is wrong in principle and should not be countenanced by the House.

I do not pretend that one or two private prisons or contracted-out managements will destroy the prison system, although I do not believe that they will do it any good. But if . . . large parts of our prisons and prison service become privatized, run by private companies for profit, it will be not just a profound error of principle but a massive and tragic waste of an opportunity to get on with the real agenda – the reform of an antiquated and outdated prison system from which this country desperately wishes to escape.

3 February 1993

All too unsurprisingly, the prison privatization programme has raced ahead under Labour. Under Jack Straw, to be exact.

Britain had ten private prisons at the latest count, housing around 8 per cent of the prison population, and the figure is rising, the privatized version being the first choice for the cost-conscious government.

Prisons – like call centres – seek out pockets of cheap labour and cheap land to build on. But, as with all PFI schemes, the shift from public service to profit-making exercise is not without effect on the standard of the service provided.

Q: Where and when is this?

Three of the girls (under eighteen) were pregnant. They were allowed to attend adult antenatal classes, as well as being given an additional pint of milk and some extra fruit each week. However, the antenatal classes coincided with the time allotted for the girls to receive their canteen goods, so they chose to receive their canteen goods instead.

Double rooms have a toilet but no screen. Hot meals were usually cold by the time they arrived. Showers were broken, there was a poor hot water supply to baths, and the washing area was infested with bugs. The girls were allowed to send to the laundry three items of personal clothing each week. Staff were unable to explain the rationale for this rule, other than to say that it was historical.

The girls had to eat out of mugs because there weren't enough bowls.

Pigeons were a menace, while cockroaches were prevalent.

Women were frequently unable to have more than two showers a week; this was the case for women who were pregnant and also for those who had recently given birth.

Most lavatories were shared, the girls using new sanitary towels as improvised seats on the stainless steel fittings.

A: Holloway Women's Prison, in 2003.

(HM Inspector's report)

Britain now has the highest proportion of its population in prison of any country in Europe, and England and Wales have one of the worst crime records in the industrialized world.[83] Two thirds of prisoners are so illiterate and innumerate that they are ineligible for 96 per cent of jobs, but the prison service has failed to reach its target that every prisoner has at least twenty-four hours per week of work, education, or training, out of their cell.

One enthusiastic bidder for penal institutes is the American company Wackenhut, founded by George Wackenhut (crazy name, crazy guy!), a billionaire former FBI agent. George, who lives in a mock medieval castle in Florida, established himself during the McCarthy era by outing the subversives. A few years later he boasted 4 million names on his list. (This was a man who once described George Bush senior as a pinko, by the way.)

Wackenhut Inc. has had a colourful history around the world. It runs internment camps in the desert in Australia; and in one of its jails in Louisiana the US Justice Department had to take the unprecedented emergency action of stepping in to protect inmates from 'life-threatening conditions' – the inmates at risk being young boys the guards were abusing.

The company is a partner, through its subsidiary, Premier Prison Services, in four private British prisons, in South Yorkshire, Nottinghamshire, Durham, and Scotland.

How did they get the business in Britain? Well, marketing helps. And in the wacky world of private prisons, marketing is a Big Thing.

How to market a jail

At a conference in Colorado several prison companies came together for the Large Jail Network Meeting.[84] A bit like the Groucho Club, but everyone is 6' 6", has a shaven head, and carries a stick. (We're guessing here.)

Among the topics: 'Exploring issues and strategies for marketing a Large Jail'; 'What does marketing the jail mean?'; and 'Identifying creative marketing opportunities'. Suggestions included tours, articles, brochures, and – one particularly well supported idea – jail websites (anyone for a dot con revolution?).

So what is at the heart of this? Simple: competition. The operators need to publicize their products in the hope of attracting more business (in this case, prisoners). Hence the need to compete and spread the message that more jails are a good idea.

OK, private prisons don't sentence. Well, not yet. And they don't run the judiciary. Yet. But, as well as cost savings, the conference's focus was how to lobby governments and what to ask them for. The answer being a bigger market. More crime, anyone?

Still, at least the prison service isn't alone in the nudge towards privatization. As well as flogging off its own property, contracting out various computer services with alarming results, and handing over the transit of prisoners to and from jail (much to the delight of the prisoners, who have managed to escape from unlocked vans at regular intervals), the Home Office, the largest department in government, set about a long overdue reform of the police force. As a result, the police are now able to acquire a part of their budget through commercial sponsorship, grants, gifts, and loans.[85]

One of the first sponsorships was by Harrods, for a Rover patrol car near its store. Transco has sponsored flying hours for a police helicopter in Nottinghamshire and Derbyshire, and has given £600 towards three electrically powered bicycles in Leicestershire. BP, in a fit of lavish spending, sponsored a police horse in Humberside and provided blankets with

The police force: Your name here

its logo on. And in Bathgate a firm of solicitors paid for a scooter for Lothian and Borders police.

Norfolk Constabulary enthused:

> Sponsorship and partnership between the police and commercial organizations represent a growth area of marketing opportunities for the business world.

The force then signed a number of sponsorship deals, including a privately funded scheme to patrol a certain area of the Norfolk Broads during the summer months.

Musgrove Park Hospital in Taunton paid for an officer to patrol the hospital site, and a car dealer within the Forest of Dean provided two Skoda Felicia estate vehicles for use by the two rural beat officers. Until October 2003 the City of London Police horses were sponsored by HSBC.[86]

All well and good. (Provided you don't mind having your local bobby kitted out in a sandwich board and handing out flyers for an upcoming trade fair.) But human nature being what it is (and, after all, without it we wouldn't *need* a police force), there are always those who go just a bit too far . . .

Avon and Somerset police had to reduce the size of the Threshers off-licence logo on a police van the company had sponsored to the tune of £10,000 after complaints from anti-drink-driving campaigners. And the normally level-headed (no, that's what it says here) Police Federation has criticized multi-firm sponsorship of patrol cars – featuring logos from Harrods, Newcastle Breweries, and Threshers – for making them 'resemble Grand Prix racing cars'. (That's the police driver's job, not the sponsor's.)[86i]

17

'I will have failed in five years' time if there are not far fewer journeys by car'

John Prescott, June 1997

He failed.

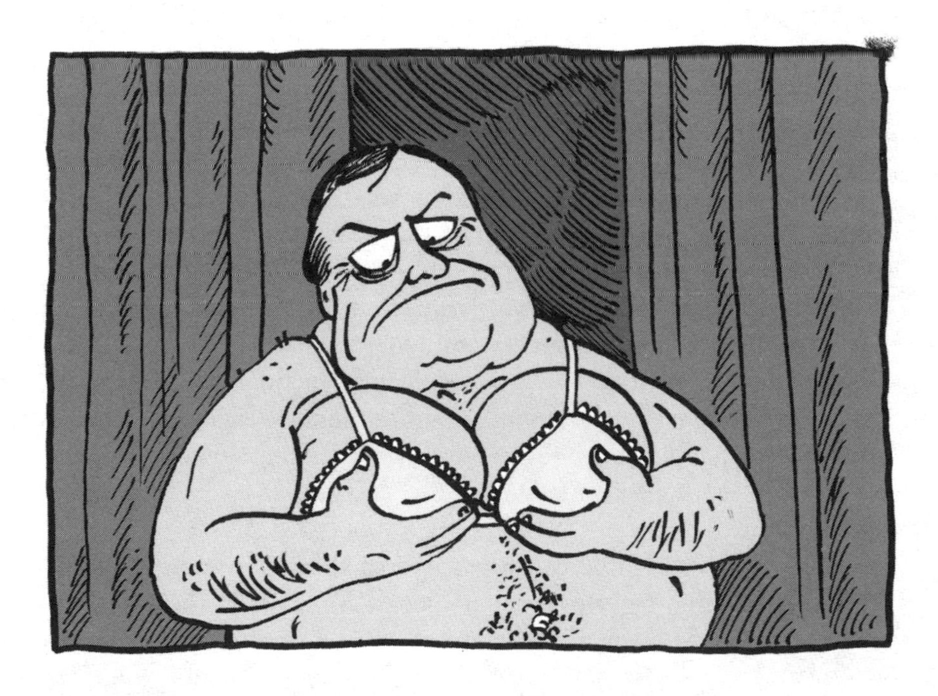

101 uses for a John Prescott

No. 34 – Tester for the first male bra, 1982

SO HOW DID HE FAIL?

In 1998, New Labour announced its flagship integrated transport policy.[87] It sounds simple, and indeed it had to be: John Prescott was in charge. But with a vibrant economy, and with the public clamouring for change after a series of rail disasters, it was hard to see how it could fail.

So in a way it's a tribute to New Labour that it did. Speed was of the essence. Two years after announcing the policy, the government worked out how to pay for it, and announced it again. And from the start, or rather the restart, they maintained they wouldn't renationalize the railways, insisting that they had to deal with the railways as they found them, not as they'd wished them to be.

The same applied to John Prescott. So Labour did the sensible thing, and removed as much as possible from his control.

But the argument didn't apply to other manifesto promises. Instead of taking their pledge not to privatize the air traffic control system as they found it, they changed it to what they wished it to be and sold off 46 per cent, thus passing the risk to the private sector. Which was fine until the private system got into trouble, whereupon the private sector passed the risk straight back to the government, which had to fork out £30 million to bail it out.[88]

Meanwhile, having decided to privatize half the Underground, the government decided that privatization was proving disastrous on the overground railway and put them into receivership, announcing a hugely expensive package of publicly funded upgrades and repairs.

Since Labour announced their policy, only one station has been opened, at Chandlers Ford – coming in at £2.5 million for a single-platform station. It boasts what must be the most expensive heating and ventilation system in the world, costing £800,000 for a building the size of a large shed.

But at least some other things have changed in the last twenty years. The real cost of travelling by train has almost doubled, while car travel is actually less expensive. So while people always say the rail system in this country is a cheap joke, they are wrong. It's not. It is, in fact, a very expensive one.

But this is not to ignore the other parts of Britain's transport system. Quite the opposite. Fed up with the lack of progress on the buses and railways, people jumped into their cars, causing such congestion that London and other cities have had to introduce congestion charging. The charges may well price poorer people out of the city while freeing up the roads for well-off drivers, but that's a socialist government for you.

Still, at least the government's policy is ahead of schedule in one respect.

Instead of failing after ten years, it failed after less than three. A far cry from John Prescott's pledge to provide people with

> a decent modern and reliable public transport system.

Still, with one failure bringing about another, it's integrated; it's certainly a policy; and it's something to do with transport. So what's the problem?

Railways

> The railway network should not be used as a plaything for bankers and speculators. It should be run for British business and the British people.
>
> Tony Blair,
> 12 December 1995

At this stage we wanted to speak to a leading industry figure. But his train was cancelled. So we made up this interview instead. (All the facts are, however, accurate.)

Sir George Parr is a banker particularly involved with the financing of the railway system. He owns the trains.

> INTERVIEWER: But surely the trains are owned by the train companies, by Arriva and Virgin and South West Trains and all the others.
> PARR: No, that's very naive, if I may say so.
> INTERVIEWER: Well, it might be naive, but it would be logical, wouldn't it?
> PARR: What's logic got to do with it? We're talking about the railways. And you know, when the system was set up it was decided by the government that there would be a group of companies who operated the trains and another group of companies that owned them. And my company is one of three rolling-stock leasing companies – called Roscos – and we lease our trains to the operating companies.
> INTERVIEWER: And this is profitable, is it?
> PARR: It is fairly profitable, yes.
> INTERVIEWER: Yes, good.
> PARR: I mean, just to give you an example: we've just supplied South West Trains with some new rolling stock...
> INTERVIEWER: Yes, and how much do you rent those for?
> PARR: For £500,000 a year.
> INTERVIEWER: Yes, yes, and what do they cost to build?
> PARR: Just over £2 million.

INTERVIEWER: So a train operator will pay you a quarter of what they cost to build every year.

PARR: Every year, yes.

INTERVIEWER: For how many years?

PARR: Well, not more than forty.

INTERVIEWER: That's a huge profit margin, isn't it?

PARR: Well, well, I hope so, jolly well hope so, but I have to emphasize most strongly here that my company does not receive one penny of taxpayers' money.

INTERVIEWER: No, no. So you're only paid by the train operating companies?

PARR: Yes, well, let me explain. Take the franchise South Central. Now their subsidy is going to increase by £342 million over the next five years. And inevitably, some of that money will come to us for new rolling stock.

INTERVIEWER: Yes, how much, well, what proportion? Ten per cent, twenty per cent?

PARR: Eighty per cent.

INTERVIEWER: And this is taxpayers' money?

PARR: No, it's taxpayers' money when it gets to the operating company, you see, but by the time it moves from the operating company to our leasing company, it's a simple commercial transaction.

INTERVIEWER: So what sort of a return are you getting on your investment, roughly?

PARR: Roughly, thirty per cent.

INTERVIEWER: Well, if you compare that with, well, a company that's regarded as being very successful – Tesco, for example – Tesco's very happy with five per cent.

PARR: Ah yes, but what you have to remember is that the three leasing companies are all owned by banks.

INTERVIEWER: Yes.

PARR: And by their very nature, banks make a lot of money.

INTERVIEWER: Yes, indeed. But since so much of your revenue actually just comes, you know, from the taxpayer, isn't it odd that the rail regulator doesn't have anything to say about this?

PARR: No, it isn't odd, no, because the leasing companies are in fact the only part of the system which is not under the jurisdiction of the rail regulator.[89]

INTERVIEWER: Yes, this whole, this whole arrangement whereby you make these colossal profits from leasing out these trains, I mean it doesn't even make sense.

PARR: Well, you see, what you have to remember is that our returns are quite large, but then we are taking a huge risk, because when the franchises were set up, the government wanted them to be very short – just five, six, seven years. But as we've discovered in this conversation, trains can rumble along for twenty-five to forty years. So if at the end of a franchise it's not renewed, then we are left holding hundreds and hundreds of trains with nothing to do with them.

INTERVIEWER: No, you aren't because they just give the franchise to somebody else and you rent the trains to them.

PARR: Not necessarily. It might happen that way.

INTERVIEWER: No, no, surely, I mean, the only risk you are taking is that if one day the government suddenly decides, for some reason, to completely tear up the whole railway system and close it down overnight.

PARR: Well, they could do that. They could do that.

INTERVIEWER: But they aren't going to do that, are they?

PARR: No, no, they might. I mean, look at it from the government's point of view. If they closed down the whole thing, there wouldn't be any more complaints about punctuality. You wouldn't have these awful accidents on the railways, and the government would save billions and billions of pounds.

INTERVIEWER: Yes. So you want to make as much money as you can while there is still a railway?

PARR: Wouldn't you?

While the Strategic Rail Authority currently sets an upper limit for some peak-time fares and season tickets (though not for much longer), other fares are unregulated, giving companies licence to raise fares despite poor performance. Even the regulated fares can rise above inflation, regardless of the quality of service.

The Government's 10-year transport plan talked of £60 billion of expenditure, split equally between the public and private sectors. These figures subsequently disappeared from the Future of Transport and Future of Rail White Papers published in July 2004, although the Government has not actually contested the increase in funding for Network Rail outlined by the Office of the Rail Regulator. Presumably, however, the money will have to be found within the total allocation for the industry.

The Spending Review did mention some more money for rail, but failed to say whether this was every year or over ten years, allowing a wide variety of interpretation. Meanwhile Hans Blix might usefully be employed looking for the presence of the £30 billion of private money.

The 10-year plan came out three months before Hatfield exposed the true state of the neglect. (True to form, the money was reannounced later.) The cost of fixing the tracks and compensating the operators was estimated to be around £1.2 billion. In response, the government offered to stump up £600 million and face being sued for the rest.

The Future of Transport White Paper (successor to the 10-year plan) says: 'The privatization of the rail industry in the early 1990s assumed that private sector discipline and innovation would drive down the railway's subsidy requirement and drive up the quality of service. In part this has been borne out'.

Rail users might well ask: In which part? The same document shows 80 per cent of trains arriving 'on time' in 2004, compared to 90 per cent in 1998. The latest National Rail Trends shows total Government support to the rail industry in 1995–96 of £431 million. For 2002–03 it was £2,588 million.

The Underground

> This is dogma gone mad
>
> John Prescott, on the Tories' plans to privatize the Underground
> February 1997

> Those who block the modernization proposals will be the wreckers, while the reformers will want to go ahead with modernization and change
>
> Stephen Byers, Transport Secretary
> January 2002

After the abolition of the Greater London Council (GLC) in 1986, the London Underground could no longer be funded out of the local rates paid by all London households. Ever since then, the Underground has had only two sources of revenue: central government grants and passenger fares. Government grants to upgrade infrastructure have declined from £398 million in 1994/5 to £160 million in 1998/9. This has resulted in fare increases of double the rate of inflation over the last decade, making London's Tube system the most expensive in Europe.

The government believed this could be solved by the part-privatization of the Underground. It projected that a PPP will make possible £7.5–15 billion of new investment, but the only indication of where this investment will come from is a prediction that passenger numbers will increase by 40 per cent over the next fifteen years. But how can such an increased number of passengers be accommodated without an immediate investment programme?

101 uses for a John Prescott
No. 11 – Bouncy castle

The Tube system spans 400 kilometres of track, 275 stations, and twelve different lines, and there is also the complex issue of who will be responsible for shared lines or interchange stations. The legal documents dealing with it are said to fill fourteen filing cabinets.

Admittedly, this may not interest people outside London, particularly as with the present system it's very unlikely they'll manage to get there in the first place.

It's the same system that was so signally successful with the railways: London Underground run the trains; the private contractors run the infrastructure; and any problems, the lawyers will sort out. (Giving new meaning to the warning 'Mind the gap'.) No wonder the carriages are full – it's all the lawyers and accountants desperate to get in on the act.

It's those privatized public services again. The people who put the Enron into electricity, the Railtrack into railway, and the Edexcel into education . . . Whatever happened to 'three strikes and you're out'?

The government love to call anyone who disagrees with them either a wrecker or a cynic. You don't have to be either to recognize that separating the running of the trains from the maintenance of the track is exactly where the last privatization went wrong. To add insult to injury, one of the new consortiums includes the company responsible for maintenance at Hatfield. That's the trouble with these private consortiums. If you try to do away with them they just go underground.

Let's go over the points:

Under privatization it costs three times as much for each mile of track. On top of all the subcontracting and regulation you've got to build in about 30 per cent profit for the private company. And they'll still get it if the service is 5 per cent *worse* than it is now.

But there is good news: the Department of Transport forecasts 'significant returns' for the shareholders, so they make money out of it; the contracts run to more than 2800 pages, so the lawyers make a packet out of it; if things go wrong there are eight layers of appeal, so the lawyers make a packet out of it (sorry, have we already said that?); and the City consultants have so far made over £100 million out of it. And the latest report on it was done by Ernst and Young, who are auditors for the contractors who'll get to do the job! You might as well commission a report on how often you should use your car from the accounts manager of the local petrol station.

In order to push this through, the contracts were drawn up without consultation, negotiations were kept secret, not just from you and me ('cos they wouldn't trust us anyway) but from the London Mayor – and when the announcement was made they had to get police with dogs to keep an eye on the crowd.

When a government disregards the lessons from all the recent rail disasters, ignores the result of the election for London Mayor, who's against the plan, ignores the Parliamentary Select Committee, which is against the plan, ignores the views of forty-five out of fifty of their own MPs who are against the plan, it's a wonder we don't take to the streets. Because with this lot running the Tube, who'd want to travel under them?

Air

> Our air is not for sale.
>
> Andrew Smith, transport spokesman
> Labour Party conference, 1996

> The reality is that change is essential if our air traffic control arrangements are to continue to meet the increasing demands on our airspace.
>
> Government response to Select Committee
> June 2001

Despite the concerns of pilots, unions, staff, and a prominent Commons Select Committee, the government went ahead with their proposed PPP for the air traffic control system. The same seven airlines that operate in UK air space are now responsible for how it is governed: there is no independent safety regulator.

In an ironic twist another PPP (or PFI project as it was then) threatens to undermine any possible benefits of the sell-off of NATS. EDS, the US computing giant responsible for horrendous delays at airports, sued NATS for over £42 million in damages after termination of its disastrous thirteen-year PFI contract to build, install and support a new transatlantic air traffic control computer system at Prestwick. Meanwhile, in 2003, the government pumped an extra £65 million into NATS to cover its debts.[90] Maybe the government was right. The air wasn't for sale; it was given away for free.

18
Education, education, education . . .

EDUCATION

'We will increase the share of national income spent on education'
Labour Election Manifesto 1997

After 1997 education spending as a proportion of national income promptly sank lower than under the Tories, although current promises are for an increase.

Education policy has now reached such a bizarre state it becomes difficult to satirise, as reality leapfrogs over parody.

Which of these is true:

(a) the Prime Minister's education policy is drawn up by a journalist
(b) four and five year olds have to be assessed on a schedule consisting of 117 separate tickboxes
(c) primary teachers are told exactly what to do every ten or fifteen minutes
(d) the government set up two committees to look into the problems of duplication?

Answer: all of them.

We're living in a world where proposals for university tuition fees (rejected as too damaging by the Conservatives twenty years ago) have been introduced by a Labour government and the Conservative election spokesman has defended comprehensives from Alastair Campbell's charge of being 'bog standard'.[91]

Labour introduced the concept of a 'failing' school. A 'failing' school has forty working days to respond to a critical Ofsted report with an action plan. If the education minister accepts this, the school then has two years to make improvements or else face government action – which may include closure or privatization. Most 'failing' schools are located in the poorest areas and have a larger than average number of pupils with behavioural or learning difficulties. A poor Ofsted report ensures a decline in pupil numbers and a corresponding drop in income for the school. This can then lead to a fall in teacher numbers in order to balance the budget, and a further drop in standards. Not surprisingly, pupils have reportedly been bribed to behave when the Ofsted inspectors come round.

And then there is the rough and tumble of market forces. When the consortium running Musselburgh Grammar School in East Lothian went bust, subcontractors impounded pupils' books in lieu of payment. There's a lesson there for everyone.

Meanwhile, the level of corporate involvement in schools has risen dramatically. Education Action Zones are collections of schools, local authorities, and businesses which are supposed to work together to help manage underperforming schools in deprived areas, a form of PPP. Companies involved include British Aerospace, Tate & Lyle, Shell, ICI, McDonald's, and Rolls Royce. Sometimes the company's involvement is very hands-on, with Shell taking a lead role in running the Lambeth EAZ. In the case of a school in the north-east, Kellogg's provides children with free food at its breakfast club – Kellogg's cereals only, of course. These privately run schools have the ability to vary the national curriculum, as well as to set teachers' pay and working conditions, and to poach staff from other schools. Presumably when Blunkett ruled out selection in 1995 he wasn't referring to teachers.

But not all schools are under private control. Take what you might call the 'bog-standard comprehensive' (if you were Alastair Campbell).

Even here, the begging bowl isn't far away. Siddal Moor High School had to raise £50,000 in sponsorship in order to get specialist status, money that was then matched by the government. Most of the money was given by JD Sports, which insisted that in return it became the sole supplier of PE uniforms and its logo was to be used on school stationery and signs.[95]

Money is needed for more sixth-formers since Tony Blair has set a target of 50 per cent of young people under thirty going into higher education by 2010,[96] the aim being to increase the proportion of young people from lower income households entering university. While 80 per cent of young people from 'professional' homes go to university, the equivalent from 'unskilled' homes is just 14 per cent. University students whose parents are classified as 'unskilled' represent just 1.7 per cent of the total.

The problems continue when they reach university, with the introduction of tuition fees. Thousands of students face expulsion for non-payment of fees; some universities excluded as many as 200–300 students in 2003. And the natural drop-out rate from those leaving university courses early is equally huge.

But at least there is an element of joined-up government in all this. With more and more pupils encouraged to stay on at school and then take up degree courses, which now come with a price tag and which many will not finish, we find ourselves desperately short of traditional tradesmen and semi-skilled workers. Which is where migrant workers (*see* later) come in.

Service Contracts

An important element of the government's part-privatization of public services is the practice of contracting out to private suppliers, the theory being that they will provide a better and cheaper alternative to the state run version.

In practice, the new service provider generally re-employs the same people who were there before, but at reduced wages. With obvious consequences for morale, commitment and standards. And then there is the profit to be earned on top. This has to be squeezed from an already shrinking pot.

But service contracts are the backbone of privatization. And schools and hospitals often have very little say in contracts directly affecting them, the deal being negotiated at regional level or above.

No longer is the school caretaker part of the fabric of the school; now he's an employee of a corporation based in, say, Pittsburgh. One headteacher rang his newly privatized caretaker to report that a child had been sick and ask him to come and clean it up. 'Sick on the classroom floor? Not in the contract, guv', replied the private buccaneer on his mobile, from the safety of his Mondeo several miles away. And the same goes for prisons, and defence establishments, and a hundred and one other newly liberated job markets.

But cutting back on, for example, cleaning staff in schools can have undesirable side effects, as recent research into 'lack of learning' in the classroom has uncovered.

This found that the pupils' concentration was often affected by their general well-being – or lack of. Dehydrated children, for instance, show noticeably less progress. The answer? Drink more. But if you drink you have to go to the lavatory, and top of the list of things that trouble children in most schools is the state of cleanliness of the pupils' toilets, which all agreed was universally dreadful.

So they don't want to use the toilets which means they don't drink, which means their concentration plummets, and they fall behind.

In 1980, professor Ted Wragg of Exeter University wrote an article entitled 'State-approved knowledge: ten steps down the slippery slope'.[92] It described how a government that was so minded could completely dictate what was being taught to the country's children.

At that time only the first step (at the level of broad intentions, like the need to provide high-quality education) had actually been implemented. At a national conference in Birmingham, a senior government official described the article as 'unnecessarily alarmist', since no government would ever dream of going beyond step three (decreeing which subjects should be taught).

By 1989 all ten steps were in place. It was the government that now decided the fine detail of the primary and secondary curriculum and how children should be tested, as well as the fact that schools should be ordered by rank in league table and that teachers failing to comply should be fired. When asked, in 2004, to come up with ten further steps down the slippery slope, Wragg declined, saying 'Today's satire becomes tomorrow's policy', on the grounds that the original ten had ended up as a blueprint, rather than an Orwellian warning.

He illustrated this by taking actual policies and assigning a step number to them. Step 14 would have been the government decreeing minute by minute how lessons should be taught. The compulsory literacy and numeracy hours introduced by Labour did precisely this by spelling out what teachers had to do every ten or fifteen minutes. Step 18 would have been that schools had to apply to the minister if they wished to innovate. The 2002 Education Act decreed that schools had to fill in an elaborate form and send it to the Secretary of State if they wished to do something new, like vary the national curriculum. Section 10 of the form requires schools to 'outline exactly who was consulted and how this consultation took place – how many individuals',[93] Even more ludicrous is the requirement that any innovation must subsequently be abandoned: 'applicants will be expected to show they have considered an "exit strategy" which allows them to revert back to current practice when the pilot project comes to an end.' Presumably Dr Christian Barnard, had medicine been subject to the same dictates, would have had to go back to his transplant patients, remove their new heart, take their old one out of the fridge, and reinsert it.

Best of all would have been step twenty – that the government's quest for control would generate so much bureaucracy it would eventually strangle itself. This is what happened when they set up two separate committees to look into the problems of duplication. Both the Cabinet Office and the Department for Education and Skills created a committee to look into reducing bureaucracy by removing duplication. Neither knew the other existed. As Tom Lehrer remarked when Henry Kissinger was awarded the Nobel Peace Prize, satire is now officially dead.

A lesson for all of us

A teacher came forward after one of our shows. He talked about his job and his work. He had been in the profession for years, enjoyed the job and had a passion for his subject, English.

But one day he decided to ignore the syllabus. The syllabus that laid down day-by-day exactly what he should be teaching and how.

Instead, he decided to read to the class from a book. A book he liked, a book he thought might educate.

And it was an enjoyable lesson: the class listened and asked questions. Then the bell rang and they went home.

Next day, the teacher was called in by the headmaster. There had been a complaint from one of the pupil's parents. The boy had apparently told them what had happened and they had written to the headmaster to point out that a lesson like this, one that wasn't on the syllabus, might cause their child to lose out on his vital learning skills come examination day.

The headmaster was apologetic, but under the school's contract he had little option but to reprimand the teacher. No it wasn't a sackable offence – thankfully, it hasn't gone that far yet – but in an instant the teacher's will to carry on was gone.

At the end of the term he handed in his notice and was lost to teaching forever.

There is now a massive pyramid structure in education. At the top stands the powerful No. 10 policy unit headed by Andrew Adonis, a former journalist. Its policies then become those of the ministers, and eventually schools, whether they like them or not.

When Labour announced its five-year education plan in July 2004, Charles Clarke said his first priority in education was to appeal to middle-class parents and get them back into the state system. He must have been mightily relieved that his own top preference coincided so closely with that of Tony Blair and Andrew Adonis.

The five-year plan was remarkable for being so close to what the Conservatives were advocating, resurrecting their grant-maintained schools and city technology colleges of the 1980s. Both main parties were proposing policies that were philosophically unsquareable. Schools were to set their own admissions policies and thus decide which pupils they would accept, but parents were told they would be given more choice (presumably a bigger list of schools to be turned down by).

Blair told parliament that the difference between the two parties was that under Labour there would be no more selection.

What he failed to point out is that, by turning all secondary schools into specialist schools, selection would increase even more, as these schools can select up to 10 per cent of their intake according to 'aptitude' in the specialist field. The government's counter that few of them act on this is irrelevant. Many do select their intake, either directly, or indirectly by rejecting those pupils unlikely to enhance their league table position – and more may do so in the future, as schools become more competitive. This power to select has been conferred by Labour.

The five year plan was a good example of empty soundbites. 'Labour to Set Secondary Schools Free' was the headline the spin doctors sought, and got. The reality was somewhat different. Schools would have to opt out (compulsory opting?) of local authority control, whether they liked to or not. They would have to become specialist schools. Pupils would have to wear uniform (Charles Clarke admitted they could not compel schools, but said they would be 'expected' to introduce uniforms). Schools would have to introduce a house system, as part of the Blair/Adonis love of public schools. Some freedom.

Labour's intention to establish 200 city academies increase was also somewhat strange, in that they want business to donate millions to sponsor them, at a likely cost of £30,000,000 plus each. Back in the 1980s and 1990s, when the Conservatives set up city technology colleges, only sixteen were ever built. Typically a donor would give £1,000,000 and the government would have to find the rest. Ironically, the person charged by Blair and Clarke with running the academies and specialist schools scheme was Sir Cyril Taylor, former deputy Conservative group leader of the GLC, the very person chosen to run the city technology college scheme by Margaret Thatcher and Kenneth Baker.[94] It was a seamless transition.

HEALTH

We needed a Queen's Speech to restore the health service *as one unified system of proper public service* in Britain.

Tony Blair
15 November 1995

It is an explicit objective of government health policy to shift towards greater *plurality and diversity in the delivery of elective services.*

Department of Health prospectus for foreign business consortia
2002

Car park

A lucrative revenue stream. With a captive market, and often no alternative, charges for patients and staff have rocketed, providing the service company and the NHS trust with valuable extra cash. Disabled parking has to be provided free, but to maximize income the number of disabled spaces is kept deliberately low. And hospitals do attract a disproportionate number of disabled users (even though most providers use the number of places at retail outlets for comparison). Unable to park or walk, the registered infirm often take a risk, only to be clamped and presented with a hefty fine. Stumping up £50 is the easy bit. What's difficult is the half-mile trip across what is often still a building site to track down the warden's office. It's little

This is a hospital

wonder that many disabled patients privately admit to abandoning their cars and dialling 999 to get picked up by an ambulance instead.

Television

Patientline provides 17,500 individual bedside TV sets to NHS hospitals. They allow patients individual choice: previously the only option was the communal set in the day room. But the one item the sets lack is an off switch. If you don't subscribe, the set remains on, punishing the patient with sixteen hours of continuous adverts for Patientline! A popular move with meningitis patients, whose debilitating headaches are much improved by the constant glare.

Mattresses

The bed and mattress you sleep on may only be rented. Many Trusts contract out their bed facilities, generating profits of anything up to 30 per cent.

Staff

While agency staff have always provided a flexible workforce, problems arise when wards find themselves largely run by temporary staff with no continuity of care, no 'local' knowledge, and no sense of belonging. Low-paid junior staff have been known to sign on with an agency to do temporary work in their time off. Staff end up on double shifts, sometimes filling in on the ward they just signed out of a few minutes before. Long hours leave nurses permanently at breaking point.

Food

Whereas staff could previously prepare simple food at a ward 'station', new health and safety regulations and PFI contracts mean that hospitals now have to limit food preparation to those holding the contract. Many hospitals are located on an out-of-town site with few (if any) other shops nearby and a fast-food outlet (for example, McDonald's) with a monopoly franchise. At the same time, the League of Friends shop which provided basic provisions at cost price has often been replaced by outlets providing the same goods at city-centre prices.

Cleaning

Cleaning services were one of the first things to be contracted out under the Tories. Very often, the new service companies would re-employ the same cleaners as before, on worse terms. Service manuals forbid staff to clean outside their designated areas; if you are detailed to clean the toilets, then a spill elsewhere cannot be dealt with until it has been cleared with a supervisor. In the end, the hospital gets dirtier, the service company gets richer, and the patients get cross-infected.

Medical records

In the interests of improving profits, your records can now be sold on to those doing research (albeit with strict rules regarding confidentiality). In effect, your illness or condition is a mini profit centre.

Hospital waste

Hospital waste needs careful handling; it covers everything from ordinary domestic waste, through medical waste, to radiological waste from X-rays and the like. It isn't quite like putting last night's curry into the wheelie bin. Which is why it is also time-consuming and expensive, with hospitals running their own incinerators. Now, if you could centralize that, shut down all those individual plants, and contract it out, you'd save a fortune.

Which is what has happened in the north of England. Hospitals within a hundred-mile radius joined together to send their rubbish to a super-incinerator in Aberdeen, which meant a huge increase in transport and environmental costs as waste lorries trundle up and down the motorway. And an increased risk of contamination. Previously, the worst that could happen was a burst bag and a spillage on the way across the car park. Now it's across half the country.

A day in the life

This is a list of common complaints at one new PFI hospital, located in the south of England, a few miles out of town on an area of inexpensive wasteland, well away from the community it serves.

- Cleaners on the weekend early shift having to pay £5 to get to work by taxi (the bus service starts at 10 a.m.), out of an hourly flat rate of £4.75 (including weekends). For the first hour or so they simply earn enough to get there. The same applies to those on the late shift.
- Nurses charged out of their salaries for parking spaces (whether or not space was available). The car park was reduced in order to build more operating theatres, the facilities having already proved inadequate.
- Nurses working unpaid extra time to ensure wards remain covered while staff on the next shift look for somewhere to park.
- A thrombolysis nurse-practitioner in A & E was unable to find a parking space when attending a cardiac emergency. Despite a note on the windscreen to this effect, the company that controls car parking attempted to clamp his vehicle and he had to leave the clinical area to move his car.
- The Volunteer Link Driver scheme closed down after drivers were regularly fined up to £50 for parking without paying at the new hospital, despite displaying their Link parking permits.
- Last year one patient at the hospital made the news when he waited a record 144 hours on a hospital trolley. He was one of 387 patients treated on trolleys in that month alone. The chief executive commented: 'Under normal circumstances we would not expect the patient to be cared for on what is technically a trolley but which, in many respects, is similar to a bed.' She later suggested that the lack of beds was a testimony to the hospital's efficiency: 'The hospital is one of the most cost-effective in the country. Around 98–100 per cent of its beds are occupied at any given time.'
- There are no private staff toilets. Male and female staff have to share the use of one toilet on the main corridor, which is often used by patients and passers-by, as the company will not allow any signs to be put on the walls for fear it might damage the decoration. That includes essential information posters, eye-charts, and other things generally related to medical matters and health care.
- If nursing staff want a shelf put up they have to get the company to do it. They were quoted up to £400 to put up a set of shelves.

- Porters carry bleeps, but there are no phones on the walls for them to ring back in response. If the bleep goes off there is nothing they can do.
- A student nurse did not know how to operate the bell system for patients to summon help.
- The IT department is now based two miles away, and the finance department is located even further away, in offices rented from Asda.
- The large Portakabins near the entrance are the builder's site offices, but the trust now rents them from the builder for office space.

The private consortium running this hospital has just been selected as the preferred bidder for another large hospital in the South of England. In its recent accounts the company concerned showed an extremely healthy rise in profits.

As well as becoming a set of profit centres, modern hospitals are encouraged to compete with each other. Extra funding and power will go to those centres of excellence that exceed targets, and those that underperform will be penalized. One critical way is through the differential pay rates that foundation hospitals will be allowed to offer; individual hospitals will be able to tease staff away from 'rival' hospitals by paying more than national rates. Some do this already. Like 'failing' schools, 'failing' hospitals will have powers stripped from them, making it harder still to match the performance achieved elsewhere.

The belief is that empowerment brings about motivation and motivation will turn the ailing health service around. The idea of a marketplace supposes that patients can and will shop around for their treatment and will punish failing hospitals by not going there.

The problem is that hospitals can't compete with each other like for like: different catchment areas present different demographics. Hospitals are services that are delivered locally. They are not footloose dot-com businesses that can chase cheap labour. The infamous 'postcode lottery' is made worse by penalizing 'failing' hospitals and diverting resources elsewhere.

What all this leads to is a bean-counter mentality. If a hospital takes up the challenge, then its success can only be judged by statistics – not the intangibles that don't show up on a spreadsheet. So, for the first time ever, there are now more administrative staff in the health service than those actively engaged in front-line care.

BLAIR: Look, I'm sorry, I can't see what the problem is.
CAMPBELL: The problem is some people might see it as turning your back on everything the Labour Party ever stood for.
BLAIR: Look, I've told you, I'm not interested what the press have to say.
CAMPBELL: I'm not talking about the press here, I'm talking about your own back-benchers.
BLAIR: Not them again. Look, I mean, I get us elected every five years, the least they could do is let me get on with things in between times – no, what really pisses me off is the fact that half the people who bellyache about all this could well afford to go private if they wanted to.
CAMPBELL: They don't see it like that.
BLAIR: Of course they don't. Look, health is a product, just like everything else. You can buy in or you can opt out. If you opt out, we'll do the best we can for you, obviously, but there's got to be a bit of personal responsibility in all this somewhere. I'm giving them a free choice, they've got more disposable income than they ever had before, all they have to do is decide what they want to spend it on. A new hip or a new iPod – it's their choice. What could be more democratic than that?
CAMPBELL: What about those who can't afford a private health plan?
BLAIR: Yeah, well, there you go; look, I'm sorry, but life's like that. They're not the people who really matter. They don't start up dot-com companies, or make a fortune setting up soft porn websites. They're not the people who we really need to appeal to, the people who really make sure this country still stands for something.
CAMPBELL: Except those people aren't worried about the state of the NHS. They all go private.
BLAIR: Exactly, they wouldn't be seen dead in an NHS hospital. Actually, come to think of it, that's about the only time they are likely to be seen in one.

Elsewhere the government has replaced the Patient's Charter with 'Your Guide to the NHS', and instead of handing over 'rights', it tells patients what they can 'expect', while emphasizing patients' responsibilities in terms of not missing appointments, doing exercise, and practising safe sex.

It's true that inpatient waiting lists have fallen, but only at the expense of outpatient waiting lists, which doubled during Labour's first term. There is a wealth of official statistics and claims, but for every figure given there is an equally unattractive one to undermine that claim. Statistics don't lie, but they don't tell the truth either.

Still, if waiting lists threaten to get out of hand, there is always one final solution: refuse to accept anyone else onto the list. That way, the figures are OK and everyone knows where they stand. Which is exactly where they were standing a year ago.

Drug companies

The Department of Health is responsible for two functions: stewardship of the NHS – ensuring the best value for money, carrying out the most operations it can, and so on – and a formal obligation, sponsorship of the pharmaceutical industry.

Under the sponsorship function comes a scheme that fixes the profit that drugs companies can make from the NHS – the Pharmaceutical Price Regulation Scheme – the general principle of which is that companies are allowed to make a specified return on their investments. Big drug companies are typically allowed to make a return on capital of 17–21 per cent through sales to the NHS. Theoretically, the difference allows them to plough money into researching and developing new life-saving drugs. However, the percentage that drug companies actually spend on R&D is very small.

Recently, companies have started setting up new smaller companies and hiving off their older and more established drugs onto them. The smaller companies are not affected by the PPRS, and the larger companies are therefore able to make greater profits on new drugs. These can be simply replacements for older drugs, offering no increased benefit apart from their 'newness'. However, the mark-up they can place on them is enormous – twenty to thirty times that on the older drugs.

One of the main criticisms of the PPRS is that it is conducted wholly in secret. The scheme should be reviewed every five years and the Labour government had promised to overhaul it. After some intense lobbying, with drug companies in and out of No. 10, threatening to pull out of the UK and possibly to ration the amount of drugs sold if they were challenged on price, the Department of Health went back on its promises.

19
The second agricultural revolution

Supermarkets run what are known as Known Value Items. Things like bread and milk, the prices of which customers can easily compare against those in other shops. These are then kept low, to entice buyers from rival outlets. (Petrol is a common example.) Other, less-familiar products can then be priced significantly higher than other stores. In addition, special offers can create temporary KVIs. The offer ends but the illusion that they are still cheaper at a supermarket remains.

In order to keep the price of KVIs low without affecting their profits, supermarkets squeeze suppliers to get a good deal, using their huge buying power to play one supplier off against another.

Milk is a good example. On average most UK dairy farmers are being paid under the cost of production, and have been for at least the last seven years.[97] So while the supermarkets use a low milk price to draw customers in, it's the farmers, not the supermarkets, who struggle to make ends meet. In 1998 food companies like Quaker and Kelloggs had profits 186 to 740 times greater than the Canadian farmers who supplied them.

One knock-on from this is that milk rounds and independent bakers have been 'eliminated' by this practice. Legislation in France, Spain, and Ireland, recognizing the economic and social consequences, forbids the sale of goods below cost price. Not in Britain. Goodwill to suppliers is itself in short supply, with stores often working on a sale-or-return basis and even demanding money up front for farmers to feature in a promotion.

To access cheap KVIs and keep other costs down, supermarkets take advantage of economies of scale. 'Compete local, source global' is the rule, with supermarkets playing off one area or country against another and then pricing to eliminate competitors in the local high street. The result is a huge movement of goods, often across thousands of miles. A study in Ludlow, Shropshire, showed that while local shops sourced much of their produce from the immediate area, the town's supermarkets sold virtually no locally produced goods.

A recent report broke down a typical Sunday lunch for one shopper.

Chicken from Thailand	10,691 miles by ship
Runner beans from Zambia	4912 miles by plane
Carrots from Spain	1000 miles by lorry
Mangetouts from Zimbabwe	5130 miles by plane
Potatoes from Italy	1521 miles by lorry
Sprouts from Britain	125 miles
Total	23,379 miles

That's very nearly once round the globe. For one meal. Not including pudding.

It takes up to 2.2 litres of kerosene to air-freight 1 pound of fruit or vegetables across the world.[98]

Out-of-season Coxes are imported 14,000 miles from New Zealand during our own apple season,[99] while British produce lies rotting on the ground. In France, 90 per cent of all the apples sold in supermarkets are produced domestically; in the UK the figure is only 25 per cent. In 1961, 36 per cent of apples used in the UK were imported. By 1999 this had risen to 80 per cent. Meanwhile 60 per cent of our orchards were destroyed, and production fell by two-thirds.

Cattle and sheep are moved around the country for pasturing in Wales or Scotland for a week or two so that they can carry the Welsh lamb or Scottish beef label. Our daffodil harvest is left unpicked because labour rates are too high and we can source imports more cheaply.

To slash costs still further, central buying and Just in Time ordering have been brought in, requiring products to be shipped round the country in large refrigerated lorries from semi-automated main depots.

It's estimated that around 90 per cent of the food we consume in this country is now bought through one of the 'big five' supermarket chains, which operate out of around 3000 superstores nationwide. The purchasing power of just 20 buyers, representing the largest food manufacturers and retailers, determine what and how 25,000 farmers farm.[100] A recent report found that all Safeway's dairy produce passes through a single depot in Warwickshire before being trucked all over the country. The food may be cheap, but the environmental cost isn't.

Then there's packaging. By virtue of its transportable nature, supermarket produce generates waste: nearly 10 million tons of discarded packaging every year, of which less than 5 per cent is recycled. The average family spends about £500 annually on the packaging alone – around a sixth of their total shopping bill. If you threw every sixth item away as soon as you got it home, that would be a fair reflection of the price we pay for having our food factory-prepared and homogenized.

Add to that the pesticides, preservatives, and additives necessary to grow homogeneous crops and to maintain denatured products in a sterile environment for a long period, and the environmental cost continues to mount.

Produce sold as 'fresh' has often been kept in vast airless containers for anything up to 18 months. The lack of oxygen means the food produces carbon dioxide, which keeps it looking fresh, but as soon as it is removed from the container the appearance will rapidly go downhill – which is why fresh fruit and vegetables that you buy in the supermarket appear to go off after a couple of days. (The same applies to MPs, incidentally.)

Just as goods have to move to supermarkets, so do people: nearly 80 per cent of supermarket trips are by car. The distance travelled to go shopping in Great Britain increased by 14 per cent between 1990 and '95.[101]

Supermarkets endlessly claim how many jobs they create. Yet their own research organization, the National Retail Planning Forum (paid for by Tesco, Sainsburys, M&S, Boots, John Lewis), provides clear evidence to the contrary. They studied areas surrounding ninety-three superstores, and found that supermarkets have 'a negative net impact on retail employment up to 15km away.' Total employment in food selling within that radius, it reported, decreased by 5.2 per cent, while nationally retail employment increased by 0.1 per cent in Great Britain outside the 15km zones.

Every time a large supermarket opens it's estimated that 276 people lose their jobs. On average for every £50,000 spent in small local shops, one job is created; in superstores, for the same result, the sum required is £250,000.

Long, unsocial opening hours and a seven-day week add to the poor working conditions. It's estimated nearly half of all workers are employed part-time and enjoy nothing like the protection offered to full-time workers. It's little wonder that, a few years ago, it was reported that almost a third of Sainsbury's staff were students earning extra money in their spare time.

But just like New Labour, who know how to spin a good story, supermarkets know the value of PR – even if sometimes it does backfire. A Tesco scheme to exchange vouchers for computer equipment for schools reportedly required over £200,000 to be spent to get a computer worth less than £1000.

Tesco

Tesco's pre-tax profits for 2003–04 were £1,600,000,000.

(That's £4.4 million a day.)

(DEFRA estimated the income of the average UK farmer at £12,211, or £33 a day, in 2002–03.)

Tesco's profits were up 17.6 per cent on last year.

UK sales reached £24,760,000,000 –
that's £500 per person per year.

At least £1 in every £8 spent with a UK retailer is spent at Tesco.

Tesco has 968 stores around the UK.

Yet this isn't part of a Europe-wide trend. The profit margins enjoyed by UK retailers are three times those of their counterparts in other European countries and the USA. As the ad says, every little helps. Particularly if you're a shareholder.

And here's another thing: the cheapest available selection out of a full list of supermarket groceries can cost up to 70 per cent more in some of the poorest parts of the country than in stores belonging to the same chain in richer areas. City centre stores often increase prices compared with their out-of-town sister stores. Why? Because the supermarkets encounter less competition in poorer areas. Same with urban sites. It's not personal, it's strictly business.

The Good News

The UK went from having no farmers' markets at all in the mid-1990s, to having over 270 at the end of the decade. In Winchester, it was found that shops reported 30 per cent greater takings on days when there was a farmer's market.

And the government's position? Well, as ministers are keen to remind us, the government's job isn't to tell you what you can and can't do with your money, it's simply there to encourage free choice in a land where the consumer is king.

And they should know, because the Prime Minister has some very good people advising him.

Tony's supermarket sweep

Supermarkets are well represented at Westminster. Lord Sainsbury (of Sainsburys) is Under-Secretary of State for Science and Technology, while Sir Terry Leahy, chief executive of Tesco, finds time to sit on four government task forces. Tory MP Archie Norman, who used to run Asda, is now an MP, so he can lobby himself. Sean Woodward, Tory defector and spouse to another member of the Sainsbury dynasty, joined Labour and in return was granted a safe seat for the 2001 election.

Other supermarket interests are well represented on several influential committees and quangos, while a supermarket trolleyful of secondments to government, always a useful way of sharing knowledge, are to be found lower down the patronage ladder.

In many ways Labour has been extremely sluggish in introducing regulations to protect its people. But in foodstuffs, egged on in part by Europe, the light regulatory touch seen elsewhere has been swapped for a mass of regulation and red tape. Not so much to protect farm workers – gang masters and poor wages have continued to proliferate – but the final produce is now extremely tightly monitored by law. This is on top of the supermarkets' own ruthless 'quality' monitoring – size and shape being deemed a quality issue.

A farmer supplying cauliflowers managed to switch from pesticide control of caterpillars to a more environmentally friendly form of biological pest control. It was far safer and cleaner but did leave the occasional dead wasp which the customer could easily wash off. The supermarket refused delivery and returned the whole crop.

In the UK less than 1 per cent of food poisoning cases are caused by dairy products, yet some of the most stringent regulations relate to them – destroying, for example, small artisan cheese makers. These laws deem cakes from the farmhouse kitchen sold directly to the consumer a health risk,[102] while two-week-old, processed yoghurt in a supermarket chiller cabinet is considered safe.

Food standards inevitably mean that only large, corporately backed suppliers can afford to stay in business. Yet ironically recent food-poisoning and safety scandals have resulted directly from large-scale mass-production methods which mean that any problem is likely to spread to the entire country.

Other things you can do in a supermarket:

- Go to church. Combined supermarkets and churches have been promoted by supermarket companies as their way of helping with Lord's Day Observance.
- Visit the police. Recently in London it was announced that many local police stations would close and the property be sold off, raising useful money to fight crime. Operations would move to voluntarily run police kiosks in supermarket foyers.
- Solicitors have moved to supermarket sites, making it possible to draw up a will if a morning searching the aisles has made you lose the will to live.
- Doctors and dentists have taken advantage of the captive market with which a supermarket presents them.

20
Business, as usual

While campaigning groups, fellow MPs, and even members of his own Cabinet complained about the difficulty of getting access to the Prime Minister during his first term in office, one man, so it was said, could be sure his calls were always returned and the door to No. 10 always open. Well, two if you include Rupert Murdoch. And the other? British Aerospace's Dick Evans.

How to sell a Hawk

Blair's Cabinet, BAe's unofficial sales force[103]

This is a log of the publicly listed occasions on which government ministers sought to push through just one BAe contract, the recent sale of BAe Hawk jets to India.

4–6 February 2003
Lord Bach, minister for defence procurement, spearheads sales push at Indian air fair.

19 July 2002
Jack Straw visits India and discusses the Hawk deal.

3 July 2002
Geoff Hoon is in discussion with the Indians about the Hawk sales.

28–29 May 2002
John Prescott raises Hawk deal at a development meeting in India.

27 February 2002
Jack Straw visits India to try and seal the deal.

4–7 January 2002
Tony Blair visits India on a peace mission and raises the sale of the sixty Hawk jets.

13–14 November 2001
Geoff Hoon is in India for talks on the Hawk deal.
At the same time Tony Blair meets the Indian prime minister in London and discusses the same thing.

July 2001
John Prescott makes a one-day visit to India to talk about the Hawk sale.

February 2001
Baroness Symons, minister for defence procurement, visits Indian air fair and supports the Hawk sale.

6–11 January 2001
Stephen Byers meets Indians and pushes for the sale to go through.

December 2000
Geoff Hoon pledges UK support for the deal at a meeting in India.

Where are they now?[104]

Michael Portillo

Secretary of State for Defence 1995–7
Non-executive director of BAe Systems

Roger Freeman

Minister of State for Defence Procurement 1994–5
Director of defence manufacturer Thales plc since 1999

Geoffrey Pattie

Minister of State for Defence Procurement
Chairman of Marconi Electronic Systems 1990–99

In January 2002, on the eve of a visit to the region, Blair pledged to have 'as strong a calming influence as possible' in the conflict between India and Pakistan. He also warned at the time of the 'enormous problems the whole of the world would face if things went wrong'.

A week later, the UK government mounted an intensive campaign to boost arms sales to India, including sixty Hawk jets worth £1 billion.[105] On 3 September 2003 India announced it would indeed be buying BAe Hawk trainer jets for over £1 billion. The Defence Minister said there were no US components on the Hawk – a key concern for the Indian government, because it is the subject of US embargoes in response to its nuclear missile programme.

'Originally some components on the aircraft were of US origin, but during earlier negotiations we had got them to replace them with British parts', a Defence Minister said.

In 2000, the government granted nearly 700 export licences for India, for deals worth more than £64 million, a significant increase over the previous year. The items covered included equipment for combat aircraft and helicopters, as well as missiles. But, to be even-handed, we also sold mortars, armoured personnel carriers, combat aircraft, production equipment for assault rifles, and machine-guns to Pakistan.

In July 2002, Jack Straw announced that UK components for the F-16 fighter aircraft would be licensed for export to the US, for the US to sell on to Israel.[106] This decision was taken despite Israel's regular use of F-16s for attacks on Palestinians in the Occupied Territories, and despite the Israeli government's admission in April 2002 that British Centurion tanks had been used against Palestinians – in breach of Israel's own assurances.

Listed in the government's latest Annual Report on UK arms exports are licences for aircraft machine guns to Indonesia; shotguns, small arms, rifles, machine guns, smoke grenades and paramilitary arms to Saudi Arabia; small arms, air-to-air missile launching systems and torpedo parts to India; and toxic chemical precursors to Pakistan. Of particular concern were £545 million of licences to embargo-restricted Iran – with the worry that dual-usage could still see equipment used to enflame already delicate border tensions – and £76 million to similarly embargoed China, the equipment this time including utility helicopters, radar, equipment for nuclear reactors and technical aid for combat aircraft. Both, countries where human rights were still of real concern.

Still, the argument was that if we supplied them, then at least we would be able to monitor what was going into service and prevent any misuse. And it has to be admitted that the government has a point here: after all, we tried this approach out with Saddam Hussein and it seemed to work pretty well.

Being Peter Mandelson

To appreciate Labour's love affair with business, and in particular American business, you need go no further than a flick through the rather attractive, hand-tooled calf leather of Peter Mandelson's travel diary.

We start in January 1999 with a trip to Paris, courtesy of BP. A few days at home, then it's off to Cologne for another meeting and a few more days away. Next month it's Milan and Johannesburg, then in March it's Madrid. In April it's a quick hop to Washington, then back to London for a change of clothes, and off again to Corfu. May sees a trip to Spain, then back to the USA (perhaps he forgot something). June is a quiet month. Just a quick pop to Portugal for the Bilderberg Conference, then over the border to Spain for a financial meeting, then back home to catch breath before it's off to the States yet again in August, a week in Aspen this time and a chance to meet Condoleezza Rice, then home for a couple of weeks before it's back to Heathrow and a trip to Frankfurt.

Then everything goes oddly quiet for eighteen months, with just a trip to Antigua paid for by that country's government in August 2000. But in March 2001 the jet-setting starts again. Madrid with the *Economist* in March, France with Unisys in August, Portugal, again with the *Economist*, in September, and then China, Hong Kong, Japan, Israel, Austria, and Germany to wrap the year up.

In 2002, Peter managed Austria and America in January, South Africa and the States yet again in February, back to South Africa (maybe he forgot something there too) and Hungary in March, then a break before Indonesia, Malaysia, Thailand, and Singapore in August. In October it's Russia; in November it's Germany and Spain for another spot of networking at the *Economist* conference. Then, with just enough time to sling a fresh pair of pants in the suitcase, it's off to India for a few days to round off the year.

And this, remember, is the man who, when he stood down for the second time, told us he really just wanted to be a back-bench MP serving his constituents in Hartlepool.

2003 sees Peter in Bahrain and Qatar at the start of the year, and Spain in March courtesy of Thompson holidays (with so much travel you'd think another foreign jolly was the last thing he needed), then it was Poland in May and Russia a few weeks later in June. Then a hop over to France and another nice winter break in the sun, this time in Dubai, before starting off 2004 with a trip to Germany courtesy of the publishers Bertelsmann. All these trips expenses paid – and all this on top of a diary full of UK speaking engagements, a monthly paid column to write for *GQ* magazine, a job on the board at an advertising agency, more paid work for the Independent News and Media group, and a part-time position at a PR consultancy.

What did he say when he resigned from office with his tail between his legs but his head held high? 'I want to be a parliamentarian rather than a minister, a good constituency MP, and someone who continues to serve the country from that base and no other.' That base presumably including Spain, Germany, Portugal, America, South Africa, Russia, Italy, Hungary, Austria, Dubai, Antigua, China, Hong Kong, Japan, Israel, Indonesia, Malaysia, Thailand, India, Poland, Bahrain, Qatar, Corfu, and Singapore.

None of which is wrong – and no doubt was of benefit to the people of Hartlepool – but it does just leave one wondering if there is such a thing as a free lunch – or, more precisely, 200 free lunches?

In July 2004, Mandelson accepted Tony Blair's offer to serve as Britain's commissioner at the European Union. Another diary, another base.

A personal message from Gordon Brown

Hello, no, don't stop what you're doing. Multi-tasking is very much a part of modern, thriving Britain and far be it from me to stand accused of sticking a spanner in the works.

In fact, my message to you, as you make the tea, watch TV, surf eBay, plump the sofa, tidy away the kids' toys, and read this book, all at the same time, is to encourage you to expand upon this spirit of endeavour even further and avoid easy street at all costs. We need you stretching yourself to the max, sorting out your bank accounts online at three in the morning, turning up at work at five so you can deal with the overnight faxes from head office in Korea, eating a high-energy snack bar at the gym in place of a sit-down supper, then popping along to the local PTA meeting to see how well the self-help group is doing decorating the year three classrooms. In short, we want busy, busy, busy.

You see, something like PFI – and I make no apologies for that, no time, too busy – demands certain things of you. After all, you did choose New Labour and when you voted us in, having been told we wouldn't put up taxes, you must have thought there had to be a catch somewhere. I mean, you're not so stupid as to think there's something for nothing in this world, are you?

Anyway, look, there's no point in going over old ground, it's too late to turn back. It's all about rights and responsibilities: you were right to vote us in, now it's your responsibility to make it work.

The thing is, if this public–private thing doesn't work out, then we really are well and truly stuffed. Look at the railway companies handing back the keys, unable to make it work, forcing us, or more precisely you, to dig deep into your pockets to make up the shortfall. Now, imagine that pattern over the entire public services. Hardly bears thinking about, does it? So we'd better make a go of it, or all those stealth taxes we've been sneaking in will go through the roof. Aye, don't think I've not got a few more up my sleeve for after the election, if we need them. A pet levy? How does that sound? So keep in line, or the puppy gets it!

See, what these consortiums and investors running our public services need is cheap money they can borrow. Take that away and they'll just tear up the contracts and be out the door like a flash.

So this is where you lot come in. We don't make a great deal these days. Our days as the workshop of the world – you remember, all those geography textbooks – well, they are long gone: too expensive, too mucky, and, frankly we just don't have the will to compete with those South-East Asian sweatshops any more. But what we are still very good at is consuming things and borrowing money.

Since we took over, incomes are up by 23 per cent, but personal debt has increased by 50 per cent. Last summer, it topped the trillion-pound mark;[107] that means you owe as much as we earn in a year. £17,000 for each man, woman and child.

Well done.

Crivens, we owe over £800 billion on mortgages alone. And it's growing fast. Hence the property boom. That money isn't coming from nowhere, it's coming from you lot popping into the local mortgage brokers and living on the never-never. And because of that, the City is thriving, and because the City is thriving the money people are happy; and that means there's sufficient confidence to keep interest rates down and give our PFI chums a fighting chance to pull it out of the bag and make it work.

So the message to you here today is very simple: Carry on moving.

And if you can't do that, then at least remortgage the place and spend the money on a frivolous foreign holiday or a new sports car. Frankly, as a man whose natural inclination is towards prudence, I shouldn't really be saying all this, but there's never been a better time to buy. Anything. And with some of the offers available, you can save yourself a bob or two and do your country proud at the same time.

And if you can force yourself to trade up the property ladder every couple of years, even if it's just down the street, well, then you are enabling us, or, rather, the companies we now rely on to run our part-privatized (we still own the bicycle sheds) schools and hospitals, to stay in business. Your selfless offer to invest in a second home is allowing them to repaint the front gate and put up a nice big shiny new sign with their name and the phone number of someone in Wisconsin if there is a problem out of hours.

So keep up the good work, and give thanks to the Third Way for providing you with the economic miracle that has got us this far and may, just may, get us a little bit further.

OK, right, well, back you go to the anvil, leafing through those property ads, and remember our new motto: 'England expects every man, woman, and child to do their duty and have a loft extension or a new patio by the start of the next fiscal year.'

Thanks,

Gordon

Debt

Total credit card lending in Britain has doubled in the past four years to £170 billion, with 4000 different credit cards available. Each adult has, on average, three different cards. One in twenty of us has over five. We spend an average of nearly £1,000 a quarter on our credit cards.[108]

The amount being sought by Britain's bailiffs has soared by 70 per cent over the past two years, to a record £5 billion.

More than 3 million people are struggling with energy bills, 4.7 million are in debt to their water companies, and more than 1 million have had their phones cut off.

Matt Barrett, the boss of Barclays, which itself reported a 40 per cent rise in pre-tax profits to £3.8 billion in January 2004, caused outrage in December 2003 when he said that he advised his children not to borrow on credit cards because they are 'too expensive'. Barrett's own goal came before the Treasury Select Committee after he was asked to explain why the interest charged on a Barclaycard was 17.9 per cent when the Bank of England's main interest rate stood at just 3.5 per cent.

21
Hard Labour

In the past seven years Labour have done a lot of work rebranding themselves as the party of business.

A key priority is attracting inward investment into Britain. That means leaner, fitter, organizations which will turn in a profit, not come begging for government bail-outs. But while a liberal climate and flexible employment laws encourage companies to come to Britain, that same flexibility makes them more inclined to make their UK workers redundant when times are bad, because the laws and financial penalties are much tougher elsewhere. As a manager at Merrill Lynch admitted,

> The main problems lie in Frankfurt and Paris; it is much easier to fire staff in London.[115]

A CBI investigation into labour markets in the six major economies of the EU showed that the United Kingdom has the most flexible economy, the highest levels of part-time and temporary work, the most flexible working hours, and the greatest freedom by bosses to set pay to suit the market. The only areas in which Britain was rated 'moderate' were in skills and the willingness of people to move house to take a job.

The normal notice required before redundancy in Britain is six or twelve weeks – shorter than in many European countries, where there is a long-drawn-out process of notification and consultation while employer and employee both consider the financial implications, and the employee seeks alternative employment. As the employer continues to pay wages during this period, they may think twice before laying workers off.

Statutory minimum redundancy payments are lower in the UK than in many other EU countries (half the EU average after ten years, in fact),[116] and there is no requirement for an employer to fund a 'social plan' in the event of major redundancies. And the current climate of flexible hours, outsourced labour, and legislation to curb union influence, makes it that much harder to protest.

The Americans have invented a new language specifically to suit new employment practices.

In Coca Cola's recent accounts, the following note appeared:

> Our company initiated a major organizational realignment intended to put more responsibility, accountability, and resources in the hands of local business units of the company so as to fully leverage the local capabilities of our system.

Which sounds reasonable enough (if a bit wordy). But read on:

> Under the realignment, employees were separated from almost all functional areas of the company's operations . . . The total number of employees separated as of December 31, was approximately 5200. Employees separated from the company as a result of the realignment were offered severance or . . .

So that's it. You're not sacked; you are organizationally realigned and separated from the company. Same thing, different terminology.

And with Britain under Blair now modelling itself so closely on America, and with what happens in the States a certainty to happen here in a few years' time, we can prepare for the moment when the call centres leave for a cheaper pool of labour in Equatorial Guinea, as they eventually will, and we can all enjoy the wholesome and fibre-building benefits of structural realigned leverage through separation. (Job losses to you and me.)

The DTI makes no secret of its employer-friendly culture: quite the opposite. The UK Trade and Investment website recently boasted the following incentives to relocate business here:[117]

- Highly competitive social costs on wage bills that are amongst the lowest in Western Europe
- A highly flexible labour market, which enables foreign investors to use a great deal of flexibility in their employment and management of staff
- UK law does not oblige employers to provide a written employment contract
- In the UK, employees are used to working hard for their employers. In 2001 the average hours usually worked per week by full-time employees

> was 45.1 hours for males and 40.7 hours for females. The EU average was 40.9 hours and 38.8 hours for males and females respectively.

And while it recognized that new European regulations might require a written agreement between employer and worker, it pointed out that there was an opt-out:

> An employer need only maintain a record of workers who have signed an opt-out [and] no further records for these workers are required.

A few months later, word leaked out that the Home Office had been equally lax in its record keeping, turning a blind eye to workers from the 'new' Europe ahead of full entry in May 2004. The government had effectively agreed to ignore immigration requirements in the hope that it might tap into a pool of cheap, deregulated labour to fill the cheap, deregulated jobs it was hoping cheap, deregulated business would exploit.

Not so much an open back-door policy as an open barn-door policy.

However, with terrorism hot on the agenda, the Home Office was at the same time peddling a new (voter-friendly) get-tough line on asylum.

Proposals included issuing asylum seekers with deportation notices, even if their claims had yet to be processed (to speed up the process), introducing measures to ensure all asylum seekers aged over fourteen would be fingerprinted, and building more privately run internment camps which could hold asylum seekers until their claims were processed.

22
Asylum

According to a recent MORI poll, on average people think that 23 per cent of the world's refugees and asylum seekers are in the UK, when it is actually less than 2 per cent.[118]

In 2001, Canada approved 97 per cent of asylum applications from Afghanistan, while for the UK the figure was only 19 per cent. Somali applicants had a 92 per cent success rate in Canada, and 34 per cent in the UK. And 85 per cent of Colombian applicants were granted protection in Canada, against a mere 3 per cent in the UK.

The UK is the tenth most popular destination for asylum seekers in Europe, when measured by the ratio of asylum seekers to the size of the host population.[119] Many do not choose their country of asylum: where they end up can depend on how quickly they flee, and by what means. But of those who do choose, asylum seekers are most likely to be swayed by the presence of members of their own community in a foreign state, rather than by any possible state benefits or standards of reception. Some asylum seekers use illegitimate means to enter, paying to be smuggled into the country. But if he is fleeing a civil war or human rights abuses, an asylum seeker is unlikely to be issued with the paperwork necessary to obtain a visa.

Dangerous countries list[120]

The US State Department issues periodic travel warnings recommending that Americans avoid certain countries because of instability, risk, or danger. At the time when the West was troubled about a flood of asylum seekers, dangerous country warnings existed for the following states:

Central African Republic
Saudi Arabia
Nepal
Iraq
Israel: the West Bank and Gaza
Indonesia
Haiti
Algeria
Libya
Colombia
Afghanistan
Ivory Coast
Pakistan
Democratic Republic of the Congo
Zimbabwe
Liberia
Nigeria
Lebanon
Sudan
Bosnia
Somalia
Angola
Kenya
Yemen
Burundi
Iran

Now, work out where the asylum seekers come from.

Dangerous countries list (II)

There was another dangerous countries list printed not long ago. This time it was commissioned by *Time* magazine in Europe and polled around 700,000 people. The result is equally illuminating.[121]

Time Europe questionnaire

Which country poses the greatest danger to world peace in 2003?

North Korea	6.7%
Iraq	6.3%
United States	86.9%

Total votes cast: 706,842

UK asylum seekers

Top ten nationalities, 2001

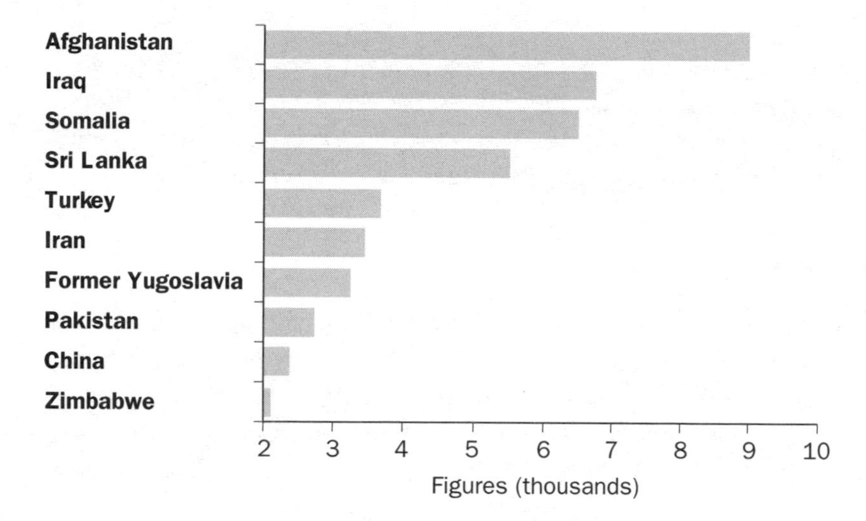

Afghanistan

On average 25 per cent of children die before their first birthday. Life expectancy is 43 years. Up to 300 people a month are killed by landmines. Sanitation is all but non-existent. Aid workers are targeted and aid dispersal spasmodic. Meanwhile, much of the country is run by violent warlords, and opium production is at an all-time high.

Iraq

It's estimated that there were at least 10,000 deaths in the twelve months following the coalition invasion.

A 2004 International Red Cross report said that coalition military intelligence officers themselves estimated that 70–90 per cent of the people they had deprived of freedom had been arrested by mistake. In most cases, no information was given to those arrested about who was apprehending them, where their base was located, or why they were being locked up. Families were rarely told anything, the arrested person simply disappearing before contact was made often weeks or months later. Hoodings, beatings, threats, and acts of humiliation (being paraded naked was common) were all part of the softening-up process before interrogation, many of the abuses taking place in the very jails in which Saddam's officers had previously committed similar atrocities. The barbarity of Saddam's regime has been replaced by bombings, sporadic fighting and threatened Shia uprisings.

Somalia

Somalia has been without a central government since 1991. The resultant fighting, combined with famine and disease, has led to the death of up to 1 million people during the past ten years. Life expectancy is 41–43 years, and the mortality rate for children under five is 25 per cent.

Sri Lanka

For the past twenty years there has been a bloody civil war in Sri Lanka. After new emergency regulations were introduced, torture, disappearances, and deaths in custody increased. Unemployment is very high and a large proportion of the population is dependent on humanitarian assistance.

Turkey

There has been civil unrest in Turkey for fifteen years. Turkey has applied for European Union membership, but the EU says it must improve its human rights record first. Political activists, Kurdish villagers, students, and children are all tortured. Writers, environmentalists, trade unionists, local and national politicians, religious leaders, human rights defenders, and other groups are imprisoned or tried for exercising freedom of expression, particularly on issues related to Kurdish rights.

Iran

Iran itself hosts the largest refugee population in the world, numbering about 2 million – it hosts 1.5 million refugees from Afghanistan alone. The war against Iraq has taken its toll economically, and all forms of opposition to the ruling elite are harshly oppressed.

Former Yugoslavia

The countries of the former Yugoslavia host over 750,000 refugees from the conflicts in the region. The number of people seeking asylum from the former Yugoslavia has declined considerably from its peak, but the situation in some areas remains volatile and members of the Serb community have been targeted.

Pakistan

The country remains under military rule, and political activities in public are banned. Torture in police custody and in jails has been widely reported.

China

China commits serious human rights abuses every year, and these have recently been on the increase. It restricts many freedoms and harshly oppresses any opposition.[122] The absence of effective social welfare provision in the country has left many facing dire poverty.

Zimbabwe

In recent years Zimbabwe has descended from relative stability into chaos. The policies of President Robert Mugabe have led to violence and to millions of people facing starvation. The authorities deny food to political opponents. Dissent is brutally repressed and torture is reported.

Once here, immigrants can find themselves exploited in some of the lowest-paid jobs in the country. Here are some examples:

Packing fruit for supermarket chain	75 p per hour
Cockle picking in Morecambe Bay	11 p per hour
Stonemasons working on West London Temple	30 p per hour
Assembly worker in electronics factory	£1.40 per hour
Clothing factory worker	£2.40 per hour

South African workers, legally allowed to come here, were lured to Britain with the promise of a weekly wage of at least £200. Not a lot, but still worth the trip.

But the deal wasn't quite that simple. The workers would have to pay their own expenses, and for this they were given £1500 to enable them to apply for visas and buy plane tickets. A generous hand-out? Hardly – the money was to be paid back in twelve weeks at 100 per cent interest. Work it out. After twelve weeks they would have earned £2400, but would have to pay back £3000.

Luckily, the gangmasters setting up the deal reworked the figures and realized they had made a mistake. The South Africans, packing fruit in Lincolnshire for a large supermarket chain, should also have been charged £55 per week for accommodation – often no more than a dilapidated caravan in a field.

Still, at least the company provided the workers with proper wage slips. That's how we know that one of them was left with just 78p for one week's work. And no chance of leaving until he had paid off the rest of the money he owed.

Which begs the question: what is it that they are getting away from that makes the alternative seem so much more attractive?

Instead, the question we are far more likely to hear is, why are they targeting us?

Once here, asylum seekers may find themselves miles away from any contact with members of their own community and support services such as specialist legal help and medical services.[123]

Under current asylum rules, you have to identify yourself to the first official you encounter. You can still claim asylum, but you must present yourself in person at the Home Office in Croydon. You will then be asked to fill in a complex form, detailing your entire life history and any evidence you have to support your claim. Although you are given an information sheet in your own language, you have to complete the form in English, and failure to do so will result in automatic rejection.

The government does not provide any legal or medical assistance. Legal advice is very difficult to get because of the shortage of trained experts. A recent exposé showed immigration officers using as translators students with a very basic grasp of the foreign language and no experience of the political situation in the country concerned. They were told the 'basic thrust' of what the applicant was saying would be sufficient.

In defence of Labour's asylum plans, it can always be argued that they are not as mad as the Tories'.

Oliver Letwin, when Shadow Home Secretary, suggested that all asylum seekers should be deported to an island 'far offshore for processing'. When asked where this might be, he gaily announced he 'didn't have the slightest idea'.[124]

Labour at least thought a second or two longer when they suggested the possibility that refugees could lodge their asylum applications in or near the country they were fleeing from. Only a second, though; any longer and they would have realized that the idea that the beaten, the tortured, and the spied-upon should form an orderly line outside the embassy gates and await their turn was unworkable. For those foolish enough actually to bother coming to an EU state to claim asylum, Labour dreamt up the idea of removing them to 'transit processing centres' just outside the EU's borders – the idea presumably being that out of sight really is out of mind. The other EU states shot this idea down; for

Germany and Greece in particular, the prospect of refugees being deported into camps in Eastern Europe evoked just too many memories.

The latest initiative is called 'migration partnerships',[125] whereby poor countries such as Kenya and Tanzania, which already have massive refugee problems, agree to take some of our asylum seekers in exchange for aid and technical assistance. So far, there haven't been too many takers.

But then David Blunkett hit on a Plan F: dump everything on the Belgians. Writing in the *People* two days before new measures to allow workers from the 'new' Europe into Britain were announced, he revealed that in future all Eurostar passengers would be checked by British Customs and Excise officials before they boarded in Brussels. In effect, he had extended our sovereign territory beyond the coast and into the heart of the Low Countries. A similar measure applies in France, where Britain now starts in Paris.

And slowly a map of new Britain emerged. Our borders start not where you enter Britain, at a port or an airport, but where you embark on your journey. New York, Tokyo, Alice Springs. The scheme has no limits. And not only does it solve the immigration problem, it means we can once again boast of controlling an empire – of sorts.

Jack Straw on asylum

Jack Straw described Iraq as one of the most vicious and evil regimes in the history of mankind, which is nice and colourful, and has the desired effect of keeping it in the frame for anything that might follow. Except that when he was Home Secretary, a long time ago, before dinosaurs ruled the White House, his department saw it differently.

In 2001 the Home Office turned down an asylum application from an Iraqi on the grounds that he had no just fear of persecution if he returned to Iraq. The Home Office expressed their confidence that

> Iraq, and in particular the Iraqi security forces, would only convict and sentence a person in the courts with the provision of proper jurisdiction

and assured the man that

> We're satisfied that if there are any charges outstanding, you could expect to receive a fair trial under an independent and properly constituted judiciary.

Another small point

Last year, of 100 million people visiting Britain, 80,000 sought asylum in the UK. Of these, just three were arrested and held under anti-terrorism measures.

New legislation that came into force in 2004 means that anyone who doesn't immediately claim asylum at their port of entry loses the right to food and shelter. Should you enter the country in a vehicle which has passed through immigration, it will make no difference if you then try and immediately claim asylum. You will be deemed an in-country applicant. Only those with the relevant paperwork, or forged documents, entering the country through an established mode of travel such as a seat on an aeroplane or on a ferry, who then approach the first immigration official they meet, will be deemed to be port applicants and therefore entitled to food and shelter.

If you are an in-country applicant, the new legislation allows for a 'reasonableness' test. However, there is no definition of what constitutes 'reasonableness'. Applicants are not allowed to claim mainstream welfare benefits. If they are destitute, the only option is to apply for support to the National Asylum Support Service (NASS), which offers a basic £37.77 per week for a single adult – 30 per cent below the poverty line.

The NHS relies heavily on foreign labour. In the last year, 13,721 nurses who had trained outside the EU were approved to work in the UK. According to the GLA, 23 per cent of doctors and 47 per cent of nurses working within the NHS were born outside the UK. In addition, in the same period, 100,000 overseas nurses received information packs inviting them to work in Britain; while the number of non-EU nurses on the Nursing Council register was up 63 per cent on the previous year, which had itself seen a huge increase in numbers.

According to a Home Office study in 2002,[126] migrants, including asylum seekers and refugees, made a net fiscal contribution in 1999–2000 of approximately £2.5 billion – worth 1p on income tax. Meanwhile, many developing countries complain bitterly about the loss of skilled and semi-skilled workers to poorly paid jobs in Britain. More than 13,000 Filipino workers left their country to find jobs in Britain – 5500 of them trained nurses. The Philippines Nursing Association complained in November that foreign agencies were creaming off all their skilled nurses, leaving Filipinos in the hands of those fresh out of nursing school.

Over three years a Catholic priest and a charity worker in London have 'rescued' over 500 Filipino nurses from the private sector, where they have been abused, forced to work for low wages, and housed in dirty and cramped conditions, often with money taken from them in fees and interest charges. Most have been found equivalent jobs in the NHS where they receive far better treatment.

23
'And I personally should be associated with it'

Blair email to Philip Gould

We are perceived as weak ... we are perceived as soft ... we're seen as insufficiently assertive. All these things add up to the sense that the government – and this even applies to me – are out of touch, somehow, with gut British instincts. The government should think now of an initiative, e.g. locking up street muggers. Something tough, with immediate bite, that sends a message through the system and I personally should be associated with it.[109]

Thus, in an email that was subsequently leaked, Tony Blair revealed his overriding concern with being seen to be doing something – anything – in order to pacify his critics. It explains how policy came to be driven by a mishmash of focus-group findings and whatever came across the No. 10 radar screen, usually via the filter of the popular press.

At the end of Labour's first term in office, the government had set themselves over 8000 targets. These were published aims – a sort of political equivalent of the Post-it note on the fridge door. They ranged from a target to 'decrease the amount of photocopying paper used in the National Maritime Museum by 300 reams in three years', to the Department of Culture Media and Sport which had a target to 'increase the number of gold, silver, and bronze medals won at major international sporting events'. Which was a close call, the only alternative target being to reduce the number of medals.

The Foreign Office had a target to improve the quality of life worldwide. Which wasn't a joke (although it later became one).

But then someone noticed a problem with targets. Very often, you failed to meet them. One solution was simply to keep moving them – except that made the people doing it a target of a different kind.

So it was decided to get rid of targets entirely – the idea of getting from somewhere to somewhere else being a real headache (especially with transport) – and replace them with the altogether more sensible idea of benchmarks.

An easy way to describe the difference between a target and a benchmark is to think of it as like the difference between a bow and an arrow. When you fire an arrow at a target and it hits, or misses, then you can say whether the bullseye has been hit or not. But a benchmark is more like the bow you use. You know it's been fired, you can tell that because there's a whooshing sound and the string vibrates, and you can tick that off as a success. But you don't need to worry quite so much about where the arrow has fetched up.

It's simpler, it's easy, and you don't miss so often. In fact, if you're good at it you need never miss.

Transport Secretary Stephen Byers demonstrated this in February 2002, when he set three benchmarks for the railways, which were safety, punctuality, and the quality of trains. The trick with benchmarks is to set them correctly – and Stephen certainly did that, his chosen benchmark being the performance of the railway system between April and June of the previous year, just after the Hatfield crash, when the network was in a state of complete disruption.

By doing this, he was able to achieve some pretty impressive figures for rail performance. In fact, the railways were able to do better than the benchmark he had set even before it had been introduced, which was a real success. They were outperforming the appalling level of service of a year earlier, when virtually no trains ran at all, and that was a real step forward.

Labour have always been keen on figures. At least, their own figures. If they have a set of figures they are proud of, they often release them three, four, or even five times. Just in case you missed them the first few times round.

Nothing But Blue Skies

Another Labour trick was the use of special advisers and 'blue sky thinkers' – often famous faces, recruited to think about the 'big picture'. By 2003, they were spending £5.4 million on special advisers – 26 for the PM alone.[110]

The Tories had invited Richard Branson to tackle rubbish, something Labour had thought risible. Apparently because it didn't go far enough. After all, why have just one famous face when you could have fifty?

The broadcaster Gus Macdonald was brought in to give John Prescott a hand, on the basis that if you were going to have one bouncer on the door then you might as well have two, while fellow broadcaster Trevor Philips was also seconded to help on the basis that ... well, he was a broadcaster. Labour maintained their love of all things show business by courting TV guru Waheed Ali, who got a knighthood and a place at the table. Alastair Campbell and Fiona Millar had the distinction of being a rare 'his and hers' special adviser team, while Paul Smith tackled ... well, Tony Blair's wardrobe mainly.

But most eyecatching was former BBC director-general, John Birt, appointed as an unpaid adviser to the forward strategy unit [*sic*]. A friend of Peter Mandelson since their days at LWT, Birt was headhunted and told to think about crime. When he'd finished thinking about crime, he was asked to think about transport.

Birt came with a reputation as more Blairite than Blair.

BLAIR: A broadcaster you can trust – now, there's a rarity these days.

Asked why the government had not considered Roger Graef, a writer and broadcaster with extensive knowledge and understanding of crime, Blair's gatekeeper, Anji Hunter, dismissed Graef's qualifications out of hand ('He's got an agenda!').[111]

You were either onside, or you weren't. What Labour wanted was special advisers – special not because they might be able to offer special advice, but because they were especially on the side of the PM.

Meanwhile policy often came down to being seen to be doing something. One such example of on-the-hoof policy making was the announcement that vandals and those guilty of street crime would be taken by the police to the nearest cashpoint machine and forced to pay an on-the-spot £100 fine.[112]

The idea surprised both the Home Office, which had hundreds of officials working on new crime initiatives, of which this was not one, and the police, who instantly distanced themselves from the whole thing.

After a few days the whole thing was quietly dropped as unworkable.[113] Several would-be vandals pointed out that they didn't often go on a car-windscreen-smashing spree armed with a wallet of up-to-date credit cards. At least, not their own.

Two months later Blair introduced the equally capricious wheeze of twenty-four-hour courts which could administer instant justice in key major cities. This time, the scheme was actually taken up, but it, too, was quickly abandoned as unworkable.[114]

While on the theme, as well as targeting taggers, fly-tippers, dangerous dog owners, vandals, rowdy tenants, and people with fireworks and airguns, the government became particularly obsessed with truants. Blair announced to the *News of the World*, now the recognized lower chamber, a scheme to make parents of truanting children carry pagers so that they could be warned if their children went missing. Which was just about as New Labour as you could get. Later the pagers would be dropped, to be replaced by a hefty fine.

No one assumes that the government has the answer to everything. Least of all the government itself. Which is why Tony Blair embarked on the Big Conversation (a Mandelsonian idea, if ever there was one). A conversation, note, not a listening exercise. Because in a conversation the government can answer back:

> Look, I've listened to all you have to say, and I'm very interested, but actually you're wrong.

An attitude already demonstrated over Iraq, tuition fees and foundation hospitals.

Still, the Big Conversation *sounds* good and democratic, even if it does cost you 25p more than normal to text in your contribution.

But even well-intentioned initiatives backfired sometimes.

A move to help deaf people at a conference by accompanying speeches from the podium with real-time surtitles came unstuck when the typist deputed to transcribe party chairman, Ian McCartney, was unable to follow his rapid, high-pitched Scots-accented delivery. What appeared on screen bore little relation to what came out of his mouth. Sensing a disaster in the making – John Prescott was due to speak the next day – officials abandoned the experiment. Ironic, as Prescott himself is hard of hearing and wears an appliance.

We're Labour

We like

Businessmen

Peter Mandelson

Sharp pencils

Partnership funding

PalmPilots

Plan for Life fitness programmes

Novelty cufflinks

Mood boards

Blue-sky thinking

Conference calls

Videoconference calls

Conference centres

Videoconference call centres (er, hang on, we're getting a bit confused here)

Hot-desking

Hot-wired teams

Hotmail

Hot anything

PowerBooks

Power breakfasts

Power runs

Power naps

Power ballads (OK, now you're just being silly)

Bullet-point lectures

Scramjet technology

Silver-blue touch-screen Korg keyboards

The *Daily Mail* (OK, the readership)

Action plans

Working breakfasts/lunches/suppers/parties/groups ... in fact, anything that works.

We don't like

Radicals

People with agendas

The *Daily Mail*

Trade unions

Peter Mandelson (no, sorry, we do again now)

Beards

Moustaches

Ken (hang on, no, we like him again now too)

Moustaches (Mandelson, Byers, Darling, Beckett . . . all shaved off now)

The *Daily Mail*

Antis – otherwise known as cynics, whingers, back-stabbers, the press

Europe (er, hang on, we're not sure about that any more)

conservatism

Conservatism

Fat people

Unfit people

The aristocracy

Fox-hunting

Hereditary peers

Thatcher (though we quite like her policies)

Chirac (although we did once)

Actually, look, it's very simple, if you're not in the first list then just assume we don't like you.

Still, ignoring the gloss, at least Labour could tell themselves, and indeed others, that they shared the social-reformist spirit of their forefathers.

Addressing a community college in 2003, just before the war started, Tony Blair managed to avoid all mention of the forthcoming hostilities, an event that was about to divide the nation, and instead used the time to lay out his Bevanite credentials, insisting that:

> Just as the 1945 government pioneered a new settlement, so today we can reinvent collective provision, and make our public services a real engine of opportunity for all our people.

After the obligatory digs at the Tories, pops at truants, asylum seekers, the Liberal Democrats, and finally the old left, he then proceeded to wrap himself up in old-left virtues, with the rousing claim that

> We need to embrace the challenge with the same zeal that led the past giants of our movement, Attlee, Bevan, Morrison and Cripps, to build the modern welfare state and National Health Service in the late 1940s,

adding, for good measure:

> As a party we have always been reformers battling against the forces of privilege and vested interests to create services and institutions that made a reality of Labour values.

Those being, it now appears, a part-privatized Tube, a health service largely run by multinational corporations, an education system that requires students to run up thousands of pounds of debt in top-up fees, a reliance on cheap foreign labour, a Prime Minister desperate to attach his name to any feelgood quick fix going, and a suspicion and a mistrust of anyone coming to the country seeking sanctuary.

24
Get back to work, you bastards!

A MESSAGE FROM GORDON BROWN

Hello, me again. Bet you didn't think you'd get two lots of me in one book. That's what I call a sales inducement.

Right, well, I've explained how we spend the money, or rather don't. Getting the private sector to do it for us. But the truth is, there are still a lot of things we have to pay for ourselves. Unfortunately.

Wars, to name but one. Thank you very much for that one, Tony. Oh, it will just be a couple of billion, Gordon, he says. Yes, and the rest, says I. And who's been proved right? And it has to come from somewhere. Which is why our tax take has been going steadily up. *No, not income tax. No, no, no, no, no.* But other taxes, they certainly can take a nudge upwards without too much bother. You drink and smoke too much anyway, so we're doing you a favour. And you can just load all those new property taxes onto the amount you borrow. And look, motorists have had it soft for too long, and you could say we're actually being environmentally very sound in pricing you off the roads.

But I'll be honest with you, and say that even with all these secret little top-up taxes things are starting to worry me a bit. You see, we in Britain earn around £1 trillion a year. That's a thousand billion in old money. And of that, maybe slightly less than half comes to me personally through taxation, to spend how I see fit. Which is why I always look so knackered.

And it's not going to get any easier, either. Because you're all getting older. Not that I'm blaming you. But it means a bigger burden. In America they have come up with the notion of 'unretiring people': you stop, you put your feet up; five years later the money runs out, and you're back in line stacking shelves with some spotty-faced youth less than a quarter your age. Frankly, I can't see the problem myself, but there you go – has a few people a little miffed. Especially those just about to duck out and rely on the weekly giro.

And if we don't want an even bigger crisis in the pensions industry, then we have to come up with something pretty soon.

And that's what I've been doing over the past few years. Basically, what it comes down to is working *cheaper and faster than ever before.* There. I've said it. Deregulation, cheap labour, cheap white goods, the whole McMuffin.

Oh, sure, consuming stuff is vital, I meant what I said back there on page whatever it was, but this is the other obligation. Oh, sorry, didn't I mention there was something else as well as going on a spending spree? Some of you may not like it. Frankly, I don't much like it myself, being an old Labour man and still having held on to my conscience, unlike some around here I could mention. But facts are facts, and frankly, handy though those PFI bods are, we still have to stump up the lion's share ourselves, and that means cracking the whip even harder.

Look, I'll be honest with you, unlike the other chap we all know, and say we can either take a larger and larger slice of the same-sized pie, until one day one poor sod is doing all the work for 50 million of us, and then he packs in and it's, oops, everyone down the plughole – or we can keep the slice the same but try, somehow, to make a bigger pie each year. A much bigger pie. A huge pie. And that's where I'm heading, and where this country is heading: a productivity boom to blast our way out of trouble. And failing that, I haven't yet ruled out raising the retiring age to eighty.

Gordon

PART IV

There's a whole world out there

25
I'm sorry, but we're going to have to mention globalization

Good things about globalization, No. 1

We can watch Thierry Henry play for Arsenal and feel proud so many foreign players are prepared to ply their trade in the English game.

Foreign players in the Premier League 2003/4[127]

45 Frenchmen	5 South Africans	2 Slovaks
29 Irishmen	4 Croats	2 Uruguayans
11 Dutchmen	4 Czechs	1 Bulgarian
9 Australians	4 Jamaicans	1 Canadian
9 Germans	4 Spaniards	1 Colombian
8 Brazilians	3 Icelanders	1 Costa Rican
8 Norwegians	3 Trinidad and Tobagans	1 Congolese
7 Danes	3 Turks	1 Grenadian
7 Italians	2 Belgians	1 Israeli
7 Swedes	2 Chinese	1 Japanese
7 Americans	2 Ecuadorians	1 Latvian
6 Argentinians	2 Ghanaians	1 Malian
6 Cameroonians	2 Greeks	1 Peruvian
6 Finns	2 Ivorians	1 Pole
6 Senegalese	2 Moroccans	1 Russian
5 Nigerians	2 Romanians	1 Swiss
5 Portuguese	2 Serbs	1 Ukrainian

Hello,

It's me, Charlie Kennedy. Chas, if you like.

No, don't get up. I won't be long. Just wondered if I could take up a few minutes of your precious time (not mine, obviously, I've nothing better to do) to have a wee word about globalization. Now, I know we're best known for our work in local government, but even on the Achnashiel parish council it's not uncommon for the subject of globalization to come up, once the washing-up's been done and the cups tidied away. It's certainly something that's kept me awake many an afternoon.

Trouble is, mention the word globalization and everyone starts to run a mile. The anarchists start putting on the face paint, the Greens get very excited and quote figures back at you ten to the dozen, and everyone else switches over to the other side to see if there's a film on. Actually, I must say I'm tempted to do that myself. But no, no, this is important, because, as Bob Dylan put it, 'the times they are a-changin' '. Or was it Shirley Williams? Not that global change is a bad thing, mind. We all like to shop around, find the best price we can. Well maybe not always, I know I will sometimes be filling up my trolley at Morrisons in Fort William of a Friday and Sarah will look over and say, 'You know you can get those lean cuisine fishcakes for 14p less at Budgens across the road' – but, ach, what the heck, we all live dangerously now and then.

And that's really all globalization is about. Competition. And choice. Fair enough, no bad thing.

But the problem is, free competition isn't necessarily free in the sense of being equal. If you're one of the big boys you can undercut everyone else through economies of scale, or by insisting your suppliers give you a better rate or you'll go elsewhere. And, as most of the big boys tend to be Western companies, and as a lot of the markets we're talking of opening up are in the Third World, at the end of the day it's the wee man that gets put through the mangle, as my auntie Hamish used to say.

Ah, but no one is forced to agree to all this, you may say. Countries can refuse if they like. Decide their own rules. All well and good in theory, to a point, but then, when has the theory ever matched the practice? Take a wee peek at our election results if you want proof of that. See, say you're a poor country in a bit of trouble with your economy. You're in debt, you've borrowed a few billion you can ill afford from the World Bank, and now you're having trouble meeting the repayments. We've all been there. Well, I know I have. When I was a student. Not several million mind, but certainly the odd tenner in hock to Mrs McTumshie for the gas or the 'leccie. But even so, the odd thing is, if you're a country with a bit of a flaky credit rating, then, strangely, they seem more willing than ever to lend you more, certainly more than a wee student looking for a sub to tide him over at the uni bar. Though I stress here I'm not speaking from personal experience.

Well, back to our Third World country, and armed with an extra few billion they can carry on a bit longer, but then eventually, that lot wasted too, mainly on interest repayments, they have to go back to the bank again, cap in hand, and really throw themselves on its mercy.

Which all too often means loan restructuring. The man from the bank likes to say yes, provided you then take down all trade barriers and put your public services out to commercial tender, no holds barred.

And before you can say Inverness Caledonian Thistle, this poor country has a fast food restaurant running its schools, a pest control company in charge of its hospitals, its water supply owned by a company from Luton that's hiked up the prices so much your average citizen has to go to his local bank just to raise enough money to have a bath (and guess who owns the bank, by the way).

Just like me at university. But that's another story. And here's another.

Mary works in London. She is employed as a live-in carer helping a frail and vulnerable old lady. Mary is kind, helpful, works hugely long hours, and never complains. Without people like her the domiciliary service of most health authorities would collapse.

Mary is paid a low wage and can just about survive. Her budget is made even tighter by the need to send some money home to Namibia. That is where Mary comes from. And where her family still live. And, of course, the money she earns in London is a lot more than she could hope to earn back in Africa. But there's another side to her story.

Mary is also a qualified commercial pilot. She trained in Namibia and is qualified to fly for the national airline there. But she can't get a job. Not because Namibia has trained too many pilots but because we in the West have. And with the global downturn in the aviation industry after September 11th a lot of Western aircrew were forced to look elsewhere for work. Such as Namibia.

It seems airlines in Namibia prefer Western crews. A posh accent and a clipped moustache still count for something. Unless you're a stewardess, of course.

The point is, because our pilots can't find work here, Mary is unable to do what she has trained for in her own country, and has to come here to do a job that no one else wants to do. Looking after old people – old people whose relatives may not be around to help because they are out in Namibia flying airliners.

Meanwhile, Mary has a daughter of her own back in Namibia who needs looking after. Luckily there's someone from Mozambique who will do the job for the minimal rate Mary can afford to pay out of her carer's wages in London.

What Mary would really like is to have the opportunity to live and work where she trained. In her own country. Instead, she has had to travel 8000 miles and work eighteen hours a day cleaning bottoms. And leave family and friends behind. Just to make ends meet.

Which is what the global economy is all about. Everyone and everything can move. And the more it can move the more it will move. And people are perhaps the most movable thing of all.

Unless you're a company relocating to another country. Because while globalization means global flows of capital, it doesn't always mean global movement of the workforce.

So employees around the world are at the mercy of their parent company in Wyoming, while in the poorer countries any hard-earned profits go to pay back debt and dividends to foreign shareholders. And that's globalization.

OK, right, well, back to your book – oh, and like I said, don't forget, if you are looking for someone to take that unwanted vote off you next time round, well, look no further than us lot. You've tried the best, now try the rest.

Thanks,

Charles Kennedy

26
The 'stans

The 'stans, a group of states that stand at the vital crossroads on the old Silk Road running between Russia, China, and Western interests to the south, are a key strategic resource as well as a huge untapped source of oil.

Here we have a collection of less than democratic, oil-rich dictatorships – not unlike Iraq – that by the current rules of combat should be high on Donald Rumsfeld's wish-list of targets. But in contrast to the line taken with Saddam, America has been remarkably lenient in the 'stans, largely due to those two great engines of US foreign policy: oil (or gas) and the War on Terror. The 'stans may boast a quality selection of mad dictators but they're sitting on a lot of energy and they're well placed to provide bases for Uncle Sam. It's the old adage, beloved by despots and estate agents alike: location, location, location.

TURKMENISTAN

Population: 4,863,169 (2004 estimate)
GDP per capita: $5,700 (2003 estimate)
Population below poverty line: 34.4% (2001 estimate)[128]

There are quite a few mad leaders in the world but Turkmenistan's president, Saparmurat Niyazov, is up there with the best of them.

In the mid 1990s, he changed his name to Turkmenbashi, which means father of all Turkmen. So far, so good. He also named the capital and the main port after himself, and lent his name to the only brand of aftershave on sale in the country. And it doesn't stop there. He's renamed various other household items after himself and his late mother. Including bread.

Giving rise to the popular expression, 'I know which side my dictator's mother is buttered.'

But it gets better. Turkmenistan's nominal legislature also passed a presidential request to change some of the names of the days of the week and the months to his first name, his new last name, and words associated with his name. Except for April, which – wait for it – he named after his mother. So you may, in an unguarded moment, point out that the dictator's mother is 'very wet for the time of year', and land yourself in jail with the local torturers and only the occasional scrap of the dictator's mother to keep you alive.

Niyazov has ruled Turkmenistan with an iron rod since he became Communist Party chief in 1985, and holds the posts of president, prime minister, commander-in-chief, and head of the only registered party. He was offered the presidency for life in December 1999 (by himself), but in a rare stroke of modesty he said he might step down and hold elections in 2010.[128i]

The first thing a visitor to Turkmenistan's capital, Ashgabat, notices (after Niyazov's image – the capital's skyline is dominated by a huge, rotating golden statue of the president) is the spectacular building boom. But the grand (and half-finished) government buildings belie Turkmenistan's economic crisis. An estimated one quarter of adults are unemployed. Meanwhile, the government enforces a strict maximum wage on public sector workers. A bank teller cannot be paid more than US$36 per month. To pay his staff a living wage, a restaurant manager must create fictional employees and disperse the extra salaries to them.

During the cotton season, soldiers have been known to board inter-city buses and abduct the passengers for weeks of unpaid work picking on the fields. And corruption hasn't helped. Diplomats estimate that Niyazov has spirited US$1.4–2 billion from the national treasury into foreign bank accounts.

Niyazov's face appears on every denomination of Turkmenistan's currency. At all times a golden profile of his face is broadcast in a corner of the screen on both of the two national television stations, while large stone Niyazovs guard the entrance to every government building.

When a gunman opened fire on Niyazov as he drove his own car in a motorcade through the capital, he miraculously escaped unharmed,[129] arousing suspicion that he had choreographed the whole incident in order to justify a crackdown against his supposed enemies.[130] More than 100 people have since been arrested, and Turkmenistan's best-known dissident, former foreign minister, Boris Shikhmuradov, was charged with engineering the attempted coup.

Foreign newspapers are banned, leaving the bulk of Turkmenistan's 5 million people cut off from the outside world, while internally Niyazov has effectively destroyed primary education. Schoolchildren study almost exclusively from a single text, a quasi-religious history written by ... the president.

Recently, video surveillance of Turkoman citizens has been intensified at key public buildings. But the kindly and wise Niyazov has a simple explanation:

> We should know if a fly quietly buzzes past.[131]

> BLAIR: Gosh, must make a note of that.

Meanwhile, he's banned gold teeth and ordered they be replaced with white ones, created a bank holiday for a melon, banned long hair and car radios ... and built several more statues of himself.

If you want to get ahead ...

Yourgi Pardett is from Turkmenistan. He's worried about proliferation of nuclear weapons. He estimates that there are a minimum of 1500 tonnes of military nuclear fissile materials scattered around the world, not least in nearby Uzbekistan, the Ukraine, and Russia.

Weapons-grade components are easily smuggled over international frontiers. Which is lucky, because Yourgi is keen to buy some. Yourgi knows what he is doing is dangerous because it increases the likelihood of a war. But he has his reasons.

> America knew Iraq had no nuclear weapons, but they thought it might in five, ten years' time, so they think, we must attack now before it is too late. Compare that with North Korea. America doesn't invade North Korea because they know they have nuclear weapons.

Eventually, Yourgi found what he was looking for in Munich and paid the standard market rate: US$1.5 million for 1 kilogram of plutonium.

Now, it's possible the Americans may never invade Yourgi's poor, landlocked country. At the moment it presents no threat to anyone, but the people of Turkmenistan are worried.

> They're very unpredictable people, the Americans. They're easily upset. One day you are oasis of stability, tomorrow you are state of concern, day after that, you are axis of evil, day after that, bang!
>
> If you actually have nuclear weapons and leader who is a little bit crazy, then people are very careful, they don't call your bluff because they don't know whether you are bluffing or not, and maybe you don't know if you're bluffing,

Yourgi explains.

And armed with a few kilograms of black-market weapons-grade plutonium and a mad dictator there's a good chance that America will think twice before attacking.

Luckily, Turkmenistan has so far denounced nuclear weapons and insisted it has no interest in obtaining the bomb. But President Turkmenbashi is real enough, and so is his eccentric behaviour, and plutonium can be bought on the black market at a price that even a small, impoverished Central Asian republic can afford.

But a state like Turkmenistan might well be advised to add a deployable nuclear warhead to its list of other essential ingredients for self-preservation, which reads:

1. A mad evil dictator
   (That's it.)

In the meantime, Turkmenistan received $16.4 million in assistance from the US in 2002.

Now, if you think Turkmenistan is an exceptional case, think again . . .

KYRGYZSTAN

Population: 5,081,429 (July 2004 estimate)
GDP per capita: $1,700
Population below poverty line: 50% (2003 estimate)

Kyrgyzstan is a rather beautiful backwater in a highly desirable, oil-rich location, with China to the east, Russia to the north, and Western interests to the south. Picture if you will that perennial doormat, Belgium, without the chocolates, but with a murderous human rights record.

National sports in Kyrgyzstan include kick-boxing and a rather jolly pastime where two teams of horsemen drag a dead goat from one end of a field to the other. We'll have the celebrity version here soon.

Head of state in Kyrgyzstan is the remarkable Askar Akaev. Crazy name, crazy guy. Akaev lists Churchill, Roosevelt, and de Gaulle as his heroes. At weekends he retires to the countryside to a traditional Kyrgyzstani tent, or yurt, to drink vodka.

He was one of the great hopes for democracy in the region until, four years ago, he lost the plot. In a snap referendum, he consolidated his grip on power and abolished one of the two houses of parliament. (Something our own Prime Minister can only dream of.) He also disqualified the other presidential candidate, Felix Kulov, on the grounds that Kulov was fluent in Russian but not Kyrgyzstani. Even though both are official languages. Kulov is now serving a ten-year jail sentence, writing out 10,000 times 'I must not oppose a despot'.

Two years ago, Akaev's security services shot dead five unarmed demonstrators, using live bullets because they'd run out of rubber ones. Other protestors face lengthy prison sentences.

The country owes US$200 million to the International Monetary Fund[133] and debt repayments account for nearly 40 per cent of the government's fiscal revenues. Kyrgyzstan is so poor that designer plastic bags given away free in the West are on sale in local markets as luxury goods. Grizzled Second World War veterans were recently spotted at one parade marching in step while clutching a range of Calvin Klein and Joseph bags.

So how does the US fit in? Very well, actually, since Kyrgyzstan agreed to host about 3000 US troops at Manas airport in order to facilitate military operations in Afghanistan. It's since been named Ganci air base, after the New York fire chief who died on 11 September. The Kyrgyz government leased them the airport, charging them US$7000 a time to take off or land. Meanwhile, the president's son-in-law makes a very good living controlling fuel sales.[134]

Now an important US ally, Kyrgyzstan received US$49 million in assistance in 2002,[135] including US$12 million for security programmes, none of it tied to progress on human rights. In addition, the US continued to provide Kyrgyzstan with non-lethal equipment and military training, despite a poll in the local Kyrgyz press claiming that 77 per cent of the population oppose the presence of US troops.

But it's obviously a very desirable neighbourhood, because last year who should move in up the road but the Russians, setting up their own military base, just twenty miles away from the Americans.[136] This would be home to 500 Russian military personnel and ten Su-27 and Su-25 jets.

All of which brings the intriguing prospect of a cut-price air war, in which the former Cold War adversaries could simply push their planes to the end of the runway and shoot at each other over the hedge.

So, while the poor people of Kyrgyzstan get by on a dollar day, their government eases its debt with millions of dollars in aid and security programmes from the Americans, the odd bottle of vodka from the Russians, and the assurance that, as long as they stay compliant, their human rights abuses are fine by us.

AZERBAIJAN

Population: 7,830,764
GDP per capita: $3700
Population below poverty line: 49%

'That's a huge pool of oil. It's time we woke up.' Brent Scowcroft, former National Security Adviser to George H. W. Bush[137]

President Ilham Aliyev is the son of the late president, Heydar Aliyev, who dominated Azerbaijani politics for three decades. Aliyev senior was head of Azerbaijan's KGB and Communist Party in the 1960s, and carefully planned his son Ilham's victory in the 2003 elections.

In April 2003, Heydar had a heart attack during a speech and collapsed, but got up and continued.[138] After a second attack he had a heart bypass operation in the USA, and it was from there that he prepared the transfer of power.[139]

Ilham Aliyev is a typical son of a leading Soviet politician. He studied at an elite international relations school in Moscow, and from 1991 to 1993 was a businessman in Istanbul. He helped run the state oil monopoly, Socar, overseeing lucrative foreign contracts, which sharpened his business acumen, if not his political one – not that that mattered. Although his CV showed little time spent in politics, he soon became president. Bit like George W., in a way.

On the night of the elections, the offices of the opposition Musavat party were attacked, and a demonstration of some 10,000 people was broken up by police, resulting in four deaths. Seven opposition leaders and 200 activists were arrested. In the aftermath, nearly 1000 people were arrested, and by mid-January 2004 more than 100 political opponents and supporters remained in detention.

The US State Department's Country Report on Human Rights Practices states that the Azerbaijani government's human rights record 'remained poor', and that it 'continued to restrict citizens' ability to change their government peacefully'.[140]

But there were extenuating circumstances. Azerbaijan's share of the oil reserves under the Caspian Sea is estimated to be worth at least US$80 billion. Construction has already begun on a US$3.8 billion pipeline from the capital, Baku, via neighbouring Georgia, to Turkey's Mediterranean port of Ceyhan. Mike O'Brien, the Foreign Office minister, told MPs in a written statement on the day before the Christmas parliamentary recess that he had approved credit cover amounting to nearly £100 million for a British-led consortium, headed by BP, to build the 1087 mile pipeline. The Baku–Tbilisi–Ceyhan Pipeline Company is now primed to pump 1 million barrels of oil a day from Azerbaijan on the Caspian Sea to Turkey on the Mediterranean.[141]

The pipeline crosses three politically unstable countries, skirting the heart of the Kurdish region in south-east Turkey, and passing within sixty miles of Georgia's lawless Pankisi Gorge. To facilitate this, all three countries had to cede territory to BP, creating a unique country, 1000 miles long and three miles wide, called simply BP.

The government agreements signed between BP and the host countries override any domestic law, bar their constitutions. Should a future Turkish state decide to pass more stringent environmental, human rights, or social laws to regulate the pipeline region, they will have to pay compensation to the construction companies.

Amnesty International claimed that up to 30,000 people will have to give up their land, and American aerial radar surveillance systems and anti-terrorist patrols may be deployed to protect stretches of the £2 billion pipeline. Campaigners fear that further militarization of the Caucasus and eastern Turkey will only serve to reignite conflicts and anger local communities.

The Azerbaijan International Operating Company (AIOC), the main foreign oil consortium in Azerbaijan, in which American firms have a 40 per cent stake, is a client of the law firm of Baker Botts, while US vice-president, Dick Cheney, was CEO of Halliburton, an oil services firm operating in the Caspian fields.

The US ignored its own criticisms as it consolidated its friendship with the Azerbaijani government through energy projects and partnership deals in the war against terrorism.

Azerbaijan had, of course, done the one thing any country in its position had to do, and got in early with its offer of help to the US after September 11th. The country granted important overflying rights for US military aircraft, and also sent contingents of troops to the coalitions in Afghanistan and Iraq.

In return, the US provided about US$913 million in security support assistance to Azerbaijan in 2002. This will include technical training of military personnel.[142]

Speaking after a meeting with President Ilham Aliyev in Baku in December 2003, Defense Secretary Donald Rumsfeld said: 'I expressed the appreciation of the American people and President Bush for the important support and contributions of this country in the global War on Terror.'

The point being that this was a war against someone else's terror, not their own.

UZBEKISTAN

Population: 25,981,647
GDP per capita: US$2600
Population below poverty line: unknown

What's the difference between Saddam Hussein and the president of Uzbekistan, Islam Karimov?

Give up?

Well, it's obvious. One of them's in custody in Iraq, while the other is still alive and well and vowing to rip the head off anyone who disturbs the peace and calm in Uzbekistan. Those are his words, not ours.

When the Soviet system collapsed in 1991, President Islam Karimov transformed himself overnight from a Communist into a national patriot. Karimov has chosen one of history's most notorious butchers as the figurehead for his police state: Tamburlaine the Great.

That apart, Mr Karimov has a great deal in common with the rest of the world's tyrants.

Like Saddam, the Uzbek president regularly has his opponents rounded up and shot (offering to do the job himself if necessary).

And like Saddam, Karimov and his security forces are also in the habit of burning down villages, persecuting religious opponents, brutalizing political rivals, maiming, killing, raping, imprisoning, torturing, defiling – you name it, he does it. Try to imagine, say, John Reid on a bad day.

Yet, until recently, Karimov appeared to have escaped Western retribution, despite some rather unattractive habits. Religious prisoners have been forced to write statements renouncing their faith, to ask President Karimov for forgiveness every day, and to sing the national anthem. Those who refused were punished with beatings, rape, solitary confinement, and denial of food and water. In August 2003, according to a forensic report commissioned by the British embassy, Karimov had two prisoners tortured and then boiled to death.

Independent human rights groups estimate that there are more than 600 politically motivated arrests each year in Uzbekistan, and 6500 political prisoners, some of them tortured to death.

Karimov recently delayed elections on the grounds that Uzbeks had better things to worry about than politics.

An Islamist terrorist network has been operating in Uzbekistan, but Karimov makes no distinction between peaceful Muslims and terrorists: anyone who worships privately, who does not praise the president during their prayers, or who joins an organization that has not been approved by the state, can be imprisoned. Political dissidents, human rights activists, and homosexuals receive the same treatment.

Now, all of this did not go unnoticed by our own ambassador in Uzbekistan, a rather plucky chap called Craig Murray. When he blew the whistle on Mr Karimov's peculiar brand of boil-in-the-bag politics, the Foreign Office immediately snapped into action, recalled him, and told him to keep his big mouth shut and stop rocking the boat.[143] Or US aircraft carrier in this case.

As it happens, Mr Karimov is already being taken care of. Very good care. Since 1999, American special forces have trained his soldiers and the State Department has granted his government millions of dollars to strengthen its security services. Not to be outdone, our own country last year granted him licence to import whatever weapons he chooses.

So why the discrepancy between Karimov and Saddam?

Well, it all comes down to geopolitics. Uzbekistan lies in the middle of Central Asia's massive gas and oil fields, and serves as a crucial link in a gas transport chain linking Turkmenistan's enormous gas deposits with Russia. Uzbekistan is also party to the parallel Central Asia Gas Pipeline project, which will bring gas from Turkmenistan and Uzbekistan to Pakistan and India, via Afghanistan.[144]

Beyond Uzbekistan lies the even more dangerous Islamic territory of Chechnya. And to the south, the largely Muslim countries of Afghanistan and Pakistan, all of which makes Uzbekistan a genial buffer zone and, by extension, makes Karimov a genial buffer.

Craig Murray

At the beginning of 2003, Tony Blair granted Uzbekistan an open export licence to import weapons from the United Kingdom. Six months later the Foreign Office recalled its ambassador, Craig Murray, from Tashkent, after he clashed with the US ambassador and openly decried Uzbekistan's abysmal human rights record in a speech in Tashkent. A senior source said the former ambassador had been put under pressure to stop his repeated criticisms of the Karimov regime – accusing it, among other things, of boiling prisoners to death. The source said the pressure was partly 'exercised on the orders of No. 10', which found his outspokenness about the compromises Washington was prepared to make in its War on Terror increasingly embarrassing. 'He was told that the next time he stepped away from the American line, he would lose his post.'

Mr Murray was subsequently diagnosed with 'nervous exhaustion', presented with a string of alleged disciplinary offences, and invited to resign.

All but two of the eighteen charges against him, which ranged from backing an overstayer's visa application to womanizing, drinking, and driving an embassy Land Rover down some lakeside steps, were later dropped. Murray has, however, according to Whitehall sources, been reprimanded for 'talking about the charges to embassy colleagues', and will have to leave Tashkent when his posting ends in 2005.

Uzbekistan has received nearly US$1 billion in US aid since 1992 (US$161.8 million in 2002 alone).[145] In exchange, the US gets a military base in Khanabad as a centre for operations in Afghanistan, surrounded by a six mile no-go zone enforced by Uzbek security services.

The State Department removed Uzbekistan from its annual list of countries where freedom of religion is under threat, despite evidence to the contrary, and in 2003 gave US$86.1 million in aid, US$30.2 million of it specifically for 'law enforcement and security services'. This to a country where, according to the State Department, 'there were continued reports of torture with impunity and unfair trials'.[146]

George Bush's letter of thanks to President Karimov was quoted in the newspapers:

> 'We are deeply grateful for your selfless contribution to the struggle with terrorism and highly value your efforts to conduct economic and political reform.'[147]

However, in July 2004, the US announced it was freezing aid to Uzbekistan, citing Uzbekistan's 'very poor' human rights record and expressing disappointment at the lack of progress towards democracy.[148] It seems they don't need the Uzbeks any more.

So if you're a crazy megalomaniac in the region, you have three ways to win friends and influence people:

1. Make sure you have a lot of oil. Or gas. Or both.
2. Have a well-advanced nuclear weapons programme.
3. Join in the War on Terror.

27
Libya

Just before Christmas last year it was announced that Libya's Colonel Gaddafi had thrown in the towel and decided to give up all links with terrorism and to hand over his weapons of mass destruction.

This was immediately seized upon by Jack Straw, peace be upon him, as a justification after the event for invading Iraq. And you think, even for Jack Straw, that's a good one.

But is it true?

Remember Senator Gary Hart, the Democrat presidential candidate who was done for philandering? No, not Clinton, the other one. Anyway, he wanted to take on George Bush senior, and they asked women who they thought would win the election, and they said: 'In my heart I know it's Bush, but in my bush I know it's Hart.'

In February 1992, Hart was in Athens, when he was approached by a naval attaché from the Libyan embassy, who told him Libya wanted to negotiate.[149] As a result, Gary Hart went to Geneva, where he met the head of the Libyan intelligence service, Yussuf Dibri, who offered to hand over the two men suspected of the Lockerbie bombing if the Americans would agree to discuss lifting sanctions.

Now, remember, this was twelve years ago, when George Bush senior was in the White House, George Bush junior didn't have a clue where he was, and Gulf War II was just a twinkle in Dick Cheney's eye.

Hart reported back to the US State Department, which replied immediately. But the Libyans wouldn't take 'Get lost' for an answer.

Undeterred, Gary Hart flew to Libya and told Gaddafi's prime minister, Abdul Salam Jalloud, that the Libyans would have to cease any support for terrorism and abandon their weapons of mass destruction programmes. The prime minister confirmed that

> Everything will be on the table.

A pretty big table, but it was clear what he meant. The Libyans wanted to come to the table and play.

Again, Hart reported this to the State Department, which once again insisted that there would be no discussions with Libya, even in exchange for the Lockerbie suspects. End of story.

Until now. Twelve years later, when George Bush is grown up, and his son's in the White House. So when his supporters, including Tony and Jack, claim that Colonel Gaddafi only caved in because Dubya whipped Saddam's ass, it seems the Libyans would have talked twelve years ago, if his dad had only had a brain, the nerve, and a Hart.

In 2002, Libya was one of the six countries denounced by George W. Bush as constituting an axis of evil. But all's fair in love and the War on Terror, and two years later, Colonel Gaddafi having declared his willingness to give up his weapons of mass destruction, Tony Blair was round offering to sell him conventional ones instead. What could be more ethical than that?[150]

The occasion was a trip to see Silvio Berlusconi in March 2004, where the pair hatched a joint plan to lobby the EU to remove the ban on arms sales to Libya as soon as possible. A leaked email revealed that Britain was 'keen to revisit the arms embargo issue in the light of Libyan progress on removing WMD', suggesting that in the meantime 'the EU could consider export exemptions on a case by case basis'.

The argument was a simple one:

> BLAIR: Look, if we don't get in there fast someone else might.

And while we might be nervous of Gaddafi's true intentions, it's surely better that we be the ones taking that risk. After all, in the world of the Big Tent – and Gaddafi has a particularly exotic one – it's better to be on the inside pissing out than on the inside pissing in.

> BLAIR: I just think, y'know, that in some way, if we were involved, then we could monitor and control the situation and make the world a safer place. I really do.

Now, where have we heard that argument before? Moustache, lived in the desert, thought he would protect us against the spread of fundamentalism . . .

But then Libya – like Iraq – does have rather a lot of oil. The fourth largest country in Africa, it is seventh in the OPEC oil cartel's top ten. Officials this year announced their belief that the reserves may be more than 100 billion barrels – three times more than currently proven.[151] It's also a potential market for British goods, and offers possibilities for the tourist trade, with 2000 kilometres of coastline as well as some of the most important ancient sites in the world. Why, it would be practically a crime not to welcome it back in from the cold.

The US severed ties with Tripoli in 1981, accusing it of supporting terrorism. In 1986, after Libya bombed a German disco, killing a US soldier and a Turkish woman, Washington bombed Tripoli and Benghazi, killing thirty-seven people, including Gaddafi's adopted infant daughter.

Twelve years of progressively tighter UN sanctions were suspended in April 1999 when Libya handed over the men suspected of planting the Lockerbie bomb. They were lifted entirely after Libya accepted responsibility and came up with a billion-dollar compensation deal.

American having dragged its feet on the sanctions issue, a few weeks after Britain announced it was lifting its ban, the US government had a change of mind and announced that it was prepared to trade with the recently labelled terrorist state. It is possible Blair's speed of action made all the difference.

> BLAIR: I just think we should draw a line in the sand. And say, OK, this side, the bit with the oil, that belongs to us; and that side, the bit with the camels, and the desert, and the things that aren't worth anything, that belongs to the latecomers. No, look, I'm sorry, George, but for once you do what I say. You know the rules: first come, first served . . . OK, how does that sound, everyone? Right, pass me the phone, I'd better call him. Wish me luck, team.

A note about the ECGD

The Export Credit Guarantee Department is the organization through which British companies are able to bid for many otherwise off-limits foreign contracts.

Underwritten by the government, it provides risk insurance, guaranteeing payment when a client – often a foreign country – defaults. The British company gets its cash, and the amount owed is added to the country's foreign debt.

Astonishingly, this is how Saddam Hussein was able to arm himself to the tune of £652 million in the 1980s. We supplied him with the arms, he defaulted on the payments, the companies got reimbursed by our government, and he went to war with us with weapons we'd paid for.[152] Soon we may reclaim the outstanding cash from the newly liberated Iraq's oil revenues.

Now, you're less likely to need backing like this for a conventional transaction. Sell buses to the French and there are any number of conventional insurance schemes on offer.

No, the ECGD really comes into its own for the connoisseur purchase: notably arms. At one point nearly 50 per cent of the deals underwritten by the British ECGD were for arms sales. After all, there's a chance if you're buying up a small arsenal that there may be something unstable about your country. As a rule of thumb, the more dangerous a sale, the more chance the British government will back it through ECGD support. And because it is never written off, simply added to the country's debt, then it accrues more money for the Chancellor through interest charges.

Of course, it's not always easy to get a defaulter to pull out the chequebook. But eventually, with the economy creaking, most countries finally pitch up at the World Bank, cap in hand, looking for a way out.

Which is usually very simple. Restructurc your economy and we'll let you off. Restructuring meaning, well, privatizing state services. It's by this process that Third World countries slowly end up handing over the keys to their key assets, hospitals and schools and water supplies, to those benevolent multinationals waiting round the corner. But, as Blair is at pains to tell us, if we didn't do it, someone else would. And at least you can be sure that when we mug someone we do it with a little better manners.

On 6 January 2004, after a twenty-year freeze, the ECGD announced that it would resume cover to Libya once an agreement had been reached on its outstanding debt. (Libya agreed to pay £20 million of the £25.4 million owed.) Welcoming the move, Trade Minister Mike O'Brien said: 'UK exporters and investors will now be able to take advantage of ECGD cover in the Libyan market, which offers opportunities in particular for the oil and gas industry.'[153]

There has not been a free election in Libya since Gaddafi came to power. Over the past three decades, Libya's human rights record has been appalling,[154] including the abduction, forced disappearance, or assassination of political opponents; torture and mistreatment of detainees;

and long-term detention without charge or trial, or else after grossly unfair trials. Hundreds of people remain arbitrarily detained, some of them for over a decade, and there are serious concerns about treatment in detention and fairness of procedures in several ongoing high-profile trials before the people's courts. Libya has been a closed country for United Nations and human rights investigators.

But it seems there may have been method in the madness.

In a series of meetings held in Britain over the past two years, which were orchestrated by MI6 and involved the CIA and Libyan intelligence. Libya agreed to hand over detailed intelligence on hundreds of al-Qaeda and other Islamic extremists, as well as pledging to abandon its WMD programme.

The key Libyan negotiator was Mousa Kousa, head of the country's security organization.[155] He was expelled from Britain in 1980 for publicly threatening to murder dissidents. (He was declared *persona non grata* by then Deputy Foreign Secretary, Ian Gilmour, amid cheers in the Commons.)

He went on to profess admiration for the IRA, and threatened to throw Libya's support behind the terrorist organization if Britain refused to hand over opponents of Gaddafi. This threat was later followed through with material support to the IRA. He was also named by the French as a suspect in the bombing of a civilian airliner over Niger in 1989 with the loss of 170 lives.

In 1995, a secret MI5 assessment accused Kousa of running agents in the UK and of presiding over an organization 'responsible for supporting terrorist organizations and for perpetrating state-sponsored acts of terrorism'.

It certainly appears that there is some sort of consistency problem in the way we deal with rogue states. In the case of Iraq we invade; in the case of Libya we embrace; and in the case of the 'stans we leave well alone. Which, upon reflection, may not be totally inconsistent, the solution in each case being determined by whatever suits the narrow political aims of the moment. Which is at least consistent.

One argument Gaddafi used to persuade the international community into welcoming him back in from the cold was the issue of Somalian refugees. He argued that with Libya about to be overrun by those fleeing conflict elsewhere in Africa – curious to think that one man's axis of evil could be another man's safe haven – he couldn't be sure how much longer he could contain them before they sought refuge in Italy. Berlusconi needed no second invitation, resuming trade links with Gadaffi in return for a tough line on the would-be job seekers (something the dictator would have few problems in pursuing).

But at least Berlusconi didn't take the line proposed by Umberto Bossi, chairman of the separatist Northern League and minister for reform, who suggested that the Italian navy should sort out the problem by opening fire on refugee boats (although his ministry did subsequently issue a statement claiming his comments had been taken out of context)[156]

> After the second or third warning, boom . . . the cannon roars. Without any beating about the bush. The cannon that blows everyone out of the water. Otherwise this business will never end . . . Illegal immigrants must be hounded out, either nicely or nastily. Only those with a job contract can enter the country. The others, out!

Thus a refugee problem can be used as a bargaining tool. Work with us, or you'll have 100,000 Somalis knocking on your door.

28
Chechnya; Or,
A brief history of crime

Let's recap.

If you are an Islamic extremist/a terrorist you are a bad guy.

Unless you are fighting Saddam, or someone else we don't like. In which case, you are a freedom fighter and therefore a good guy.

Except that for many years Saddam himself was the good guy, so that made you the bad guy again.

But if you were fighting the old USSR (in Afghanistan, say), then you were definitely the good guy and the Communists and the warlords who fought alongside them were bad.

Until the fall of Communism, at which point the warlords became regional leaders, and you were bad again.

Which is the situation as it now stands in Afghanistan.

Or, at least, it certainly was when we last looked.

And as in Chechnya, where you are definitely bad, because you kidnap and torture and kill.

Unlike the Russian army, who also kidnap and torture and kill, but they are good, because they are now our friends . . . well, at least they were until they refused to back our war against Saddam, at which point they became . . . well, at present no one really knows.

Tony Blair pointed all this out when he told us that he always raises the issue of Chechnya with President Putin,[157] but in a way that recognizes how Russians have suffered at the hands of Chechen terrorists.

Which is true. Particularly after the devastating tragedy at Beslan.

And what of the Chechens themselves? Not the fighters, but the ordinary Chechens.

Who have been shot at and attacked by the Russians.

And shot at and attacked by the Chechen rebels.

Who weren't our friends, but then were, and then weren't again.

They are 'the unfortunate victims caught up in all this'.

But not so unfortunate as to warrant Western intervention.

Which is a pity, because if you had been an Iraqi it would have been imperative that we did something to avert a wholesale human catastrophe.

And bombed you.

During the First Chechen War, in 1996, the Council of Europe bent the rules to allow Russia to become a member despite well-documented human rights abuses.

During the Second Chechen War, in 1999, Western leaders did at least express concern, but nothing more, despite refugees on the Ingushetian border pleading 'they are killing us, we are cold, help us'. Instead, they were encouraged to return to their homes, only for the nearby town of Grozny to be raised to the ground a few months later, with widespread stories of atrocities.

Later unwillingness to become involved might just possibly have been connected with the need for Russian cooperation in Kosovo. Others might point to the Bush–Putin strategic oil partnership, part of a US plan to reduce dependency on OPEC oil. Still others might point to a more obvious problem – namely, that with Afghanistan, Iraq, and any number of other problems to sort out, picking a quarrel with Russia over the same issues that pre-empted action in Iraq and Afghanistan could have resulted in the one war no one wanted.

Meanwhile, if you are a Wahhabi leader, like the Saudi Arabian warlord Khattab, who set up terrorist training camps with the aim of exporting jihad across the region, then you are definitely bad.

Unless you are the London-based Chechen rebel envoy Akhmed Zakayev, whom Russia has accused of murder, torture, and masterminding terror attacks,[158] who is refusing to leave Britain on the grounds that he could be tortured and murdered if he was sent to Moscow to stand trial.

At which point we have to admit we are a little confused and wish the whole thing would just go away.

It seems that after the fall of Communism, and the end of the Cold War, and September 11th, and the Iraq War, we are really not at all sure how the Russians fit into things any more.

Unless you have a lot of money and want to buy a football team, in which case we know exactly where you fit in.

So, to sum up. If you are a poor, innocent Chechen farmer, caught up in all this and suffer random killings and endure rocket attacks, sniper attacks, and bomb attacks, and have perhaps the worst quality of life of all the countries in the region – Afghanistan, Iraq, the 'stans, wherever, all included – then you probably have good reason to feel pretty let down. But then under Stalin your entire population was carted off to central Asia in boxcars and a third of you never came back, so you're probably used to this sort of thing by now.

So that should be a bit of comfort at least.

29
Africa: A scar on the conscience

In his 1997 manifesto, Tony Blair wrote,

> With a new Labour government Britain will be ... an advocate of human rights and democracy the world over ... Labour wants Britain to be respected in the world for the integrity with which it conducts its foreign relations.

> The state of Africa is a scar on the conscience of the world ... But if the world as a community focused on it, we could heal it. And if we don't, it will become deeper and angrier.
>
> Labour Party Conference, October 2001

So what was our solution?

Under Labour, Britain has overtaken the US as the biggest supplier of arms to Third World countries.[159] The UK made £422 million worth of arms sales to African countries between 1999 and 2002, with the US making £66 million worth in the same period. In 2002, the UK sold £2 billion worth of weapons to developing nations. In total, Britain earned £2.8 billion from overseas arms sales last year.

Between 1999 and 2002, we earned almost £10 billion from arms deliveries to the Third World. In 2002, arms sales to developing nations made up 87.5 per cent of all UK weapons contracts.

The Labour government's 2001 annual report showed that it had granted arms export licences to thirty-one of the forty-one poorest countries in the world. Since 1997, Labour has sent arms to some of the most notorious trouble spots in the world, including Colombia, Sri Lanka, Algeria, and Zimbabwe. Labour's ethical foreign policy stumbled at the first hurdle, in 1997, when it supplied Indonesia with Scorpion tanks, water cannon, and Hawk jets. Despite assurances from Indonesia, the equipment was used to crush those supporting a legitimate claim for independence in Aceh province. British arms sales to Indonesia subsequently rose from £2 million in 2000 to £40 million in 2002.

One of the most striking single examples of the UK's attitude towards Africa is Tanzania. In 2001 the government agreed to grant an export licence for a £28 million BAe Systems military air traffic control system for the East African state, failing to take into account that the country has barely any aircraft.

One of the poorest countries in the world, average annual income per head in Tanzania is £170. The deal, branded a waste of money by the World Bank (and they'd know), added half a year's worth of debt to the country's already crippled economy.

But not everyone thought it was a bad decision. Andrew Turner, MP for the Isle of Wight, where 250 jobs rested on the contract, said,

> It would have been a tragedy and disaster for Cowes and the island if the government were not to grant the export licence.[160]

And while less than half the population of Tanzania has access to clean water, Dick Evans of BAe had complete access to Tony Blair.

But we hadn't finished with Tanzania yet.

Confronted by the same wave of Somali refugees that President Gaddafi had used as a bargaining chip, Britain was looking for a makeshift solution which didn't involve opening up her borders.

Out in Dar es Salaam, a Home Office team floated the idea of Tanzania becoming a 'host' state for Somali asylum seekers.[161] A figure of £4 million was floated and, perhaps not surprisingly, with a large carrot dangled before them, the Tanzanians didn't say no.

Britain obviously thought that, as the Somalis were coming from a war-ravaged, desperate country, Tanzania, with an infant mortality rate of 25 per cent would be something of a step up.

Britain would be rid of the problem, the cash would help the Tanzanians keep up the repayments on the white elephant air traffic control system, and 250 people in Cowes would get their Christmas bonus. So everyone's happy.

Well done, the Somalis, for making it all happen.

And well done, Tony Blair, who in November 2003 dismissed Oliver Letwin's proposals for offshore holding camps by asking the House to imagine the conversation:

The British Foreign Office: 'Hello, are you a very impoverished nation? You've got to be really impoverished. How do you fancy a few thousand British asylum seekers?' A piece of cake. That is not Fantasy Island but a fantasy policy.[162]

UK-issued export licences, 2002

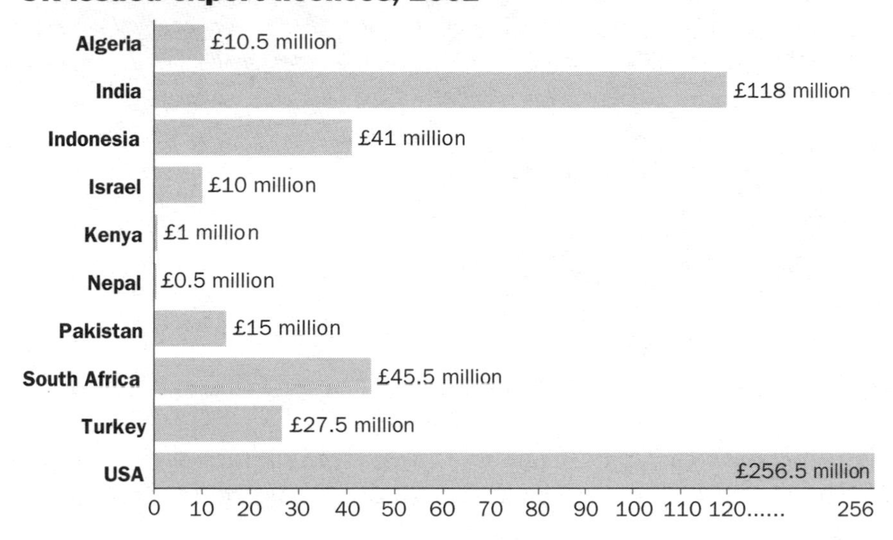

UK arms exports, 1980–2001

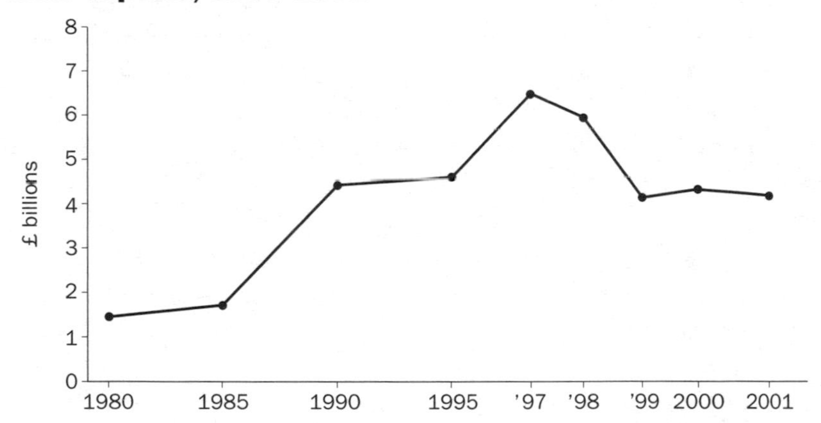

In January 2000, Blair overruled Robin Cook and approved the export of spare parts for disabled Hawk fighter jets to Zimbabwe. Zimbabwe had 11,000 troops in the Congo. We also provided components for military vehicles and military air-traffic control radar. Yet publicly the Foreign Office minister, Tony Lloyd, said, 'We have made it clear that there can be no military solution [to the conflict in the Congo] . . . Britain is working hard for peace.'[163]

Small arms[164]

Britain's recently introduced arms control legislation fails to outlaw the activity of British arms brokers who work outside the UK, despite a manifesto commitment (for what that's worth).

The vast majority of people who have been killed in violent conflict since the Second World War – about 2 million over the past decade alone – have been the victims of small arms, handguns, and rifles, not weapons of mass destruction. Small arms were the only weapons used in forty-six of the forty-nine conflicts since 1990. They have been handed out to an estimated 300,000 children aged under eighteen in the last ten years.

THE CONGO

On paper the Democratic Republic of Congo is one of the richest countries in the world. It is rich in gold and diamonds and other rare mineral resources.

Its people should all be millionaires.

It is also believed to have the world's largest reserves of the ore columbite-tantalite or coltan:[165] the Congo is the biggest supplier of coltan outside of Australia, Brazil, and Canada.

Coltan is refined to produce a heat-resistant powder: tantalum.

This makes it a vital resource in the electronic and telecommunications industries: capacitors for mobile phones, computer chips, game equipment, and camcorders all rely on coltan.

Without coltan there would be no telecommunications industry.

A little tantalum goes a long way. Over 4 million pounds of tantalum are used each year.

Coltan has reached a high of US$50 per kilogram on world markets.[166]

So annual tantalum sales reach around US$2 billion a year.

Not a lot for the one thing keeping a multi-trillion-dollar industry afloat.

Meanwhile, the Congo has been at war for the last seven years. It's a messy complicated war, involving seven countries. There are more than 10,000 child soldiers fighting, and 3.5 million people have died already as a result of the conflict.

While 2.25 million more have been driven from their homes.

Instability and war mean the coltan mines are controlled by local militias.

They use the cash from coltan to help fund their activities, including looting, raping, and pillaging on a massive scale.

Living conditions for the Congolese are some of the worst in the world.

Over half the population has no access to safe drinking water.

Infant mortality rates have reached over 40 per cent in parts of the country.

Coltan miners can earn up to US$50 a week.

This puts them on high wages for the Congo, where the average annual income is US$90.

So jobs in the coltan mines are highly prized and fought over. Literally.

Even though they are dangerous, with landslides and collapsing mines commonplace.

And cramped conditions.

Which is why many coltan miners are children.

Well, it's either that or a front-line job with the army.

There is little alternative employment available.

And the Congo isn't quite like here in terms of human rights.

Besides, the mines are run by people with guns.

By supporting the different factions in the war, Western governments have prolonged the conflict.

And conflict has been good for the mining business.

Because of regional instability, coltan from the Congo is much cheaper than from mines elsewhere in the world.

And Congolese coltan may pass through many hands before it reaches the final user, so tracing the origin of any shipment is practically impossible.

National parks and wildlife have been destroyed in the search for coltan and other minerals.

Meanwhile, the UK taxpayer received a £21 billion rebate thanks to the windfall tax on the sale of radio wavebands.

Which are used by the new generation of mobile phones.

Mobile phone companies now post some of the largest profits in the world.

And, remember, mobile phones all use coltan.

Nearly a million children have been orphaned by Aids in the Congo.

In 2001, Tony Blair told those gathered at the Labour Party Conference: 'The International community could, with our help, sort out the blight that is the continuing conflict in the Democratic Republic of Congo, where 3 million people have died through war or famine in the last decade.'

Since then, very little has been done and the situation has got considerably worse.[168] Unless you own a mobile phone. Or a mobile phone company.

Some good news

In February 2004 Tony Blair launched The Commission for Africa. Intended to coincide with the UK's chairmanship of the G8 and the EU (late 2005), it seeks to address the challenges facing the country and to generate ideas and action towards the implementation of the UN Millennium Development Goals.[169] On 27 February Bob Geldof told Somaliland Net:

> These are highly geared-up people, and the mix [nine of the seventeen commissioners are from Africa] suggests it will not be a commission of yes-men. The brief will be far wider than economics. It will look at the cultural and philosophical framework which explains what really drives the way the world works – and why it leaves Africa behind.

30
Leading by example: The USA

GUANTANAMO BAY

> Is an enemy so execrable that though in captivity his wishes and comforts are to be disregarded and even crossed? I think not. It is for the benefit of mankind to mitigate the horrors of war as much as possible.
>
> Thomas Jefferson
> 1779

> Guantanamo Bay's climate is different than Afghanistan. To be in a eight-by-eight cell in beautiful sunny Guantanamo Bay, Cuba, is not inhumane treatment.
>
> Donald Rumsfeld
> 23 January 2003[170]

The US has classed the 500-plus detainees at Guantanamo Bay as 'illegal combatants' rather than prisoners of war, denying them rights enshrined in the Geneva Conventions. As long as the prisoners never touch US soil – and the naval base is not considered part of the USA – they are denied the rights guaranteed to criminals under the American Constitution, such as a presumption of innocence and a trial by jury. In October 2003, three Afghans were sent home. Two were pensioners in their mid-seventies. The third was fourteen years old. In March 2004, five of the nine Britons held there were also flown home. All were released without charge a day after they arrived.[171]

> This is a very highly classified area, but I have to say that all you need to know [is]: there was a before 9/11, and there was an after 9/11. After 9/11 the gloves come off.
>
> Cofer Black
> Former head of CIA counterterrorism centre[172]

According to the *Washington Post*, the US government has sanctioned interrogation methods that violate human rights.[173] These offences are occurring in a number of secret detention centres. One is the US-occupied Bagram airbase in Afghanistan; another is Diego Garcia, an island in the Indian Ocean which the United States leases from Britain.

The United States

Of the 1200 people detained in the wake of September 11th, 750 were held on 'immigration charges' (and 80–100 of these are still being detained),[174] 110 have been charged with unrelated offences, and between eighty and 100 are still being detained. Getting information about many of them is almost impossible. The last time prisoners were held and interrogated in such a way was during the American Civil War, when nearly 8000 Confederate prisoners were detained and questioned.

The International Criminal Court[175]

Q: What does it do?

A: It does what it says on the tin. It's an independent court which countries sign up to and which allows cases of unlawful conduct against any member to be heard.

Q: When was it founded?

A: It was discussed by the international community after WWII, but Trinidad and Tobago was the first country to raise the possibility at the UN, in the early 1950s.

Q: Trinidad and Tobago?

A: The same.

Q: So when did people get round to sorting things out?

A: 1998.

Q: Busy, were they?

A: You could say that.

Q: Meaning?

A: Well, it took a while to persuade the Americans.

Q: Not enthusiastic?

A: They thought it might end up with them in the dock.

Q: But they signed up in the end?

A: Hmm. Well, they did. But then they wouldn't ratify it unless they could control which cases the court looked into.

Q: But at least they're sort of signed up.

A: Were. In 2002 they repudiated their own signature, pointing to their American Service Members Protection Act which says the US may use 'all necessary means' to return anyone detained by the ICC to the US.

Q: They can bomb an international court set up to try terrorists and bad guys.

A: You read what it said: 'all necessary means'.

Q: Wait a minute, this sounds like the start of the *Magnificent Seven*?

A: Now you're just being flippant.

Q: So they went it alone?

A: Not quite. They also said they would deny military aid to states that had ratified the Rome statute (that's the key piece of legislation that spelt out the terms of the court).

Q: They would punish countries that agreed to abide by the law?

A: That's about it.

Q: Anything else?

A: No. Oh, yes, they have been reaching their own private, bilateral agreements about what is and isn't legal with countries like East Timor and Israel and Romania and Tajikistan.

Q: Their own International Criminal Court?

A: See, they do abide by the law. Provided it's their law.

Q: And would a genuine International Criminal Court help?

A: Well, terrorism is a crime, not an act of war (the rules on that are already governed by the Geneva Conventions) and if there is a universal, internationally supported court which can prosecute and sentence anyone caught, and is above national interests, then of course it helps.

Q: And the alternative?

A: You tell me, because I'm buggered if I know.

Q: Except you're even more buggered if you want the USA to play by the same rules as everyone else.

A: Exactly.

THE US AND THE UN

Thirty years of vetoes, 1972–2002

The Second World War certainly left one lasting legacy. Only the big five on the Security Council – Russia, China, Britain, France, and the USA –

have the right of veto in the UN. For the first twenty-five years of the UN, the USSR constantly used its veto, to the fury of the USA. For the second twenty-five years, the roles were reversed.

During this period the US blocked moves to:

urge the permanent members to ensure UN decisions on the maintenance of international peace and security

call for developed countries to increase the quantity and quality of development assistance to underdeveloped countries

end all military and nuclear collaboration with apartheid. Support the oppressed under apartheid

inquire into the living conditions of Palestinians in the Occupied Territories

help negotiations on disarmament and cessation of the nuclear arms race

call for protection for developing countries' exports

call for alternative approaches for improving the enjoyment of human rights and fundamental freedoms

oppose intervention in the internal or external affairs of states

support a United Nations conference on women

safeguard the rights of developing countries in multinational trade negotiations

attempt to establish a new international economic order to promote the growth of underdeveloped countries and international economic cooperation

endorse the programme of action for the second half of the United Nations Decade for Women

support non-use of nuclear weapons against non-nuclear states

emphasize that the development of nations and individuals is a human right

call for the cessation of all nuclear test explosions

call for the implementation of the Declaration on the Granting of Independence to Colonial Countries and Peoples promote cooperative movements in developing countries

affirm the right of every state to choose its economic and social system in accord with the will of its people, without outside interference

condemn attempted coup by apartheid South Africa in the Seychelles

call for action in support of measures to prevent nuclear war, curb the arms race, and promote disarmament

urge negotiations on the prohibition of chemical and biological weapons

support prohibition of chemical and bacteriological weapons

condemn Israeli invasion of the Lebanon

declare that education, work, health care, proper nourishment and national development are human rights

call for the setting up of a World Charter for the protection of the environment

set up a United Nations conference on the succession of states in respect to state property, archives, and debts

support nuclear test bans and negotiations on nuclear-free outer space

support a new world information and communications order

develop a new international law

protect against products harmful to health and the environment

declare that education, work, health care, proper nourishment and national development are human rights (again)

protect against products harmful to health and the environment (again)

develop the energy resources of developing countries

support international action to eliminate apartheid

support resolutions about cooperation, human rights, trade, and development

support measures to be taken against Nazi, fascist, and neo-fascist activities

call on all governments to observe international law

support a resolution about cooperation, security, human rights, trade, media bias, the environment, and development support measure to prevent international terrorism, study the underlying political and economic causes of terrorism, and convene a conference to define terrorism and differentiate it from the struggles of people for national liberation

support resolutions concerning journalism, international debt, and trade

support opposition to the build-up of weapons in space

support opposition to the development of new weapons of mass destruction

oppose nuclear testing

oppose the acquisition of territory by force

set up the International Criminal Court.[176]

UN veto league table[177]

Number of vetoes by the big five in the last thirty years; or, why China is the most tolerant country in the world

USA	68
UK	29
France	14
Russia/USSR	14
China	4

Vice-President Dick Cheney's voting record in Congress[178]

Opposed Equal Rights Amendments

opposed resolution to urge the release of Nelson Mandela from a South African prison during the apartheid era

opposed federal Safe Drinking Water Act

opposed Clean Water Act

opposed authorizing funds for Head Start

opposed plastic gun ban, but changed his mind after law enforcement groups lobbied him opposed federal funding of abortions even in cases of rape, incest, or when a woman's life is in danger

opposed Endangered Species Act

opposed spending more on Superfund environmental clean-ups

supported oil-drilling in Alaska's Arctic National Wildlife Refuge

opposed gas and oil leasing in his home state of Wyoming and sought to designate 650,000 additional acres in Wyoming as wilderness areas

supported Star Wars, deployment of MX missile, and production of new chemical weapons

supported military aid to Nicaraguan Contras

supported raising the social security retirement age from sixty-five to sixty-seven

opposed bussing to achieve racial desegregation in public schools

supported prayer in public schools

opposed limiting contributions by political action committees

opposed long-term home care for the chronically ill under Medicare, and voted against a measure that would have shielded Medicare beneficiaries from bills for catastrophic illnesses and provided prescription-drug coverage under Medicare.

31
Aid

> Every gun that is made, every warship launched, every rocket fired, signifies a theft from those who hunger and are not fed, and those who are cold and are not clothed.
>
> Dwight D. Eisenhower
> 16 April 1953

Among the tireless work being done by aid agencies, there remain some alarming trends.

Global inequality is rising. Most African and many Latin American countries are worse off now than they were at the beginning of the 1970s.[179] With Afghanistan and Iraq in urgent need, what money there is is now spread ever more thinly.

In November 2003 the Department for International Development diverted £100 million of aid money to Baghdad.[180] One country to suffer as a result was South Africa, where HIV/Aids programmes faced a cut as the situation in Iraq worsened. The government's reasoning was that it should take money from middle-income states like South Africa and Honduras in order to target lower-income countries. But in Honduras 44 per cent of the population aged 25–35 lives on less than US$2 a day.[181] Middle income, like everything else, is a relative term.

In terms of aid budgets, Britain comes about midway down the list of Western countries in per capita donations. Not particularly great, but not the worst. The position of top penny-pincher goes to the USA, and a good proportion of the aid it does give goes to Israel for arms purchases.

But when we look into the fine print of our own aid donations, an equally alarming picture emerges: not in the amount given, but in the way it is dispersed.

The Organization for Economic Cooperation and Development has moved towards relaxing the definition of aid, allowing 'security measures' to be described as 'development'.[182] In practice, what this means is that money that could otherwise have been used for humanitarian purposes can now be redirected towards beefing up defence-related contracts. Comforting, perhaps, for foreign tourists visiting these countries, but not necessarily a top priority for local people.

By way of example, Pakistan's position as a pariah – in 1998 it had tested a nuclear weapon and been subjected to a raft of sanctions as punishment – was lifted just days after September 11th, and aid to the country (much of it military based) greatly increased. Both Britain and the US were key players in this: both stood to gain from the contracts offered by the Pakistani defence ministry.

But this isn't the only way aid money is being used to boost Western exports.

Across in the Indian state of Andhra Pradesh, £324 million has recently been allocated as an aid package. This is a huge amount, far more than we spent on the Ethiopian famine or to help the dire situation in the Congo.[183]

In return, Andhra Pradesh had to restructure and reform (i.e. privatize) its public services.

At a recent conference in Cancun to discuss how global trade barriers could be removed and markets opened up still further, three ministers from Ghana, Barbados, and Malawi were wheeled out to describe how such liberalization had helped their respective countries escape the poverty trap. Sam Mpasu, the Malawian minister for commerce and trade, was first to speak, and surprised the G7 delegates with his candour:

> We have opened our economy. That's why we are flat on our back.[184]

In Zambia, less than £1 million of aid money went on improving nutrition, but £56 million went towards privatizing the copper mines.

Meanwhile, the Americans have also been using aid not just as a lever, but also to open up markets for unwanted products.

Aid in the US comes with tax breaks. Companies can make money by dumping old stock they can't get rid of at home on to Third World countries. And often they aren't too choosy. Old clothes may not harm anyone, and old electrical goods that can't run because of the voltage difference are more of an inconvenience than a health hazard. But other donations are less benign.

Pharmaceutical companies have been known to offload short-dated drugs anywhere there is a relief effort. Appetite suppressants have ended up in the Sudan. Treatments that require a full course of drugs if they are to be effective often have to stop short because the aid agencies have only got half the consignment. Wrongly labelled drugs, and drugs that can't be used but cost a fortune to dispose of, add to the misery of countries that have come to depend on handouts, only to discover that one day the handouts don't come.

Such are the ironies of 'humanitarian assistance'.

PART V

So here's the bill . . .

32
The cost of freedom

> ### *A modest proposal*
>
> Intelligence
>
> In 2003, just forty-eight hours after a ring of steel had been imposed around Heathrow airport in response to a specific threat of an attack by Arab extremists, a Venezuelan of Bangladeshi origin arrived at Gatwick, thirty miles away, on a flight from Colombia in South America – not an obvious hotbed of Arab extremism – carrying a hand grenade.[186]
>
> In MI5's defence, there is a tricky balance to keep: on the one hand, they can tell the public absolutely nothing; on the other hand, they should, if possible, tell them everything they know.
>
> But here, at least, we are in luck, because in MI5's case, the two often amount to the same thing.

In America, post-September 11th, there was only one agenda: the War on Terror. And that meant not only tightened laws, and cutbacks in freedom of information, and xenophobia, and increased NRA membership, but also that everything else slipped down the list of things to do. The environment – never the biggest of deals, as Kyoto clearly showed – now became little more than a footnote in the appendix to the errata.

America's own social problems continued to manifest themselves outside the glare of publicity.

Ritalin, the behaviour-altering drug, which was barely talked about a few years ago, is now given to as many as 20 per cent of children in some areas.[187]

American infant mortality, promoted by an unhealthy lifestyle and a nation that needs to consume, rose to a rate that put it eighteenth out of twenty-one developed nations. Even one of Bush's terrorist states has a better figure.[188]

But as obesity and health problems mounted, together with the growth of GM foods, continued global warming and mining in Alaska, Bush's crusade on terror was pushed relentlessly as the only issue that mattered. Not the state of the economy, not the state of the world, not even the state of Dick Cheney.

And where America leads we now follow.

In Britain, the War on Terror gave the government licence to tighten our own laws and to embark on a huge expansion of the security service – the very people whose credibility Iraq had compromised.

Secretly tapped phone calls can now be used as evidence in trials of terrorist suspects. Foreigners can be detained indefinitely without trial, despite this breaching the European Convention on Human Rights.

MI5 will soon be back up to Second World War staffing levels.[189] Other measures announced in the Civil Contingency Bill allow ministers to ban access to sensitive sites, evacuate designated areas, and stop public gatherings without Parliament's approval.[190]

In November 2001, David Blunkett announced that we had opted out of Article 5 of the European Convention on Human Rights, which states that you're forbidden from detaining a person and putting them in jail without charge or without trial. The European Convention allows us to do that only if you declare a national state of emergency. Which, of course, we did.

However, Article 5 says you're only allowed to declare a state of emergency if there is a war or other public emergency threatening the life of the nation. Although there was no genuine emergency when Mr Blunkett made his announcement, eighteen months later, after we'd attacked Iraq, there certainly was more of a risk. Which proves that anything that Mr Blunkett says can turn out to be true, if you're prepared to wait long enough.

Two and a half years after September 11th, Britain remains on a high state of alert. Many of the freedoms we used to take for granted are now under attack from an organization about which we know little except for its ruthless opposition to Western liberal values. The greatest threat to our way of life is not Saddam Hussein, but the as yet uncaptured individual whose bearded face is a regular feature on our television screens. David Blunkett.

Who I hate

By David Blunkett, aged 47

(A list of Mr Blunkett's published or quoted bugbears)

Hooligans, the press, university researchers, the police, lawyers, judges, the chattering classes, Harold Shipman, teachers, the politically correct, Somalis, anti-war protesters, asylum seekers, the BBC, the middle classes, the Church, people on the school run, anti-homework campaigners, the monarchy, Harold Shipman, the work-shy, bleeding-heart-liberals, muggers, TV programme makers who expose racist police, the Police Federation, terrorists, rebel MPs, the Conservatives, civil rights campaigners, anyone opposed to ID cards, Harold Shipman, refugees, truants, vagrants, left-wingers, right-wingers, prisoners, juvenile offenders, BMW drivers, anyone opposed to any government plans, Yardies, scroungers, benefit cheats, single mums, delinquents, chief prison officers, Kosovans, Afghanistanis, Kurds, the Archbishop of Canterbury, Harold Shipman.

Mr Blunkett is Home Secretary.

Mr Blunkett's current or proposed legislation includes the power to detain individuals, not on proof of involvement beyond reasonable doubt but on the balance of probabilities. Trials may be held in secret in front of a vetted judge (no, not Lord Hutton, that was just good luck). The evidence may not be revealed to the defendant, in order to protect intelligence sources (to protect anonymity, presumably, but this wheeze could prove useful in saving embarrassment; after all, it has not been unknown in recent history for information gathered by the security services to be wrong). Foreign nationals can be – and are being – held without charge on the basis of evidence they cannot see. After a recent ruling by the Court of Appeal, they can now be tried on the basis of evidence extracted under torture, so long as no British agents were involved in the actual torturing. The European Convention on Human Rights doesn't apply (we've opted out). Meanwhile, under a new extradition agreement, the Americans can request extradition of a British citizen without the need for proof of their offence. Though this doesn't apply the other way round (it's called a special relationship, remember).[191]

But you can see Blunkett's point: unless we have detention without charge, secret trials, and less stringent criteria for arrest, how can we fight those who would take away our freedoms?

Katherine Gunn was only able to fight her case because, in rewriting the Public Interest Disclosure Act, the law lords had thankfully made provision for public servants to blow the whistle if they felt that by so doing they were preventing unlawful loss of life. This defence may not help others with information to disclose, but, as war becomes the norm, who knows?

Without Katherine Gunn's revelations we would not have known that we had been asked to spy on other countries' embassies and eavesdrop on the United Nations. But the government will still pursue hers and similar cases (albeit unsuccessfully) as a matter of policy – *pour décourager les autres.*

Not everyone agrees that government secrecy is a good thing. Some even question whether it is needed at all.

> The problem is at present the government grants information when it wants to. What is needed is a change in culture and a statutory obligation to make it a duty to release information to the people who elect the government.

Or,

> There is still far too much addiction to secrecy and wish to conduct business behind closed doors.

Or even,

> We want to end the obsessive and unnecessary secrecy which surrounds government activity and make government information available to the public unless there are good reasons not to do so. So the presumption is that information should be, rather than should not be, released.

Guess who? Tony Blair. In 1996.[192]

The War on Terror has given licence to clamp down, spy, and control, to a government that has already shown that it needs no further invitation.

We have more spies, more security measures, more CCTV surveillance, more police, more clamping, more parking restrictions, more curfews, more anti-social behaviour orders, more jails, more stop and search, more everything. And that's without ID cards. Although the fact that we all carry Reward cards, which tell anyone all they need to know, does suggest that the civil liberties lobby has rather missed the boat.

Yet the problems remain.

Far from putting off louts, city centre TV cameras seem to provide something of a captive audience to perform to when falling over drunk at two in the morning.

In November 1995, following yet another Tory vote in which Major's rebel wing was brought in line and forced through the lobbies, Tony Blair spoke out in Parliament in sympathy with the

> whipless wonders expelled to the darkness for daring to defy the Prime Minister.[193]

Yet that is exactly what happened here once we signed up to American foreign policy.

As Labour cranked up for the war debate, Blair's own whips went off in search of his rebels. Chief whip Hilary Armstrong took a prominent role in this, calling in many back-benchers and demanding support for the leader. One of those confronted was Paul Marsden, MP for Shrewsbury. He had the presence of mind to record the conversation, revealing just how extreme the new darkness would be for anyone who dared defy the Prime Minister.[194]

> ARMSTRONG: Paul, we are all comrades together in the Labour Party and we are all supposed to be on the same side. I want to improve your communication skills.
> MARSDEN: What do you mean?
> ARMSTRONG: I want you to join the mainstream of the party.
> MARSDEN: What do you mean by the mainstream?
> ARMSTRONG: Look, Paul, let me put it another way, those that aren't with us are against us.
> MARSDEN: Name names.
> ARMSTRONG: We don't really know each other do we? We haven't had a chance to speak properly in the last four years. [Marsden mentioned three previous meetings.] Oh yes, I remember now. [She picked up an inch-thick brown file and waved it in his face, opening it to reveal articles written by Marsden for his local *Shropshire Star*, speeches he had made, transcripts of radio interviews he had given.] I want a guarantee that you will not talk to the media unless you speak to me first.

MARSDEN: I won't do that. I believe it is my right to speak to whoever I choose.

ARMSTRONG: I have been looking at your file, you are clearly very inexperienced and your attendance record is poor. [Between 1997 and 1999 Marsden had spent a lot of time away from the Commons. His wife had given birth and was seriously ill. Ex-chief whip Nick Brown gave him compassionate leave.]

MARSDEN: I take great offence at that. I am not inexperienced and my attendance record is certainly not poor. My wife was being cut open in the operating theatre and Nick Brown kindly allowed me extra time at home. You must know all that. What the hell has it go to do with all this?

ARMSTRONG: Your attendance record was not good last year either. You missed more votes than most others.

MARSDEN: That is not true. We were fighting a general election and you lot told us to go home and campaign to win it.

ARMSTRONG: You made a complete fool of yourself the other day when you got up in the Commons. [Armstrong was referring to Marsden's question to Blair in a Commons debate, when the MP said the decision to go to war should be approved by a vote of all MPs, not by the Prime Minister alone.] You just don't understand the rules here, you're too inexperienced.

MARSDEN: There's no need to insult me. I know the rules, I consulted the speaker's clerk about voting procedures.

ARMSTRONG: In fact, we may well hold a vote, but if we do, it will be whipped.

MARSDEN: That is outrageous. You won't even give us a free vote on whether we go to war, it is an issue which should be a matter of conscience.

ARMSTRONG: War is not a matter of conscience. Abortion and embryo research are matters of conscience, but not wars.

Whoa, whoa, whoa, hold on, hold on, wait . . . What did she say? Can we repeat that? *War is not a matter of conscience. Abortion and embryo research are matters of conscience, but not wars.*

So that's it, then. Blair was right. You can be unprincipled and principled at the same time. Principled enough to support your party, but unprincipled enough to surrender your own principles.

Paul Marsden challenged Armstrong.

MARSDEN: Are you seriously saying blowing people up and killing people is not a moral issue?

ARMSTRONG: It is government policy that we are at war. You astound me. We can't have a trusting relationship if you keep talking to the media without permission.
MARSDEN: It would help if your deputy didn't send me snotty letters disciplining me.
ARMSTRONG: I did leave a message at your office on Monday night saying to call me.
MARSDEN: Are you sure?
ARMSTRONG: Yes. Why?
MARSDEN: You couldn't have phoned the Shrewsbury office because you didn't leave a message on the answer machine. You can't have left a message in London either, because I was in the office and there was no voicemail left there.
ARMSTRONG: But I spoke to someone and left a message with them.
MARSDEN: You didn't. I checked the telephone log and there are no messages left.
ARMSTRONG: Er, perhaps I got the wrong number.
MARSDEN: Let's get this straight. You did not call me.
ARMSTRONG: Anyway, you must stop using the media.
MARSDEN: That's a bit rich coming from people like you and Downing Street when Stephen Byers's spin doctor, Jo Moore, says September 11th is a good day to bury bad news.
ARMSTRONG: Jo Moore didn't say that.
MARSDEN: That is exactly what she said in her email.
ARMSTRONG: We don't have spin doctors in No. 10 – or anywhere else.
MARSDEN: You aren't seriously telling me that you don't have spin doctors and they don't exist. You are losing it, Hilary.
ARMSTRONG: You wait until I really do lose it. I am not going to have a dialogue with you about that. It was people like you who appeased Hitler in 1938.
MARSDEN: Don't you dare call me an appeaser! I am not in favour of appeasing Bin Laden, I simply disagree with the way the government is going about stopping him. That's the official line now, is it? We are all appeasers if we don't agree with everything you say?
ARMSTRONG: Well, what would you do about Bin Laden then?
MARSDEN: I think we should indict him on criminal charges. It could be done very quickly, and then the UN should take charge of the military action, not the USA. It would be much more effective. By all means send in the SAS, but let's get the UN onside first.
ARMSTRONG: The trouble with people like you is that you are so clever with words that us up north can't argue back.

MARSDEN: Do you mind? I am a northerner myself. I was born in Cheshire. I spent four years at Teesside Polytechnic, near where you come from.
ARMSTRONG: You do realize that everything that is said in here is private and confidential, don't you? You cannot go out and tell the media.
MARSDEN: I haven't got the media outside and I won't go to them. But if they come to me I will talk to them.

33
Back on planet Earth . . .

When the Labour government signed up to the Kyoto Agreement to cut global emissions, they'd hardly spent anything on developing solar or wind or any other sort of green power, even though the UK has more than five times the potential offshore wind resources of any other European country. So that left us with just one realistic solution: nuclear.

On average, the government spends around £10 million per annum researching renewable energy resources. Compare that with the £650 million we recently spent bailing out just one bit of the nuclear industry. Yet our energy surplus is actually greater than the total generated by nuclear. So why, then, consider building up to twelve new nuclear reactors, as we did at one point?

As one critic of the policy reflected,

> What is unbelievably depressing about the government's response is that they see in the evidence about greenhouse gases, or acid rain, not an opportunity to promote the environmental concerns, but a chance to make the case for nuclear power . . . radioactive waste is itself a major environmental problem and one for which we have no easy answer at present.[195]

Tony Blair again, talking not about his government but that of Mrs Thatcher.

Yet even she didn't try to argue that going nuclear was our environmentally friendly way of saving the planet.

Still, better an old Tony Blair than an old John Prescott:

> Look, it may not be quite what everyone thought it would when we said we intended to honour our commitments and cut pollution, but frankly, as the man who guided Kyoto through, I've just got to say, our

101 uses for a John Prescott
No. 44 – Judge in a doughnut-baking contest

> Pauline goes nuclear every Friday night when I get home, and we've nearly always cleared up the fallout by Sunday lunchtime.[196]

The MoD objected to over half of the 800 applications to build onshore wind farms lodged in the last year or so, claiming the spinning blades could confuse radar scanners and allow enemy planes to hide behind them. Apart from the obvious visual similarity between a small, sleek, fast-moving object, and a large, tall, stationary object with a giant fan on the front, it is hard to see how the two things could be mistaken. It doesn't seem to pose the same problems abroad. While the MoD has asked for a minimum of fifty miles' separation between any radar site and any wind farm, in Europe the only country to set any restrictions is Germany, and there the ban is set at less than five miles.[197]

What's more, a software package to sort out any glitches is available and already used in Denmark, where there is a large wind farm a few miles from Copenhagen airport.

al-Qaeda undoubtedly presents a threat to Britain, and to many other countries, but the prospect of their sneakily deploying wind turbines as a shield for an attack does seem a little outlandish.

The Day After Tomorrow was a Hollywood scare-pic released in summer 2004, telling the story of a climate shift some time in the future. A combination of smoke and gases disrupts the ocean currents and leads to an instant ice age. The president is flash-frozen and, in a twist on the immigration debate, the United States has to plead with Mexico to allow American refugees to travel south to the warmth.

The scare reached NASA, who promptly emailed dozens of scientists the following message:

> No one from NASA is to do interviews or otherwise comment on anything to do with this film. Any news media wanting to discuss science fiction vs. science fact about climate change will need to seek comment from individuals or organizations not associated with NASA.[198]

The email was sent on 1 April so there's a possibility it was a joke. Or there's a possibility it was serious, in which case it was an even bigger joke. What definitely was a joke was that at US$125 million, the movie's budget exceeded the money that the US has spent looking into and dealing with climate change.

So, there you have it. While climate change may not amount to big bucks, fictional climate change certainly does.

How to sell smog

It's often assumed that because the USA never signed up to Kyoto, it is less progressive than other countries when it comes to pollution. Contained in the Kyoto agreement was an energy emissions policy whereby high polluters would pay a fine while low polluters would receive a rebate. In effect, you can buy off your environmental obligations by finding a country that's keeping its house in order to take your waste. But it's a start, and it would have been nice if America could at least have signed up like everyone else.

But the Americans, working on a federal basis, were way out ahead, cutting it their way.

Under the Texas Clean Air Act, companies can trade their emissions through an emissions reductions bank. In one two-year period, 2000 tons of nitrogen oxides were 'bought' and 'sold' in this way.

The free market rides to the rescue again.

But, more recently, companies have cut out the bank and started trading directly in discrete emission reduction credits. This is a permissible system, where two firms get together to trade smog.

Where there is a market solution, there is a market. If you run a fleet of clean vehicles, it's in your interest to encourage someone else to pollute, so you can sell your quota to him.

It's not driven by environmental concern; pollution has become just another stock to trade. You gamble on futures and make money out of predicting how much pollution will go up or down. It doesn't really matter which way things go so long as there is trade in the market.

While Kyoto is still underperforming, the Texas Clean Air Act – ten years old – is doing fine. And all those people selling clean air, for someone else to grub up, are doing even better. Clean air isn't a right, it's just another product.[199]

The ghost fleet

Q Put the following countries in order of importance: Britain, USA, Portugal, India, Turkey, Greece.

It's all to do with dismantling rotting WWII warships sent by the USA to Britain for scrap. So America is first on the list.

As the convoy approached the Azores, the Portuguese, these being their territorial waters, sent a gunboat to force the ships back out to sea, afraid of the environmental risk the asbestos-leaking vessels posed. So Portugal second, and Britain, where the boats eventually arrived to dockside protests, grudgingly third.

But it doesn't stop there, because we then dispatched a ghost fleet of our own even more dilapidated warships for dismantling in Turkey. Except that Turkish environmentalists intervened when the vessels arrived, forcing them to turn back to Greece, which said thanks but no thanks, and sent the toxic armada back out onto the high seas. Finally, they fetched up at Alang, in India, where they were beached and broken up by hand, by an army of barefoot workers with no protective clothing and little more than a lot of sledgehammers and will-power.[200]

No matter how poor your environmental record may be, there is always someone worse off than you are. But it does still leave the question of what the Indians do when they have some old ships they want broken up?

THE EXTRAS

We earn around £1 trillion a year and spend about half that on running the country. The war in Iraq cost around £6 billion but that figure is rising. Here's where the rest goes:

Nuclear weapons clean-up, £32 billion[201]

According to the MoD, the future cost to the taxpayer of cleaning up Britain's ailing nuclear defence installations will be £32 billion. The expensive and complex process of decommissioning military nuclear facilities once they have passed the age of safe use is generally costed when they are built. In June 1999, the MoD claimed that the cost would be only £10 billion, but a recent review by the Treasury calculated that the figure had tripled in five years and advised that three times the original sum be set aside.

One possibility is a PFI. That would keep the cost off the balance sheet, storing it up for later. But one thing private companies aren't very keen to acquire is risk. Especially long-term risk. Who would, at that price and with costs ballooning? Funny how just when you need them, all your friends in the City desert you.

Trident, £2 billion per annum (indefinitely)[202]

The annual cost of maintaining Britain's nuclear weapons is estimated to be about £2 billion. Britain's four Trident submarines are each armed with American missiles, carrying a maximum of forty-eight 100 kiloton warheads capable of devastating a built-up area 15–30 kilometres across.

Devonport dockyards, £1 billion[203]

The cost of building earthquake-resistant docks to refit Britain's semi-redundant nuclear submarines, a legacy of the Cold War, has soared to

£933 million – almost double the original estimate – and may rise more, according to a National Audit Office report. The contract was given to DML, a company whose main shareholder, Brown and Root, is a subsidiary of Halliburton, the American oil services company formerly chaired by the US vice-president, Dick Cheney.

General Ministry of Defence write-offs, £482 million[204]

In its latest annual accounts, it was revealed that last year the MoD wasted millions of pounds on write-offs, including £118 million on a computerized inventory scheme which was scrapped before going into operation, and £77 million on the development of a new radar system for the Sea Harrier before it was decided the plane would be taken out of service.

Aldermaston, £2 billion[205]

The Ministry of Defence is investing more than £2 billion in a project that would enable Britain to produce a new generation of nuclear weapons. A huge expansion plan for the Atomic Weapons Research Establishment at Aldermaston in Berkshire would provide scientists with the capability to design and produce 'mini-nukes', or nuclear warheads for cruise missiles. A sort of must-have for the warmonger who has everything.

New GCHQ building, £337 million

In September 2003, GCHQ's staff began moving into their new 'doughnut' building. By December, it was revealed that staff have to hot-desk because they have already run out of space, and many are being told to keep their cars at home because of a lack of parking spaces. The assorted spies and secret agents have been told to use a park-and-ride scheme to come to work. Not so much 'licensed to kill' as 'licensed to park anywhere onsite'.

The final cost has been officially put at £337 million. Originally, GCHQ had estimated the cost of relocating computers at £20 million. Later this was revised to £40 million, an estimate that Edward Leigh, MP, chairman of the Public Accounts Committee, said 'may be the most inaccurate I have ever seen.'[206] In June 2004 it was increased to £450 million – over ten times more than anticipated, and twenty-two times more than the first estimate approved by Whitehall in 1997.[207]

Scottish Parliament building, £430 million and counting[208]

The building of the new Scottish Parliament at the bottom of the Royal Mile in Edinburgh has been dogged by delays and spiralling costs. In September 1997 the cost was estimated at £10–40 million. This has now increased to more than £430 million,[209] and the completion date has slipped by four years.

A report into the mess was published in September 2000, but its findings were not made public. It stated that the contractor, Bovis, had not been appointed in a 'fair, transparent, and accountable manner', that the company had won the contract on the strength of a 'comfort-factor' relationship with a senior Scottish Office official, that the late architect of the building had benefited from a 'substantial overpayment of fees', and that there had been a 'blatant disregard of Treasury/Scottish Office guidelines in the procurement of consultants, construction manager, and some individuals within the Holyrood project management team'.

Welsh Assembly building, £55 million and counting[210]

Not to be outdone, the Welsh stepped in with a white elephant of their own. In July 2003, contractors were finally given the go-ahead to build the new debating chamber for the Welsh Assembly on a site in Cardiff. The projected cost is currently put at £55 million, almost five times the original £12 million estimate. And that's before work has even started.

Libra court computer system, £318 million[211]

A new computer system for magistrates' courts in England and Wales is still unfinished after years of spiralling costs, condemned as a 'shocking waste of taxpayers' money' by Edward Leigh, chairman of the influential Commons Public Accounts Committee, in January 2003. He said the Libra scheme was 'one of the worst IT projects' he had ever seen, and that 'it may be the shoddiest PFI project ever'. Costs have more than doubled, and courts will be able to use the system for two years less than planned. The £146 million PFI deal signed with ICL (now Fujitsu Services) in 1998 has risen to £390 million.

And finally – well, in this list; there are plenty more that could have been added had we wanted to –

Channel Tunnel rail link, £9 billion[212]

The National Audit Office confirmed in April 2003 that the taxpayer could be exposed to more than £9 billion in loans and other guarantees to get the Channel Tunnel rail link completed. Successive governments have always claimed that the financial risk lay with the private sector, but the government has already had to bail out the developer, London and Continental Railways, on more than one occasion, and the taxpayer may foot the bill for more liabilities in the future.

34
Fighting fit

In July and August 2002, the biggest war game of all time, the US$250 million Millennium Challenge 2002, took place. The combined might of the American armed forces took on what was called a militarily powerful Middle East nation on the Persian Gulf, ruled by a crazy but cunning megalomaniac.

The part of Saddam – I'm sorry, the part of the enemy – was played by retired Lieutenant General Paul Van Riper. Using a flotilla of civilian ships and planes, and messages broadcast from the minarets of mosques, he succeeded in sinking sixteen American ships and wiping out thousands of marines before the Americans decided they wanted their ball back. The Pentagon, furious at the way it had gone, simply ordered all the dead troops back to life and refloated the sunken ships. The referees then told Van Riper that his communications had been destroyed, and ordered him to turn off his air defences whenever the Americans were about to attack and move his forces away from areas where they wanted to land. Not surprisingly, Van Riper gave up and refused to play any more. But, luckily, for the real thing the Americans also had the might of the British army.[213]

The curious thing is, as arms companies' profits go up courtesy of the biggest defence-spending spree since the Second World War, the kit doesn't necessarily get any better. That's assuming it actually turns up in the right place. And that it works when it gets there.

In August 2002 the National Audit Office published its report into Exercise Saif Sareea (Swift Sword) II in Oman, a joint exercise designed to test the military's readiness for war.[214] Among the problems it found were the following.

Challenger II main battle tank

Of the sixty-six Challenger II tanks deployed to Oman, nearly half broke down. This type of tank was originally designed and procured during the Cold War for use in north-west Europe. They were used in the Gulf War and it was decided they needed to be modified to suit desert conditions. In Europe the air filters had an average life of twelve months. In Oman it was four hours. The problem was addressed by airlifting in a further 55 tons of spares, effectively exhausting the global supply of air filters.

AS90m self-propelled guns

The AS90m was designed in the expectation that it would be used exclusively in Europe. The air filters melted in the desert, causing two units to be withdrawn from the exercise. One caught fire. They were modified in the field by engineers, but even then the guns were restricted to moving only at 25 kph and at night.

Container handling rough terrain system

The container handling rough terrain system is used to move containers from ships or trains to land transporters or within depots. Of thirteen vehicles in service, eight were deployed to Oman. Because usage is limited to these types of operations, experience of operating the equipment is low and it is easily damaged. Unfortunately, the five-year maintenance contract with Kalmar applies only to the UK and Germany. To overcome the shortage of functioning vehicles, cranes were used instead. Containers moved in this way took about forty to fifty minutes to move, compared with about four minutes if a container handling rough terrain vehicle is used.

Older vehicles

Older vehicles' engines overheated so much that, in order to keep them running, drivers had to switch on the heaters, which meant they could drive only for very short periods.

Helicopter fleet

Designed for use in – wait for it – northern Europe, the rotor blades on the Lynx helicopters had a life expectancy of 500 hours. In Oman this was reduced somewhat to twenty-seven hours. Which came as a surprise, not least to the pilots.

Communications systems

The army's tactical communications system, Ptarmigan, was designed, once again, to operate in European conditions, and is susceptible to dust and sand. Furthermore the army's Clansman family of radio systems hit the same problems that have arisen in the past. The systems failed completely in the heat and dust of the desert. The NAO report states: 'Tank Squadrons, for example, were unable to communicate effectively with each other, and were frequently forced to interrupt manoeuvres in order to consult on orders for ongoing training. Whereas military units were able to use mobile phones as an expedient in Kosovo, the lack of coverage in the Omani desert ensured that this was not an option during the exercise.'

Clothing and supplies

There were insufficient desert combat suits and footwear. Some boots quickly fell apart, others melted. A shortage of desert boots led to some soldiers buying 'suitable footwear at their own expense'.

However, on a more positive note, the report recognized that 'the standard of food provision on the exercise was generally excellent'.

Apache helicopters

The army has an order in for Apache helicopters, but they cannot be used to fire their Hellfire anti-tank missiles because debris from the weapons system could hit the rotor blades, causing the aircraft to crash. The cost of each helicopter is around £30 million. The US has restricted its Apache helicopters to firing missiles only during wartime, and to launching them only from the right-hand side of the aircraft to try and ensure that the rotor blades aren't hit.

SA80-A2 standard army rifles

These are lethal weapons. Not least if you happen to be using them. The original SA80 rifles were recalled in 1999 for modification as they kept jamming in extreme weather. A total of 300,000 have been modified, at a cost of £92 million. However, the new rifles have severe maintenance problems. They were tested in Afghanistan by the Royal Marine Commandos, who found that the rifle has a tendency to jam in dusty conditions. This can, of course, be avoided if, every time you fire the weapon, you then take it apart and oil it. And if there is no time, well, you have to *make* time.

Royal Navy – on the rocks

In July 2002, the 3500 tonne naval destroyer HMS *Nottingham* hit a clearly charted rock off Australia. Two years previously, in September 2000, HMS *Grafton* ran aground after hitting rocks off Norway, and in 1995, HMS *Brazen* ran aground in the South Atlantic.[215]

Stockpiling

Last year the NAO reported that the MoD had valued 1175 brass nuts at a total of £83, when they were actually worth £1.17. The MoD had also valued 159 special personal computers in its stockpiles at £192 million, when their real worth was less than £2 million. The report also pointed out that the RAF was holding 1775 aircraft refuelling tanks, enough to last for 440 years.

One of the main lessons learnt from Operation Swift Sword was clear: if we were to fight Saddam Hussein properly, we would have to persuade him to come to northern Europe.

35
And the other big winners . . .

THE A–Z OF LIFESTYLE ENHANCEMENTS UNDER NEW LABOUR

0% finance
118 118 (infuriatingly)
1471
2 passport-sized photographs, utility bill, proof of ID
24/7 News
4 remote controls
7 working days (how come when everything else is faster, cheques now take even longer?)
911 (what happened to 999?)
absinthe
adding attachments
affordable liposuction
air con (never air conditioning)
alcopops
Aqua Libra (how many health drinks do we need?)
Apple computers (being cool again)
Atkins
automated lawn-mowing systems

Babington House
BabelFish translator (now everyone can speak thirty-seven languages)
bagels with thirty-four choices of fillings
bedbugs (numbers soaring now under New Labour)
bite-size
Bluetooth, WAP, GPS
Boden catalogue (perfect for the countryside march)
bottled water
Botox (how did we live without it?)
Budgens (back from the Tory eighties' dead)
Burberry (who'd have thought country chic would make it?)

cable telly
Caesar haircuts (now out again)
cameraphones (multi-billion-pound industry so we can take photographs of girls' breasts in the pub)
car insurance for women only
Channel 5 becoming the new Five
Channel 4 becoming the old Five
Chapman brothers

chip/hologram security on bank cards
ClipArt
colonic irrigation
compact edition broadsheets
courtesy cars
credit (we now have a super range of credit cards in our pocket)
cybersex

DAB digital radio
Daily Mail (how did that get in there?)
default (general computer excuse for stepping in where not wanted)
designated non-smoking areas (next to smoking tables)
designer anything
digital (everything)
'Done a . . .' (as in 'Done a Beckham', 'Done a Barrymore', 'Done a Gazza')
downloadable ringtones
downloading music illegally, then legally, then illegally again
downsizing (the nineties' version of dropping out)
drug-resistant bugs
DVD-R

e in front of anything (e-4, eBay, e-commerce)
easy-anything
egg (the credit card not the food)

factory outlet shopping
family car (finally cheaper than New Zealand but still cheaper on the Continent)
foreign football managers
filtered tap water
flat screen
fly-by-wire
Forbidden Planet
Freeview/serve/dom/etc.
FCUK (so predictable, but what was the Church doing rebranding itself JCUK?)

gluten
Go Large!
Google
Googling someone
GPS
Grayson Perry original
gun culture (formerly 'carrying a gun')

hardwood flooring
having something 'to go'
head lice (numbers have rocketed in the last seven years)
hip hop (Eminem really)
home shopping
home shopping channels
horoscopes (on the mobile, naturally)
Hotmail
hyperdrive (move over, floppies)

I think you're calling for Odeon Manchester, is this correct?
Ibiza
If you know the number of the person you are calling . . .
inbox
intelligent cruise control
Intelligent Finance
interactive
Internet Banking
Internet dating

iris recognition
irony
ISAs (PEPs out)
It looks like you are typing a letter . . .

Jimmy Choo Shoes
Jonny Wilkinson
Jordan (the model)

Kit-Kat Chunky
Kompressor (it has to be spelt with a 'K')

lactose intolerance
lads' mags (techno-porn)
laser eye surgery
lastminute.com
lifestyle
lifestyle magazines
lifestyle makeover
lifestyle programmes
lifestyle programme presenters
liposuction
loft living (has there ever been a newspaper property section without at least one article about it?)
login
Lotto rollovers
low fat/ultra-low fat/virtually fat free/no fat
low-cost loans (on all day on cable channels)
Lulu Guinness handbag

maxing it (credit card, sugar-free cola, sex, anything)
memory stick
minicabs for women only
mobile gaming
mocha-chocca-latte-triple-espresso shot-cinnamon-sprinkled drinks
moist, lemon-scented cleansing squares
moisturizer for men (plus make-up)
Monsters of Rock (also Rock Legends, Classic Rock, Rock Gold)
metrosexuals
MP3 players
MSN
multiplex
muffins

The new iPod (wouldn't be seen dead with the old one)
nip 'n' tuck
no-claims bonus protection
no-win no-fee lawyers
Nokia
number withheld/private number

openly gay police officers/chiefs
opt-out clause (of holiday entitlement/overtime regulations)
Oyster, Nectar, loyalty, store cards

PalmPilots (oh no, sorry, they've gone out of fashion since we started writing this list)
parking fines (for anything and everything, any time of day or night, anywhere, from mass armies of swarming parking rats)
pashminas
passwords
passwords with numbers in
password reminders
pay as you go
peanut allergies

personalized number plates (for south-east England)
Philippe Starck
PIN numbers
pixels
plasma screen
plastic surgery
predictive texting
printer not found
private health care (the patient will see you now, doctor, ah, sorry, I'm going to have to go outside and scream at something)
public inquiries

rats (have just begun to outnumber humans in the UK this year)
-rage (road, trolley, golf . . . please add as appropriate)
Real Madrid
reality TV (*Big Bro, I'm a Z-List Celebrity, Pop Idiot, Ant & Dec, Davina McCall*, Jade from *Big Brother* . . . see how it catches on)
Red Bull (mixed with vodka, under a certain age)
reflexology/acupuncture/Swedish massage/facials/frangipani wraps, etc. (for men, too)
renta-presenters
retail therapy
Ritalin
Rooney, Wayne
rugby (who'd have thought it would be cooler than football?)
RSI (repetitive strain injury)

sat-nav (in cars)
shabby chic
scooters (of all kinds, including Segway)
scratch cards
screensavers (especially goldfish)
selling your useless endowment policy
server/ISP
Sex in the City (nineties' version of *Tropic of Ruislip*)
shock jocks
SIM cards
skateboards (they just wouldn't go away)
Sky
slang/text/binary/machine code/hex
smoke detectors and car alarms which don't go on for ever once triggered by mistake
snail mail
spam (the computer version, the sandwich filler ironically being a casualty of New Labour's term in office
speed cameras (now helpfully yellow and detectable for 300 quid)
spas
speed-dating
sports utility vehicles
Starbucks (or what used to be known as coffee bars)
stretched limos, otherwise known as stretchies
Sunday opening (apart from supermarkets after 5, helpfully)
super-size fries
surf shops (in Ealing?)
surround sound

Take a note of your table number (and order your food at the bar)
Tesco Metros

texting
Thai (the food, not the bride)
The Big Read
The Bloody Gadget shop (43 branches nationwide)
The London Mayor
The phrase 'bear with me'
The phrase 'I hear you'
The use of the word 'like' as oral punctuation (after America)
thalassotherapy
This item may contain traces of nuts
timeout (computers/magazine/life)
TiVo
things
To return the call, press 5
top-up (cards/fries/coffee/mobile phone cards/drugs)

Ugg boots
ultra-violent (rated movies)
username

videophones
virtual reality
voice-activated
voicemail
voicemailbox number
voice recognition
Vorderman (any TV presenting/diets/word/number expert)

water coolers
water-cooler moments
Wayne Rooney
widescreen
workspace living
wraps (the new sandwich)

Yahoo!
You are the weakest link (as a punchline to any conversation)
You have 16 new messages
Your call is held in a queue
Your call is important to us

zip codes (formerly postcodes)

36
And yet . . . a ray of hope

One of the lasting legacies of the 1945 Labour government was its part in ratifying the founding Charter of the United Nations. And just as the 1945 manifesto aspired to create a better Britain, so the UN's Millennium Declaration sought to inspire a better world, with the UN itself leading the way.

> The United Nations is the indispensable common house of the entire human family, through which we will seek to realize our universal aspirations for peace, cooperation, and development.[216]

The document encouraged cooperation between nations:

> Only through broad and sustained efforts to create a shared future, based upon our common humanity in all its diversity, can globalization be made fully inclusive and equitable.

Dealing with transnational crime, the elimination of weapons of mass destruction, and justice for all, the declaration even squeezed in the intention

> to promote peace and human understanding through sport and the Olympic ideal,

adding,

> We recognize that, in addition to our separate responsibilities to our individual societies, we have a collective responsibility to uphold the principles of human dignity, equality, and equity at the global level. As leaders, we have a duty to all the world's people, especially the most

vulnerable and, in particular, the children of the world, to whom the future belongs.

So what went wrong? Well, September 11th, of course.

The heads of state gathered together to sign the declaration at the UN in New York in September 2000.

It is chilling to think that if they had looked out of the windows of the UN's downtown HQ just over a year later, they would have been perfectly placed to see the two planes crash into the Twin Towers.

The damage done to the United Nations in the three years since has left the declaration's vision looking more remote than ever. And yet we forget that the UN (through its Security Council) did *not* authorize war. The majority of countries opposed it. The very people (let's call them George and Tony) who argued that the UN's authority was at stake if it did not sanction military action were the ones who broke ranks and went to war regardless. It was they who damaged the UN's authority, not the UN.

For Tony Blair, as ever, the ends justified the means, whatever the cost.

The world did change after September 11th. It's possible that, had the declaration been written one year later, the text would have changed in the light of the 'War on Terror'. But the need for cooperation and collective will is greater than ever before, and the UN remains the only body that can provide an international solution. Why else do Britain and the US call for the UN to come and clear up the mess?

So, what of the future? Amongst the heady aspirations of the Millennium Declaration, a document light on figures but rich in emotion, one firm pledge is made:

> To halve, by the year 2015, the proportion of the world's people whose income is less than a dollar a day and the proportion of people who suffer from hunger and, by the same date, to halve the proportion of people who are unable to reach or to afford safe drinking water.

We have now got eleven years left, and the figures have got worse, not better.[217]

And if the consequence of the War on Terror is that the UN is sidelined, its aims and ambitions relegated to clearing up after another war in another corner of the world, what price the high hopes of 2000?

37
A DIY guide to the future

Ten modest proposals to solve the world's problems.

1. Swap Cuba with Israel

The Cubans want missiles and have historical links with Russia. Israel wants to be closer to America and as far away as possible from the Palestinians. What could be simpler? Straight swap. One weekend, easyJet. So the Cubans get Jerusalem, but just look what a great job they've done opening up Havana to tourism, and think how good Yasser Arafat would look doing salsa.

2. Close all the schools down for ten years

Saves a lot of money, plus we'd have a generation of thick, lazy people to do all the thick, lazy jobs no one else wants to do.

3. A second Russian revolution

Everyone was happy when Russia was the way it used to be. Except the Russians. And let's face it, they never are, are they? Now, look at the place. Twenty years of capitalism have done what decades of the Cold War failed to do, and break the country up. But there is hope. Russian cities are still littered with the remains of the last regime. It's all there: New Stalinism – traditional values in a modern context. And with the return of the Cold War we could forget about counter-terrorism and spend our money on a proper arms race again.

4. Build a big wall around anyone we don't like . . .

Already being done.

5. Offer death incentives

The greatest threat to the world isn't al-Qaeda, or terrorism, or George Bush, or even the hole in the ozone layer, it's old people. They're living longer, consuming more, asking for bigger pensions, and health care is frankly a nightmare. Then there's the tricky business of inheritance. Solution: incentivize death. Capital tax relief, plus a cashback bonus for anyone going early. Sliding scale, start at sixty. Who wants to stick around with crime and council tax rises? Imagine the look of joy on your children's faces as you tell them what you've got planned and their inheritance is not going to the cats' home.

6. Join al-Qaeda

No, no, hear this one out: we all join. Not so easy to mount attacks with so many members around the world. Here's the motto: you're never more than fifty feet from an al-Qaeda cell. And it solves another problem. Infiltrating al-Qaeda has always been impossible – their language, their customs, their beards. But if enough people sign up we can bring about change from within. It just needs a populist touch, a PR push. A few celebrities to sign up. What's Mick Hucknall up to these days? He's got the beard.

7. Diet for life

Every time you would have had the extra chocolate bar or the second helping, stop. Put it back. Now make a mental note of how much it would have cost and how much you have saved. Keep a running total. At the end of the month, write out a fat cheque for this amount and send it to one of the charities working in the Third World. They're easy to track down. Now you really do have a reason to slim. By losing a few pounds you will have saved lives, maybe your own as well.

8. 29 February Day

Every four years we get an extra day. That works out at an annual 0.75 per cent windfall. It doesn't sound a lot, but it's still £7.5 billion. Enough to make a difference. So, if we don't take it as pay but put it into the Leap Year Fund, well, there's enough there to build a few hospitals, or tackle poverty, or start a small war in the Middle East. We wouldn't notice if for one day in every four years we were not paid. But someone else might, and apart from allowing women to propose, what else are you going to remember it for? Make it worldwide among the G8 nations and there should be around US$100 billion (roughly the estimate for rebuilding Iraq). Sorted.

9. Trickle-down economics

Not something that happens late at night in the pub after you've had a few, but a rather smart Victorian idea: all the country's wealth is given to one man of power, who in turn spends it wisely on those around him, who in turn pass it on, and so on and so forth. He hoards, no one works; we die, he dies. Dispersement is in everyone's interest. Clearly open to abuse, but it would certainly make the *Sunday Times* Rich List a lot more interesting.

10. Do nothing

Why intervene when it just makes things worse? In business studies, one of the models is called the 'Spaghetti Organization', credited to the Dane Lars Kolind.[218] Companies are encouraged to engineer-in disorder – to act randomly, to go against better judgements – in the hope that out of chaos creative solutions that no systems analyst could ever have predicted will emerge. It would make for entertainment and is just as likely to work as the McKinseyesque flip charts, focus groups, bullet points, and starched white shirts of current policy making. And it works for al-Qaeda too.

38
The Little Book of Britain

Wealth

By 2010 there will be 760,000 millionaires in Britain.[219]

1 per cent of the population holds nearly 23 per cent of Britain's wealth.[220]

The average property price in Kensington and Chelsea is £702,553.[221]

The average income for the whole of Britain in 2003 was £16,796.[222]

Nineteen of the top twenty richest areas are in south-east England.[223]

Britain's richest man is worth £7.5 billion.[224]

A garage in Devon went on sale for £135,000.[225]

64 per cent of students have loans.[226]

It is predicted that the average student will be £17,561 in debt by 2006.[227]

And they are likely to be looking at a mortgage of six times their salary.[228]

One in three pensioners lives in poverty.

Over a third of the population earn less than £6 per hour.

Nearly 25 per cent of the population lives below the poverty line.

Total credit card transactions amount to £113 billion per annum.

Consumer debt stands at £168 billion.

4 million children live in poverty.

2 million families have severe financial difficulties.

The total of those living below the poverty line has doubled in twenty years.

Children are more likely to live in poverty than adults.

Almost half of children in London live in poverty.

One third of families have no savings at all.

TS15 in Middlesbrough is Britain's poorest postcode.

45 per cent of households in this postal district have an income of less than £10,000.[229]

More than one in five adults are routinely refused credit.

Nearly half a million adults do not have a bank account.

1 per cent of companies account for nearly 90 per cent of retail trade.

Work

7 million adults are not literate enough to cope with modern life.

Trade union membership has fallen by nearly 2 million.

Less than a third of all workplaces are unionized.

UK employees work the longest hours in Europe.

One in ten men is still in employment after the age of 65.

1.6 million people are temporarily employed.

A quarter of employees work over forty-eight hours per week.

1.7 million people are unemployed.

Housing

14 per cent of households in England live in 'poor housing'.

30 per cent of tenants in England live in 'poor housing'.

85,000 households were living in temporary accommodation in 2002.

Lifestyle

Over £6 billion is spent on alcohol every year.

The average is £1272 per person, more than anywhere else in Europe.

Over £2 billion is spent on air travel every year.

2 per cent of household expenditure goes on cigarettes.

We spend more on food than on housing.

The average Briton travels 893 miles a year just to shop for food.

In the last five years fifty specialist shops closed each week in the UK.

Over 20 per cent of the population is obese.[230]

11 per cent of children in England are overweight.

Over £8.6 billion is spent annually on soft drinks.

£5 billion is spent on fast food and ready meals.

3.5 million glasses of soft drinks are drunk every hour.

£750 million is spent annually on alcopops.

A third of young women drink to excess.

Nearly 40 per cent of young men drink to excess.[231]

A third of young people have recently used drugs.[232]

Over 35,000 children are on child protection registers.

There are more than 1.5 million legally held guns in Britain.

The UK has the highest imprisonment rate in Europe, incarcerating 139 per 100,000 members of the population.[233]

There were over 130,000 warrants issued for repossession in 2003.

Carbon dioxide emissions from traffic have almost doubled in twenty-five years.

Children spend £3796 million per year.

8 million people shop online.

22 million prescriptions for depression were written last year.

2.1 billion text messages are sent every month.[234]

Single parents are four times more likely to be burgled.

10,000 children were permanently excluded from school last year.[235]

101 uses for a John Prescott

No. 83 – Bar steward on the 7.47 GNER London–Leeds express

The volume of waste produced in the UK in one day is enough to fill Trafalgar Square up to the top of Nelson's Column.

In 2002 on average one school playing field was sold off each week.

One in 1000 people commits suicide.

POSTSCRIPT BY MICHAEL HOWARD

Hello. I see I made it then. Just. For a moment, I thought I was going to miss out. Still, as my old grandmother always used to say to me, 'Michael, if you can't be heard, be last.' And that's what I propose to do.

Now, it would be easy, wouldn't it – very easy, in fact – to trawl through the archives, and search the cuttings, to see what I said in the past, and make a pretty convincing case for saying I've no right to talk. And you'd be right. I admit it. I don't. I've said some awful things in the past. Dreadful stuff about asylum seekers and criminals and beggars and goodness knows what else. 'Prison works', remember that? Damn. No, no, please, take me out and shoot me, I deserve it. Of course, Labour are still saying the same things we were saying, making the same mistakes, which would suggest, would it not, that they were very, very easy mistakes to make, and therefore quite understandaBLE. But I'm using that as an excuse. It could be, but no, let's remain humBLE. We got it wrong.

And in admitting my party's many faults – and I'm happy to list them for you, if you like – I hope you will appreciate a rather remarkaBLE thing has happened: we have become human.

It's taken seven years. And it hasn't been without its cost. And here I'm thinking particularly of William Hague and Iain Duncan Smith, both fine leaders of the party. But joking apart, the party needed a caretaker for a few years, and in that role of the man in the brown coat with a bucket and mop, they were both perfect. True, they were never going to get us elected, but then, frankly, neither was anyone else.

But in the meantime a rather interesting thing has happened, and I'd like to tell you about it. You see, people's perception of politicians as a whole has continued to sink since we were booted out. People have come to expect little of their politicians, and that's something we can deliver in trumps.

Being raised in Swansea and serving as MP for Folkestone, it is perhaps only natural that I should support Liverpool Football Club. And somewhere in the canon of English football chants is a refrain that we would do well to adopt. It goes something like this (I've adapted it slightly, as you'll see):

> We're shit, and we know we are.

Roughly speaking, for those more accustomed to the Carlton Club, it translates as 'We're honest enough to admit our limitations and for that reason we are really rather likeaBLE.'

We say foolish things, we wear funny clothes, we still look like a bunch of oddballs at a Home Counties wine and cheese party, and apart from everyone discovering they are gay, we still haven't got that far with integrating the party. But, and this is the point, it doesn't matter.

PeoPLE's expectations of us are so low that if we try to raise them they will only become suspicious and mistrust us even more. So let's not go there. Let's play up to the contempt they have for us and provide them with a reasonaBLE supply of half-baked, warmed-up, or discredited policies that chime with the electorate's low opinion of us.

You never know, it might work.

People won't feel threatened by any sense that we are in some way superior to them. And we don't have the strain of constantly thinking, how on earth can we appeal to your better judgement? Instead, we can concentrate on firing off a range of risiBLE ideas without the remotest chance of them being workaBLE or properly costed. You know we're not serious, we know we're not serious; what could be fairer than that?

So that's the plan. For the next year and a half, or sooner if Mr Blair's nerve cracks – as, indeed, I am sure it will – I will present myself in a series of ever more preposterous ways. The fact that this is all part of a cunning plan will remain a secret between you, me, and anyone who has read this far.

And we will guarantee transparency: we appear useless and, in fact, behind the scenes, we are useless. After all, we've tried practically every other route back to power, so why not go for broke?

So, if you see us, spare us a thought. We won't be asking you to vote for us, but if you did decide to give us your support, perhaps as a joke, or maybe as a bet amongst friends, then we'd be delighted to accept. We're not choosy. It's a fun thing to do, and you're guaranteed at least a few years of the freaks and oddballs running things, rather than that tiresome, priggish Mr Blair.

And if you're looking for a little method in the madness, then you need look no further than the increasingly wild-eyed and batty world of my friend Boris Johnson, who has been playing the role of the laughaBLE fool with ever greater success, with his bike, and his mane of foppish hair. People flock to him for a burst of incoherent rambling and on-the-hoof, homespun philosophy based on no more than a pick-'n'-mix collection of right-wing observations and a dose of good old-fashioned self-deprecation. And, like prison, it works. Give a shrug, raise one's shoulders, and admit you haven't a clue, then trot out a few jokes with a bit of political mumbo-jumbo thrown in, and there's just a chance we have enough of a pot-pourri to tickle your fancy.

Right, well, that's me done; I've taken up enough of your time I'm sure. I could list what the Labour government are doing wrong, but by now you're probably pretty well up on that; and I could list all our faults too, but that would take even longer, and you can probably remember a lot of them from the last time.

Sorry you had to wait around till right at the very end for a dose, but hopefully it was worth it. I did try to get in earlier, but they explained there wasn't any room, and, like Granny said, if you can't leave them wanting more, then leave them wanting less.

So relax, admit that although you might vote for the Conservative Party you don't expect anything from us, and I promise we won't disappoint.

Thanks,

Michael

PS Oh yes, and remember the fun you had kicking us out in 1997? Well, if you vote us back in, you'll be able to kick us out all over again in five years' time – and that *has* to be something to look forward to.

39
Who's next?

(Originally written by Tom Lehrer in response to nuclear proliferation in the 1950s and 1960s, he very kindly gave us permission to adapt it for the War on Terror. Forty years on, the words may have changed but the message hasn't.)

First we had the bomb, and that was OK,
'cos we ruled the world that way.
But 9/11 changed the plan,
show time for the Taliban.
Who's next?

War on Terror that's the aim.
Groups or countries just the same.
Iraq don't have the bomb, they say,
well, let's attack them anyway!
Who's next?

Syria and Sudan too,
soon we're coming after you.
Declare jihad, you'll get what for,
instead of peace it's Holy War.
Who's next?

Those Arab guys have got us pissed.
Iran and Yemen on the list.
After Somalia, Cuba, and Libya.
Burma may have changed it's name,
but what the hell, we'll find it just the same.
Who's next?

From Texas to Afghanistan
a rocket-powered Marshall Plan.
Smart bombs by the megaton
will hit the house next door but one.
Who's next?

Korea and Israel have their own,
I guess we'll leave those guys alone.
Once they've got the bomb you see,
we'll have to use diplomacy.
Who's next?
Who's next?
Who's next?
Who's next?

Notes and References

A NOTE ON THE SOURCES

In many cases the references given are not our original or primary sources of information, but they are supplied to support the material contained in this book and provide a guide for further reading.

PART I: THINGS CAN ONLY GET BETTER?

1 *Edinburgh Evening News*, 9 January 2004; see also Lambeth Environment Directorate Parking Services
2 '"Big Brother" Britain to get more cameras', CNSNews.com, 14 August 2001
3 UK Election Statistics 1945–2000. Commons Library Research Paper 01/37, 29/3/01
4 Quoted in prnewswire.co.uk, 6 March 2001
5 BBC News, UK Politics, 30 June 2000; 3 July 2000
6 *Breakfast with Frost*, BBC, January 2000. BBC News, UK Politics, 5 December 2001
7 Government spending forecast, Spending Review, July 2002
8 Inaugural Fabian Society Annual Lecture, the Old Vic, 17 June 2003
9 Ibid.
10 Quoted by Anthony Sampson, *Who runs this place?*, John Murray, 2004, p. 78
11 'Since 1997, the rich have continued to get richer and inequality in disposable income appears to have slightly increased since 1997'. IPPR Social Justice Factfile, August 2004
12 BBC News, 23 February 2003
13 'UK selling arms to India', Richard Norton Taylor, *Guardian*, 20 June 2002
14 See later in chapter 'What happened next'
15 Alan Travis, *Guardian*, 9 June 2004
16 'Army can't go to war for five years', *Daily Telegraph*, 25 March 2004
17 Hutton Inquiry transcript, 18 August 2003
18 Quoted by Peter Oborne, *Spectator*, 5 April 2003
19 'Labour link to Berlusconi cash probe', *Observer*, 16 February 2003
19i It was – though not in the sense he meant.
20 BBC News, 7 April 1998. bbc.co.uk (with audio link)

PART II: DRAWING A LINE

21 Quoted in *Daily Telegraph*, 30 January 2004
22 Quoted in the Heritage Foundation website, 19 March 2003. See also the press release by US Ambassador to Mexico (usembassy-mexico.gov/releases)
23 Robin Cook, *Point of Departure*, Simon & Schuster, 2003
24 BBC News, 26 February 2004
25 Thalif Dean, *New Internationalist*, December 2002
26 Daily Headlines, www.lse.ac.uk, 1 March 2004
27 Kristol and Kaplan, *The War over Iraq*, Encounter Books, 2003
28 Yale Bulletin and Calendar, October 2003
29 National Review Online, 20 September 2001
30 Bob Woodward, *Bush at War*
31 www.newamericancentury.org/iraqclintonletter.htm
32 pbs.org website
33 'Rebuilding America's Defenses: Strategy, Forces and Resources for a New Century', PNAC, September 2000
34 Ibid.
35 Quoted by Nicholas Lemann, *New Yorker*, April 2002
36 Richard A. Clarke, *Against All Enemies*, Free Press, March 2004, p. 31
37 Ranjit Bhushan, *Outlook*, New Delhi, 17 September 2001
38 *New York Times*, 13 April 1991. Quoted at slate.msn.com
39 *Meet the Press*, NBC News, 16 March 2003
40 Writing as President of the Air Council, 1919
41 George H. W. Bush, Raytheon Plant, Andover, Mass.
42 'The Ghosts of 1991', P. Galbraith, *Washington Post*, 12 April 2003
43 See Robert Baer, *See No Evil*
44 Hutton Inquiry, CAB/11/53
45 The September 11th Commission later confirmed there was no link ('Al Qaeda–Hussein link is dismissed', *Washington Post*, 17 June 2004
46 *Vanity Fair*, July 2003
47 BBC News, 10 December 2002
48 Butler, Review of Intelligence on WMD, July 2004, paragraphs 410, 434, 436
49 Interview, *Observer*, 25 January 2004
50 Joseph Curl, *Washington Times*, 27 September 2002 (quoted in *Intervention Magazine*)
51 *Face the Nation*, 14 March 2004. Full transcript at cbsnews.com
52 'So much for the peace dividend', *Guardian*, 22 May 2003
53 Speech on Corporate Responsibility, New York, 9 July 2002
53i These were 'absolutely enormous' deals for the government a National Audit Office report noted adding 'you don't usually see numbers like these outside health and defence' which of course are two other areas in which companies like Bechtel have a keen interest. Those numbers, by the way, are a projected return for shareholders of around 18–20 per cent a year, limited downside risk thanks to a 95 per cent government 'cash back' offer in the event of termination, together with a

£450 million payment to be shared by the bidding companies to reimburse them for the cost of putting in the bids.

54 Speech to NATO, Russia summit, Paris, May 1997
55 Quoted by John Kampfner, *Blair's Wars*
56 Transcript online at BBC News, 5 March 2004
57 Quoted in *New Yorker*, 1 April 2002
58 Transcript: 'The Blair Doctrine', pbs.org 22 April 1999
59 Speech to Labour Conference, 2 October 2001
60 Printed in *Observer*, 7 April 2002
61 'Campbell defends dossier role', BBC News online, 19 August 2003
62 For transcripts of testimonies and documents from the Hutton Inquiry, see the *Guardian's The Hutton Inquiry and Its Impact*, Guardian Books 2004
63 Speech, 5 March 2004
64 Quoted in *Guardian*, 19 August 2003. Also in Appendices to the Hutton Report
65 Butler, op. cit. and comments at press conference
66 'The PM is in denial', Robin Cook article, *Independent*, 15 May 2004
67 Social encounter with RB
68 Social encounter with RB
69 *Democracy Now*, 7 August 2003
70 See 'Blueprint for a mess', David Rieff, *New York Times Magazine*, 2 November 2003
71 Chalabi disputed the fraud charges, but also faced warrants issued by the new Iraqi regime on a charge of counterfeiting (BBC News online, 8 August 2004). No action was taken when he visited Iraq this autumn, and he himself said that the charges had been dropped (BBC News online, 1 September 2004).
72 See Antonia Juhasz, Foreign Policy in Focus Policy Report, July 2004
73 Colette Flight, 'Silent Weapon: Smallpox and biological warfare', BBC History
74 Chemical and Biological Arms Control Institute Dispatch 154, September 2001
75 'Israel planning ethnic bomb', *Sunday Times*, 15 November 1998
76 'Police sniff out mother of all stink bombs', *Observer*, 24 February 2002
77 'Science that stinks', *American Scientist* online, May/June 2002
78 Remarks to Senate, byrd.senate.gov/byrd-speeches

PART III: THE HOME FRONT

79 Speech to CBI, Birmingham, 17 November 2003
80 BBC News UK Politics, 29 November 2000
81 See 'NATS Privatisation financially flawed', BBC News, 5 December 2001. The government also had to save British Energy with a £650m cash injection in 2002. Chairman Robin Jeffrey left with a reported 'golden goodbye' of £336,000 plus a £150,000 annual pension.
82 Speech to Prison Officers' Association Conference, April 1996
83 World Prison Population List (4th edition), Home Office
84 US National Institute of Corrections, July 2000

85 See also *Herald*, 11 February 2003
86 City of London Police website
86i A fair point, the only surprise being that the Police Federation have themselves gone into the business with their own online motoring store, complete with sales hotline, new and used offers, special deals, finance and servicing departments. To quote from their website: 'The only crime is how low our car prices are!' The only crime being that crime has been reduced to a slogan to sell cars.
87 'A New Deal for Transport: Better for Everyone [*sic*]' Government White Paper, July 1998
88 NATS Privatisation financially flawed', BBC News, 5 December 2001
89 This has now been addressed. The Office of Rail Regulation (the successor to the Rail Regulator, abolished in July 2004) can now investigate and take enforcement action (including fines of up to 30 per cent of turnover) against the ROSCOs if they engage in anti-competitive behaviour or abuse their dominant positions in the rail market.
90 'High Court deal for NATS and EDS', *Computer Weekly*, 2 May 2002
91 Ted Wragg, *Guardian*, 3 September 2002
92 'State-approved knowledge? Ten steps down the slippery slope', E. Wragg, *in The Core Curriculum*, ed. Gilbey, Perspectives 2, Exeter University, May 1980, pp. 11–20
93 Official DfeS Form schools and LEAS have to fill in under the 'Power to Innovate' section of the Education Act 2000
94 See *Independent*, Education editor, 2 July 2004
95 'Education Sponsorship – a slippery slope?', BBC News, 12 October 1998
96 'New types of specialist school', BBC News Education, 8 February 2001
97 Source: FARM
98 Robert Egli, citing Lufthansa
99 George Monbiot, 'The Mailed Fist of the free market', *Evening Standard*, 2 May 1996. See also Monbiot's book, *Captive State*, Pan Macmillan, 2001
100 Source: Friends of the Earth
101 Source: FARM
102 Hospital bosses at Uttlesford Primary Care Trust banned the WI from supplying cakes to patients in Saffron Walden Community Hospital 'after reviewing potential risks to patients'. *Scotsman*, 28 July 2004
103 Source: 'The political influence of arms companies', Campaign Against the Arms Trade, April 2003
104 Ibid.
105 '£1bn arms push to India', *Guardian*, 12 January 2002
106 'Straw defends arms sales change', BBC News Politics, 9 July 2002
107 'Household debt tops the trillion mark', *Guardian*, 24 July 2004
108 Press Association, 19 July 2004
109 BBC News, Politics, 17 July 2000
110 *Scotsman*, July 17 2003
111 Private information
112 BBC News, Politics, 30 June 2000

113 Though David Blunkett returned to the idea of spot fines, addressing the Police Federation in May 2003
114 See also 'Talking tough. falling short?', BBC News online, 12 July 2002
115 Quoted by Paul Convery, Centre for Economic and Social Inclusion Working Brief, 10 January 1999
116 *Management Issues*, 2 June 2003
117 UK Trade and Investment website (www.uktradeinvestusa.com) See also 'The real reason we should fear immigration', Polly Toynbee, *Guardian*, 11 February 2004
118 'Attitudes towards refugees and asylum seekers: A survey of public opinion' (MORI). See also CRE website, cre.gov.uk
119 Source: CRE
120 US Department of State (travel.state.gov/travel/warnings)
121 TIMEEurope.com
122 Source: Human Rights Watch
123 This section draws on information from the Refugee Council, amongst others.
124 'Letwin pledges to keep asylum seekers out', *Guardian*, 8 October 2003
125 Commons Standing Committee B, Asylum Systems, 21 April 2004
126 'The migrant population in the UK: fiscal effects', Home Office RDS Occasional Paper 77, 2002, iii

PART IV: THERE'S A WHOLE WORLD OUT THERE

127 Bremner, Bird & Fortune, series 5, show 5, broadcast 29 February 2004
128 Source: CIA World Factbook 2004
128i At the time he said 'The people respect me so much I can not sleep'
129 *Eurasia Insight*, 25 November 2002
130 Op. cit., 7 January 2003
131 Eurasianet.org, 26 February 2004
132 See BBC News online, 30 May 2002
133 International Monetary Fund website, 15 July 2004
134 GlobalSecurity.org
135 US State Department, 11 February 2002
136 'Kyrgyzstan agrees Russian base', BBC News online, 22 September 2003
137 Quoted in *Washington Post*, 6 July 1997
138 Azeri leader collapses on live TV, BBC News online, 21 April 2003
139 Obituary, BBC News online, 12 December 2003
140 US State Department Report on Human Rights Practices, 25 February 2004
141 'Caspian pipeline dream becomes reality', BBC News online, 17 September 2002
142 US State Dept., 6 June 2002
143 See 'The envoy who said too much', *Guardian*, 15 July 2004
144 www.worldpress.org
145 US State Dept. 11 February 2002
146 US State Dept. Commission on Human Rights, 25 March 2004
147 Press Service of the President of Uzbekistan, 2 September 2002

148 'US freezes aid to Uzbekistan', BBC News online, 14 July 2004
149 See 'My secret talks with Libya, and why they went nowhere', *Washington Post*, 18 January 2004
150 'Britain's secret bid to end Gaddafi arms embargo', *Scotsman*, 11 March 2004
151 'Libya reports high potential for oil reserves', Middle East online, 21 April 2004
152 See *Sunday Herald*, 9 June 2002
153 ECGD website, 6 January 2004
154 Source: Human Rights Watch
155 *Al-Zamaan daily*, quoted on africast.com, 29 October 2003
156 'Italy in "fire on immigrants" row', BBC News online, 16 June 2003. The Bossi ministry statement can be found on that page.
157 See 'Putin defends Chechnya war', BBC News online, 18 April 2000
158 See www.gazeta.ru/2003/11/13/Britainrejec.shtml
159 'Britain leads sale of weapons to poor', *Sunday Herald*, 28 September 2003. Under the Tories, arms to Africa made up 1.6 per cent of all British arms to the Third World. By 2000 it had grown to 19 per cent.
160 'Tanzania row escalates', BBC News online, 19 December 2001
161 'UK plans asylum camp in Tanzania', BBC News online, 26 February 2002
162 Hansard, 26 November 2003, column 30
163 Hansard, 1 December 1998, column 160
164 Saferworld Briefing, 6 November 2003, 'The Government's proposals for secondary legislation under the Export Control Act and wider export control policy'
165 abcNews.com, 21 January 2002
166 'A Moral Minefield', *New Scientist*, 7 April 2001
167 See World Bank News Release, 'World Bank Resumes Support to the Democratic Republic of Congo', 13 June 2002
168 See 'Chaos and Cannibalism under Congo's bloody skies', *Observer*, 17 August 2003
169 Commission for Africa website
170 'Rumsfeld lashes out at critics', BBC News online, 23 January 2002
171 'Life after Guantanamo', BBC News online, 27 July 2004
172 See 'The Roots of Torture', John Barry, Michael Hirsh, Michael Isikoff, *Newsweek*, 24 May 2004
173 'Pentagon Approved Tougher Interrogations', Dana Pries and Joe Stephens, *Washington Post*, 9 May 2004
174 'Court calls for open detainee hearings, US chastised on immigration case secrecy', *Washington Post*, 27 August 2002
175 See 'Presidential Determination 2004–17', 30 December 2003, available at usinfo.state.gov
176 Partial list of US vetoes in the UN, printed in *Guardian*, 20 March 2003
177 See 'Subjects of UN Security Council Vetoes', available at www.globalpolicy.org/security/ membship/veto/vetosubj.htm
178 'Cheney on the issues', *USA Today*, 26 July 2000
179 UN Human Development Report 2003, available at http://hdr.undp.org/reports/global/2003/

180 '£100 million in aid funds diverted to Iraq', *Guardian*, 7 November 2003
181 'Poverty and exclusion among Urban Children', Unicef, November 2002
182 'A Development Co-operation Lens on Terrorism Prevention', OECD 2003, available at http://www.oecd.org/dataoecd/17/4/16085708.pdf
183 'On the edge of lunacy', George Monbiot, *Guardian*, 6 January 2004
184 Quoted by Larry Elliott in 'Policy made on the road to perdition', *Guardian*, 12 December 2003
185 For transcripts of testimonies and documents from the Hutton Inquiry, see the *Guardian's The Hutton Inquiry and Its Impact*, Guardian Books, 2004

PART V: SO HERE'S THE BILL

186 BBC News, 17 February 2003
187 'The Extent of Drug Therapy for Attention Deficit-Hyperactivity Disorder Among Children in Public Schools', G. B. LeFever, K. V. Dawson and A. L. Morrow, *American Journal of Public Health*, September 1999, vol. 89, pp. 1359–64
188 'US infant mortality rises 3%', *Washington Post*, 11 February 2004
189 'MI5 expands to meet terror threat', BBC News online, 22 February 2004
190 'Emergency powers plan published', BBC News online, 7 January 2004
191 See http://www.liberty-human-rights.org.uk/
192 Speech to Freedom of Information awards ceremony, 25 March 1996
193 Hansard, 15 November 1995, column 18
194 Transcript appeared in *Guardian*, 22 October 2001
195 Hansard, 6 April 1989, column 369
196 I'm afraid we made that one up. But thank you for checking.
197 'MOD asked to withdraw objections to new windfarms', *Guardian*, 1 March 2004
198 'NASA curbs comments on Ice Age disaster movie', *New York Times*, 25 April 2004
199 'Carbon emissions trading', Ross Gelbspan, *Ecologist*, 22 June 2002. See also www.tnrcc.state.tx
200 www.greenpeace.org
201 'Nuclear weapons clean-up cost taxpayers £32 billion', Nick Paton Walsh, *Observer*, 31 December 2000
202 'Yes, but why do you Brits need nuclear weapons?', Kevin Myers, *Daily Telegraph*, 27 July 2004
203 'MOD: The construction of nuclear submarine facilities at Devonport', National Audit Office, 29 November 2002
204 'MOD "footnote" reveals £1.7 billion written off in failed projects', *Daily Telegraph*, 9 November 2003
205 'MOD plans £2 billion nuclear expansion', *Guardian*, 18 June 2002
206 www.edwardleigh.net
207 'GCHQ underestimates cost of relocating by £430m', *Computer Weekly*, 15 June 2004

208 'Damning Holyrood Report', BBC News online, 8 April 2003
209 'Holyrood Price Tag rises to £430m', BBC News online, 24 February 2004
210 Nick Bourne, Welsh Conservative Leader, quoted at ePolitix.com, 2 March 2004
211 'Court's Libra system "is one of the worst IT projects ever seen"', *Computer Weekly*, 30 January 2003
212 National Audit Office, quoted in 'Passengers may lose out on link', BBC News online, 10 April 2003
213 'Wake up call', *Guardian*, 6 September 2002
214 http://www.nao.org.uk/publications/nao—reports/01-02/01021097es.pdf
215 'Whoops!', *Guardian*, 9 July 2002
216 'United Nations Millennium Declaration', September 2000, available at http://www.un.org/millenniumgoals/
217 'World Failing Poverty Pledges', BBC News online, 23 April 2004
218 'Spaghetti Organisation', *Guardian*, 18 October 2001
219 'House prices boost millionaires', BBC News online, 1 March 2004
220 Inland Revenue Personal Wealth Report, 31 October 2003
221 'Property prices soar', BBC News online, 9 August 2004
222 'Inequality and living standards in Britain: some facts', Institute for Fiscal Studies Briefing Notes, December 2002
223 'How postcodes put the wealthy in their place', *Observer*, 20 June 2004
224 'Chelsea owner "UK's richest man"', BBC News online, 18 April 2004
225 'Garage for sale', BBC News online, 14 November 2002
226 'A debt mountain to climb', *Guardian*, 16 August 2003
227 Ibid.
228 'Help at hand for first time buyers', *Daily Telegraph*, 27 February 2002
229 Ibid.
230 'Children's diets must improve' BBC News online, 27 May 2003
231 'More women are drinking too much', BBC News online, 29 July 2004
232 'Drug information', Drugscope, available at http://www.drugscope.org.uk/druginfo/home.asp
233 'Judges blamed for prison boom', BBC News online, 1 July 2003
234 'Text messaging reaches new high', BBC News online, 27 April 2004
235 'Pupil attacks: thousands excluded', BBC News online, 29 July 2004